a–z of housing

professional keywords

Every field of practice has its own methods, terminology, conceptual debates and landmark publications. The *Professional Keywords* series expertly structures this material into easy-reference A to Z format. Focusing on the ideas and themes that shape the field, and informed by the latest research, these books are designed both to guide the student reader and to refresh practitioners' thinking and understanding.

Available now
Mark Doel and Timothy B. Kelly: *A–Z of Groups & Groupwork*
David Garnett: *A–Z of Housing*
Jon Glasby and Helen Dickinson: *A–Z of Interagency Working*
Richard Hugman: *A–Z of Professional Ethics*
Glenn Laverack: *A–Z of Health Promotion*
Glenn Laverack: *A–Z of Public Health*
Jeffrey Longhofer: *A–Z of Psychodynamic Practice*
Neil McKeganey: *A–Z of Addiction and Substance Misuse*
Steve Nolan and Margaret Holloway: *A–Z of Spirituality*
Marian Roberts: *A–Z of Mediation*
Fiona Timmins: *A–Z of Reflective Practice*
David Wilkins, David Shemmings and Yvonne Shemmings: *A–Z of Attachment*

a-z of
housing

David Garnett

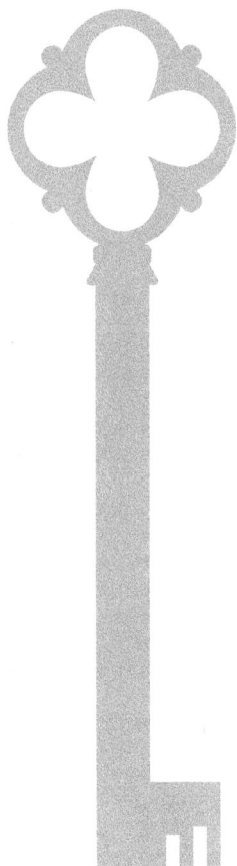

BLOOMSBURY ACADEMIC
LONDON • NEW YORK • OXFORD • NEW DELHI • SYDNEY

BLOOMSBURY ACADEMIC
Bloomsbury Publishing Plc
50 Bedford Square, London, WC1B 3DP, UK
1385 Broadway, New York, NY 10018, USA
29 Earlsfort Terrace, Dublin 2, Ireland

BLOOMSBURY, BLOOMSBURY ACADEMIC and the Diana logo
are trademarks of Bloomsbury Publishing Plc

First published 2015 by PALGRAVE

Reprinted by Bloomsbury Academic

A catalogue record for this book is available from the British Library.

A catalog record for this book is available from the Library of Congress.

ISBN: PB: 978-1-1373-6673-3
ePDF: 978-1-1373-6674-0

To find out more about our authors and books visit
www.bloomsbury.com and sign up for our newsletters.

contents

acknowledgements vii

how to use the book viii

regional references x

introduction xiii

accountability 1

accounts 2

affordability 6

allocations 9

anti-social behaviour 12

asset management 16

audit 19

business planning 22

capital and revenue 26

care and support 31

choice 36

community 39

continuous improvement 41

cost of housing 45

culture 46

development 51

diversity 56

dwellings 60

equity 62

finance 66

fuel poverty 70

governance 73

home ownership 77

homelessness 80

housing law 82

housing market 83

inclusion and exclusion 89

leasehold 92

low cost home ownership 95

low income households 101

merit goods and services 108

mortgages 109

need and demand 116

nudge theory 120

participation 126

partnerships 131

performance monitoring 134

planning gain 137

private renting 138

proprietary interests 144

quality 149

regulation 152

rent 156

risk and uncertainty 159

social enterprise   166

social housing   169

social returns   170

subsidies   175

sustainability   184

tenancy agreements   190

tenure   194

value   197

value for money   202

welfare   209

bibliography   213

index   223

acknowledgements

I am indebted to a number of people who provided help and advice in the production of this collection of key terms. In particular I would like to thank Barry Thompson and Garry King for taking time to read and comment on much of the material. I am also grateful to those who have guided my reading and understanding of some of the entries. In particular I would like to mention Jon Rae, Amanda Lewis, Professor John Pitts, Justin Cartwright, Dr Lorcan Sirr, Professor Paddy Gray and Jason MacGilp. Most of all I owe a debt to my wife Julie for her time and tolerance in checking and commenting on the early drafts. Finally I would like to thank all those present and past students and colleagues who allowed me to share and thereby develop my fascination with etymology.

David Garnett

how to use the book

The main entries generally focus on broadly themed topics that have long-standing relevance to policy and practice debates. Current and more specific rules, laws, approaches and practices then appear in the index and are referenced under Key Texts that follow each entry. The index plays a crucial part in how to engage with the text and on many occasions it will provide the reader's initial point of entry.

Although, in order to illustrate or amplify arguments and debates, historical and regionally specific policy initiatives are sometimes made reference to, an effort has been made to keep clear the distinction between theory and practice. Readers interested in understanding current (regionally or locally specific) policies should do so by referencing key sites on the internet (see below for a guide to these sites).

The organization of the text is intended to enable the reader to look up certain key entries in the index and, as well as finding a referenced explanation of the term itself, be directed to related topics. This facility should help both essay and report writers to research topics and coordinate their thinking. Where appropriate, entries consciously link operational regulations, procedures and practices to an associated academic literature. An example would be 'universal credit' and 'housing benefit' both of which, as well as being linked to each other, are cross-referenced to the wider literatures on 'low income households' and 'subsidies'.

Although current data and factual material are included throughout, the entries have been written with an emphasis on the underlying conceptual, non-changing aspects of housing rather than on current, highly specific (and inevitably temporary), definitions. More emphasis has been given to the ongoing socio-political debates surrounding topics than a detailed description of their current legal and financial status. This means that the text provides what the internet fails to provide – a way of thinking about housing policies and practices.

The further reading guides are indicative only. Many of the suggested texts themselves contain extensive reading suggestions. These provide a good starting point for further reading and research.

regional references

International and regional differences have always existed in the creation and application of the policy responses relating to the key words discussed in this text. Over the years these have been constantly reviewed, amended or reformed. Since the referendum on Scottish Independence, all the main British political parties have made clear their intentions to implement further significant devolution of decision-making powers. These will apply not only to Scotland but also to the other national regions of the United Kingdom. There is also a political commitment to enhance the powers of city and regional authorities that will allow them to implement fiscal and service provision decisions that would better reflect local knowledge and preferences. The decentralization of power and budgets will result in increasingly different local policies and practices. This means that the reader who wishes to keep up-to-date on the details of housing operations will need to make constant reference to local sources of information. In an electronic age there is no shortage of facts regarding local housing policies. The problem is in deciding where to look for information that is relevant and trustworthy. The websites of the following authorities, agencies, charities and voluntary organizations provide a reliable gateway to such information.

key gateway information sites and references

United Kingdom
- http://www.almos.org.uk/
- https://www.gov.uk/government/topics/housing
- http://www.cih.org/
- http://www.housing-ombudsman.org.uk
- http://hqnetwork.co.uk

- http://www.statistics.gov.uk/
- http://www.tpas.org.uk/
- http://www.bshf.org
- BSHF_Perspectives_on_housing_FINAL_WEB%20(1).pdf

England

- https://www.gov.uk/government/organisations/department-for-communities-and-local-government
- http://www.homesandcommunities.co.uk/
- National Housing Federation: *The Lyons Housing Review*. http://www.yourbritain.org.uk/uploads/editor/files/The_Lyons_Housing_Review_2.pdf

Scotland

- http://www.scotland.gov.uk/Topics/Built-Environment/Housing/
- www.scotland.gov.uk
- www.scottishhousingregulator.gov.uk
- www.careinspectorate.com
- www.cih.org/scotland
- www.cih.org/housingreport
- www.sfha.co.uk/
- www.gwsf.org.uk
- www.cosla.gov.uk/
- www.alacho.org
- www.existinghomesalliancescotland.co.uk
- www.rihafnews.co.uk/rihaf-email/articles/
- www.scotland.shelter.org.uk
- www.homelessactionscotland.org.uk
- www.tpasscotland.org.uk
- www.tis.org.uk
- www.rics.org/uk/about-rics/where-we-are/uk/scotland
- http://www.rics.org/Global/The%20RICS%20Scottish%20Housing%20Commission%20%e2%80%93%20Building%20a%20Better%20Scotland%20%e2%80%93%20July%202014.pdf

Wales

- http://wales.gov.uk/topics
- http://chcymru.org.uk/
- http://wales.gov.uk/topics/housing-and-regeneration/?lang=en

- http://wales.gov.uk/topics/planning/?lang=en http://www.cih.org/cymru
- Welsh Local Government Association – Housing Updates, Policy Documents, Consultation Responses, etc. http://www.wlga.gov.uk/housing http://www.chcymru.org.uk/
- Welsh Housing Quarterly magazine. http://www.whq.org.uk/main/index.php

Northern Ireland

- Paris, C. (ed.) (2001) *Housing in Northern Ireland – and Comparisons with the Republic of Ireland* (Coventry: Chartered Institute of Housing). http://www.niassembly.gov.uk/
- http://www.nihe.gov.uk/
- http://www.dsdni.gov.uk/
- https://www.planningni.gov.uk/
- http://www.nihe.gov.uk/
- http://www.nifha.org/
- http://www.housingrights.org.uk/ (good for private rented policy)
- http://www.cih.org/NorthernIreland

Republic of Ireland

- Kenna, P. (2011) *Housing Law, Policy and Rights* (Dublin: Clarus Press)
- Norris, M. and Redmond, D. (eds) (2007) *Housing Contemporary Ireland: Policy, Society and Shelter* (Dordrecht: Springer Science)
- O'Connell, C. (2007) *The State and Housing in Ireland: Ideology, Policy and Practice* (New York: Nova Science)
- Redmond, D. and Norris, M. (2014) 'Social Housing in Ireland' in D. Redmond and M. Norris (eds), *Social Housing in Europe* (London: Wiley-Blackwell)

International policy perspectives

- European Network for Housing Research. http://www.enhr.net/
- Lowe, S. (2011) *The Housing Debate* (Bristol: The Polity Press)
- Maclennan, D. (2005) *Housing Policies: New Times, New Foundations* (York: Joseph Rowntree Foundation). Available at http://www.jrf.org.uk/sites/files/jrf/1859353622.pdf
- Redmond, D. and Norris, M. (eds) (2014) *Social Housing in Europe* (London: Wiley-Blackwell)

introduction

Politicians and cultural historians constantly draw attention to the fact that a dwelling is more than a building – it is a 'home'. Our homes influence our well-being, our sense of worth, our ties to our families, communities and work. The nature of housing affects physical and mental health, educational attainment and social behaviour. For the average household, it absorbs about a fifth of total weekly income. Housing is also an important part of the nation's total private investment: it represents by far the most valuable single asset class, accounting for some two-thirds of the country's net worth (2014). Along with such engineering investments as roads, sewers and flood defences, the £5 trillion plus worth of dwellings also constitute part of the nation's social infrastructure and, as such, how we invest in it and how we treat it is of crucial importance to future generations. In short, housing is no ordinary commodity and as a topic for debate and study it embraces many disciplines, including politics, sociology, ethics, economics, finance, law, psychology, social history and technology. Clearly a comprehensive 'a–z of housing' would require the creation of a library rather than a single text. This means that the reader needs to be clear about the limitations as well as the uses of the current volume.

As a keyword reference, this text is not intended to be a definitive reference book, nor can it be a comprehensive summary of the multifarious academic literatures that make reference to housing. Although this book includes references to current thinking about 'best practice', it should not be treated as a practice manual. The keyword entries are intended to provide a grid of meaning within which the historical and political contexts of current professional terms can be located and appreciated. By taking an etymological approach, I have sought to emphasize that many of the entries contain words and phrases that have experienced significant shifts in meaning. In many cases they can be seen to be the semantic sites of contested concepts, complex ideas and political debates.

The book is primarily directed at those who wish to acquire a coherent overview of the current discussions and debates surrounding housing policy and practice. It provides a reference source for all those who are currently working in the housing field as well as those who are seeking to work there whether in a professional, voluntary or political capacity. I have paid particular attention to the needs of that growing group of people who engage with housing organizations as lay members of boards of management and governance committees, including tenant and resident activists and elected representatives of local authorities.

In both the local government and voluntary housing sectors there is a strong culture of staff training and education. Some of this activity involves in-house programmes designed to enhance corporate coherence. This volume will support such work as well as supporting employee induction programmes. It can be used by experienced staff moving into new fields or pursuing a programme of continuing professional development. It also provides contextual information for those practitioners who are required to write reports on strategic issues for board or executive meetings.

As well as serving the needs of students who are following qualifying or exempting diploma and degree courses that lead to membership of the Chartered Institute of Housing, the Royal Institution of Chartered Surveyors and the Royal Town Planning Institute, the book will be of interest to those following academic courses in social and public administration and to the general reader concerned with issues relating to community development, citizenship, the built environment and public affairs. Students will find the text a useful resource in planning essays and dissertations and for initiating a literature search.

The length of an entry should not be regarded as a measure of its importance. Some of the longer entries are those where the ideas or information are in common use but often poorly understood (e.g. *capital and revenue* and *value for money*). Some are more emergent than established, and therefore more difficult to engage with, or are more philosophical and theoretical, and therefore require a more discursive commentary (e.g. *affordability, anti-social behaviour* and *culture*). Where detailed facts are readily accessible on government or other established websites, or where things are constantly changing (e.g. prices, rates of interest, regulations), the reader is normally directed to current sources rather than being provided with data and information that will become out of date.

Although the primary focus is on social housing, key aspects of all housing sectors are included. This is not only because social housing professionals and their clients often have to engage with the other sectors, but also because social housing policy is, to some considerable extent, determined by what is happening in the wider world.

The multifaceted nature of housing means that reforms or changes in one policy area are likely to impact on other policy areas. The transformation of theory into practice is a politically managed transition: one that often results in the creation of unintended consequences. It is not simply that the 'devil is in the detail', but all too often there are also unexpected 'imps in the implementation'. A common criticism of much recent policy change is that it is not 'joined up' or properly thought through. An effort has been made to cross-reference entries so that the theoretical and operational links between policies and practices can be better understood.

To aid discussion and debate, much of the content is organized around generic themes such as 'affordability', 'value for money', 'diversity', 'quality' that are constantly used by policy makers and practitioners and have come to have particular meanings in the context of housing policy and practice. The text consciously complements rather than replicates the function of an internet search engine. It is more than an arbitrary list of referenced terms and definitions. The selection of entries encourages its use as a tool for learning, research and further reading rather than as a simple dictionary and jargon buster. Most entries relate the practical/operational to the conceptual/theoretical.

a

accountability

SEE ALSO accounts; allocations; audit; choice; finance; governance; housing market; participation; regulation; social housing

Social housing is, by definition, an administered arrangement and market forces cannot be relied upon to hold landlords to account for the ways in which they build, allocate and manage their homes. The question is 'Who or what should hold them to account?' Housing association and arm's length management organisation (ALMO) policies and practices are steered and monitored by boards of management that may include nominated members of a local authority (LA) and tenants as well as independent appointees. Because they receive some support from public funds, local authorities, ALMOs and registered housing associations are also subjected to systems of external *regulation*.

Those social landlords who borrow a proportion of their *development finance* from private sources need to demonstrate to lenders that the borrowed money is properly managed and that they have adequate collateral to cover their debts.

During the second half of the twentieth century, there was much debate amongst politicians and academics about the extent to which social landlords should be accountable to their tenants. This housing debate should be seen in a broader context in which society's attitude towards *welfare* provision, in general, gradually changed from one of outright paternalism to one of managed consumerism. Paul Reeves (2005) has made the point that in the early decades of the century the idea that welfare recipients should be seen as active 'customers' or 'clients' with rights to have some say in how publicly funded (or subsidized) services should be managed would have been seen to be inappropriate: as 'applicants' they were regarded as passive receivers of services defined by others. With the introduction of 'co-regulation' in 2010, the position of residents as an 'accountable authority' has been formally strengthened.

KEY TEXTS
- Reeves, P. (2005) *An Introduction to Social Housing* (London: Elsevier Butterworth, Heinemann)
- Reeves, P. (2014) *Affordable and Social Housing: Policy and Practice* (New York: Routledge)
- http://www.housing-ombudsman.org.uk/http://www.tpas.org.uk/
- European network for Housing Research: http://www.enhr.net/

accounts

SEE ALSO **accountability; capital and revenue; governance; value**

The word 'account' has been in common use since the thirteenth century and over time it has accumulated various shades of meaning. In its financial context, it carried a sense of 'narration' so that account records were seen to tell a story of how money flows were received and spent. In its simplest conception, this 'telling a story' in figures is still the function of accounts. Recorded number calculations were, from an early stage, seen as the key to monitoring the activities of those who held money in trust or were in some way responsible for the good management of financial resources. The word was eventually extended from specific explanations of money transaction to wider narratives of justification, leading to the notion that people and organizations in public life need to 'give an account' of their overall activities and behaviour.

Today we live in a money economy and every commercial, charitable or voluntary organization needs to acquire and spend money in order to achieve its purposes. The production of audited accounts is a crucial part of the procedure by which those who manage an organization are made accountable for their actions to some authority such as a body of shareholders, a management committee, councillors, a funding agency or local tax payers.

types and styles of accounts

Most organizations produce annual accounts and some are legally required to do so. During the year, the organization will record all of its financial transactions and at the end of the year these records will be used to produce the final accounts. In a purely commercial business, the total income minus total expenditure in a given accounting period is called a 'profit' or 'loss'. In a not-for-profit business, it is called a 'surplus' or 'deficit'.

The final accounts consist of records that show the income and expenditure for the year and a balance sheet that lists the assets and liabilities held by the organization at the year-end. An asset is a resource that results from past activities and from which future economic benefits are expected to flow. The assets held will include such things as buildings and land, stocks of goods and debts owed to the organization. Liabilities are current obligations arising from past activities, the settlement of which are expected to result in an outflow of money from the accounts. The liabilities will include the amounts owed by the organization to others in respect of capital (e.g. loans outstanding) and revenue commitments (sundry creditors).

Although all organizations produce accounts and balance sheets, this does not mean that these all look alike or contain the same sort of information: the style of the accounts used will be determined by the needs of the organization. For example, the accounts of a company will contain details of its trading activities, profits made and distributions to shareholders. The accounts of a local authority will detail expenditure and income associated with the various services that it has a duty or power to provide, together with local tax receipts and Exchequer *subsidies*. Owner-occupiers are not required to keep accounts as they are not responsible to others for their housing decisions, but they may choose to keep records for their own information.

Basic Accounting Concepts and Principles
See also 'depreciation' and 'impairment' under the entry 'capital'.

prudence
Accounts are prepared according to the prudence principle. This means that, as far as possible, accountants work with facts rather than opinion, and with past events rather than with future ones. Most accounts are prepared on an historic basis and use market-related values. The period for which the accounts are prepared (usually a year) is called 'the accounting period'. Because accounts do not deal

with the future directly, those wishing to make use of them for planning purposes can only refer to them to identify trends from transactions that have taken place in previous accounting periods.

consistency

Accounting consistency across any particular economic sector or industry is managed by reference to a Statement of Recommended Practice (SORP). To ensure a degree of consistency across national barriers, the SORPs take some account of international practices, but their intention is to provide recommendations for how accounts should be kept, how financial reports should be presented and how to account for nationally focused, sector-specific transactions.

SORPs are issued and regularly updated by bodies recognized by the Financial Reporting Council (FRC) for that purpose. The FRC is the United Kingdom's independent regulator responsible for promoting high-*quality* corporate *governance.*

Accounting for registered social landlords is a specialist activity and SORPs for the sector are issued by the National Housing Federation (NHF), Community Housing Cymru, the Scottish Federation of Housing Associations (SFHA) and the Northern Ireland Federation of Housing Associations (NIFHA). The Dublin body is the Irish Council of Social Housing (ICSH).

clarity and precision

Housing associations are now (since 2013) required to implement new 'component accounting' rules that require them to keep financial account of constituent components for discrete subgroups of properties. This means that the accounts must distinguish the values and depreciation rates between different elements such as windows, doors, boilers and so on, for different property types.

effectiveness and relevance

In the early part of the twenty-first century, as part of its 'modernizing programme', the government introduced reforms to its own accounting procedures that put them more in line with those operating in the private sector.

At the heart of these reforms was a shift in emphasis away from 'cash accounting' to 'resource accounting'. The reforms were intended to make departmental spending more 'business-like' by taking account of the real resource implications that follow from financial decisions. This approach has now been extended to local government and all organizations or agencies that received financial support from the Exchequer.

The idea of resource accounting (and budgeting) is that the accounting records should be kept in such a way that the information they contain helps organizations in making decisions about how best to allocate scarce resources between competing ends. That is, resource accounting seeks to present information in a way that will enable managers to make optimal decisions about the use of the valuable and limited resources under their control. Optimal decision-making requires clarity about the objectives of the decision-makers. It cannot be understood simply by reference to the records of cash flows that have been made in a given accounting period: it needs to consider the real results of spending and investment decisions. In particular, it requires managers and auditors to be able to assess the actual outcomes of their decisions against the planned-for outcomes. Resource accounting seeks to provide information that will help the organization to judge the extent to which its investment of funds has been effective. In this context, the notion of 'effectiveness' has a particular meaning (see *value for money*).

matching

In a commercial setting, 'profitability' is widely used as the measure of successful resource budgeting. Housing agencies, however, are usually more concerned with managerial effectiveness than with crude commercial profitability. In assessing the extent to which it is optimizing the use of its resources, an organization needs to match inputs and outputs and effort with accomplishment by comparing what was planned for to what actually happened.

accruals

As well as embracing the 'matching principle', the effective measure of commercial or social profit and loss also requires accounts to be kept in accordance with the 'accruals concept'. This states that to acquire a true profit and loss picture for a specific period (e.g. a financial year), revenues and costs should be recognized as they are earned or incurred, rather than as they are received or paid out (as occurs in the cash-flow approach). For example, if it costs £50,000 a year to *rent* a building, then an expense of £50,000 has to be recognized each year regardless of how or when the rent is paid. If, for example, it is paid biannually in advance, the accruals principle states that it would be inappropriate to charge £100,000 as an expense for year one. An 'accrued charge' is an expense that has been incurred at a particular date but not yet invoiced or paid. An accrued revenue is an income that has been earned but not yet recorded.

The accruals principle requires the impact of investing in a capital asset to be discounted over the asset's useful life. Accruals accounting has the effect of reducing the recorded cost in the first year of investment and enables a longer-term rational view of the investment's financial viability to be taken (see *capital and revenue*).

KEY TEXTS
- Atrill, P. and McLaney, E. (2012) *Accounting and Finance for Non-specialists* (Hemel Hempstead: Pearson). This is a popular, well-received text that is regularly updated. It provides the layperson with a clear introduction to the basics of accounting and structure of standard accounts
- Most social landlords also publish simplified summaries of their spending and investments in their annual reports to stakeholders
- Smith and Williamson (2014) *Finance Demystified: A Guide for Housing Association Board Members and Non-finance Executives* (London: NHF)

affordability

SEE ALSO **low cost home ownership; low income households; merit goods and services; mortgages; need and demand; planning gain; proprietary interests; rent; subsidies; welfare**

Although the notion has long been at the forefront of the housing policy debate, there is no universally accepted definition for 'affordability'. Without such a definition, it is not possible to produce any officially accepted statistics measuring the number of households living in 'unaffordable' housing.

The question of affordability arises from the fact that, for many people, good *quality* housing is expensive relative to their 'disposable incomes'.

Affordability only became a policy issue when the State began to pass housing and public health legislation that defined minimum levels of housing provision as part of national policy. If the State was prepared to allow those on low incomes to live in mean, insanitary and over-crowded hovels, the affordability question would not arise.

There are three broad ways of analysing affordability. These are

1. the ratio approach;
2. the benchmark approach; and
3. the residual approach.

The ratio approach considers the proportion of household income devoted to housing costs. The benchmark approach considers what is affordable by reference to some fixed level of expenditure that is assumed to be reasonable. The residual approach considers the financial resources that remain available to a household once the *rent* or *mortgage* payment and other housing costs have been met.

affordable housing

The phrase 'affordable housing' is often used fairly loosely to mean housing that people in low-paid employment can afford to rent or buy. At different times attempts have been made to stipulate some sort of guide figure but no government, academic or professional agency has ever established a clear, unambiguous, lasting definition as such. In European countries attempts at a definition have tended to use some percentage of the market price or rent. Housing experts make the point that affordability is not simply a rent/price issue and that a home's running costs (particularly its energy costs) should be taken into account.

affordable home ownership

A crude house price-to-earnings ratio is sometimes used as a general measure of affordability in this sector. Reference to such a measure helps to emphasize the cyclical nature of inflation in house prices and shows that the point at which the household gained access to the *tenure* in part determines the costs of *home ownership*. However, because most owners acquire their first homes by taking out a variable interest mortgage loan, interest rates as well as purchase prices affect the month-by-month costs of occupation. Indeed, to make meaningful cross-tenure or inter-household comparisons, it is necessary to conceive of the costs of owner-occupation not so much in terms of the purchase price but rather in terms of the week-by-week outgoings that the household has to pay in order to maintain its occupancy. In addition to loan interest payments, these outgoings will include building insurance premiums. The costs of owner-occupation might also be considered to include the opportunity costs of any capital invested in the property and some actual or notional annual sum that is (or is assumed to be) set aside for repairs and maintenance. To avoid problems such as negative *equity* and repossession, new Financial Conduct Authority Affordability Rules requiring viability appraisals to take place were institutionalized into mortgage agreements in 2014.

implications for practice
- What counts as 'affordable housing' is largely defined locally under the guidance of the National Planning Policy Framework (NPPF). This highly generalized guidance was introduced in 2012 and it abandoned all attempts to provide an overarching official definition.
- As well as simplifying the planning system, the new approach is intended to shift the emphasis away from central prescription to local perception. There is now an anticipation that, to a large extent, the definition and provision of affordable homes be left to local planning authorities that are expected to develop a Local Planning Framework (LPF). As part of its LPF, an authority may produce Local Action Plans (LAPs) that focus on the housing needs (both market and social) of specific communities.
- From April 2011, the government made significant changes to the rules around *social housing*. One of these changes involved the introduction of rents that are nearer to market rents. These are called 'affordable rents' and are intended to be higher than typical social rents and lower than market rents. Social landlords who wish to continue to receive grant funding to help develop and build homes for future residents are now required to enter into a contract to agree to let newly built homes and a proportion of existing homes at an 'affordable rent'. This tenure allows associations to charge up to 80 per cent of local market rent on new homes built as part of the 'affordable homes programme' and on some homes converted to 'affordable rent' when they become vacant.

- Increasingly, there is an appreciation that 'affordability' is not simply a rent-related factor. In particular, social landlords, as well as architects and builders, are now seeking to instigate design features and propagate behavioural changes that will reduce domestic energy costs.

KEY TEXTS
- For a clear and concise summary of the political background to the affordable housing debate, see the latest edition of Lund B. (2011) *Understanding Housing Policy* (Bristol: The Polity Press)
- For a complete discussion and further reading on the private sector's contribution to the provision of affordable housing, see the Montague Report, DCLG (2012)
- For an overview of the new arrangements regarding 'affordable rents', refer to Wilson, W. (2011) 'Affordable Rent Model', House of Commons Library, Social Policy Section, Standard Note SN/SP/5933, DCLG
- Most local authorities outline their approach to current planning regulations on their websites
- Oxley, M. (2004) *Economics, Planning and Housing* (Basingstoke: Palgrave Macmillan), Chapter 8

allocations

SEE ALSO **choice; culture; housing market; need and demand; subsidies**

The word 'allocate' comes from the Latin 'ad-' 'to' + 'locare' 'to place'. In its original meaning, it carries both a sense of active positioning and some form of dependency relationship – 'I allocate this to you.' This authoritative approach to distribution is well entrenched in the history of subsidized and *social housing*. Ancient alms house trusts were typically set up by wealthy benefactors who stipulated allocation criteria that identified needy (and often 'worthy') individuals who might qualify for residency by virtue of being destitute, old, or possessing some other characteristic such as a craft affiliation or religious allegiance. Some of these foundations predated the Elizabethan Poor Law system that incorporated both outdoor relief and residential support for the destitute. Because the Poor Law and its subsequent arrangements were financed by parishes, residency qualifications became a prominent feature in the early history of social housing allocations.

After the First World War, the emerging council housing provision was administered by local authorities. The excess of demand over supply in most areas meant that authorities needed to apply rationing processes to their allocation systems. This typically produced a dualistic approach that incorporated a queuing principle in the form of a waiting list, coupled with a needs assessment principle in the form of priority points that were weighted to reflect the intensity of an individual's needs. Local authorities retain a responsibility for assessing the housing needs in their areas and most continue to exercise allocation rights to *dwellings* managed by stock transfer housing associations.

Arguably one of the most subtle, value-laden shifts in modern social housing policy is the move from 'needs-based' to 'choice-based' lettings for affordable rented housing. Since the 1980s, British governments have gradually adopted an allocation approach to a range of publicly supported services (notably health and housing) that emphasizes user *choice* and is associated with the notion of 'New Public Management'.

In the owner-occupier and private-rented sectors, allocation is largely determined by the interplay of market forces.

implications for practice
- Within the social housing policy debate, there is a long-standing discussion about the role that local connections should play in the allocation of homes. As mentioned earlier, under the old Poor Law arrangements, it was the parish that paid for the relief and this fact established an early concern that resources should be targeted at people who could demonstrate an allegiance to the locality. This 'political instinct' that 'foreigners' (including non-locals) should not be given priority remains deeply seated in the social psyche of some established communities and is often discernable in the popular and local media. Local connections are still given consideration but, in a modern economy, mobility of labour is often regarded as an important economic issue, and for this reason it is sometimes not given a high priority. 'Local connection' is defined in Part VII of the Housing Act 1996.
- Prior to the 2011 Localism Act, almost anyone could apply to live in social housing. As social housing is in great demand

and priority is given to those most in need, many applicants had no realistic prospect of ever receiving a social home. The previous arrangements encouraged false expectations and large waiting lists. The Act gives local authorities greater freedom to set their own policies about who should qualify to go on the waiting list in their areas. This means that they are now able, if they wish, to prevent people whom they judge to have 'no need' of social housing from joining the waiting list. Authorities are still obliged to ensure that social homes go to the most vulnerable in society and those who need it most.

- Choice-based lettings (CBL) schemes are designed to introduce an element of choice for people who apply for council and housing association homes. It is an initiative supported by the regional governments that is designed to allow people applying for a home (including existing tenants who want a transfer) to bid for properties that become available on a points-based system. The fundamental theory behind CBLs is that applicants need to take the initiative in securing a dwelling.

- No CBL system is exactly alike but there are some common features of those currently operating. Typically, applicants first register with the landlord or regional scheme (i.e. group of landlords). The scheme administrators then assess the applicant and award a 'priority pass'. All properties are advertised as they become vacant and applicants who are interested in the property inform the administrators. An individual list is made of all bids received for each advertised property and then an assessment is made that considers all applicants interested in the property. The property is offered to the applicant with the highest priority pass. If two applicants have the same priority pass weightings, the home is offered to the applicant with the oldest pass. Landlords or their agents give feedback on lettings outcomes to help applicants understand their likelihood of success when bidding for other properties.

KEY TEXTS

- Bramley, G., Munro, M. and Pawson, H. (2004) *Key Issues in Housing: Policies and Markets in 21st-Century Britain* (Basingstoke: Palgrave Macmillan), Chapter 8

- Reeves, P. (2014) *Affordable and Social Housing: Policy and Practice* (New York: Routledge)
- Local authority websites

anti-social behaviour

SEE ALSO housing law; nudge theory; partnerships

The government defines anti-social behaviour as any aggressive, intimidating or destructive activity that damages or destroys another person's *quality* of life (Home Office, 2013). Such behaviour may or may not be criminal: the point being that it is likely to cause harassment, alarm or distress to members of the public. In housing practice, it is the common term used to describe incidents or actions that cause damage or affect the quality of people's life in a *community*. These include vandalism, graffiti, abusive language and other instances of intimidation. It also includes a range of minor neighbourhood nuisances such as dropping litter and dog fouling in public places.

Arguably, the most famous and most often-quoted approach to policy formation in this field was Tony Blair's prosaic pronouncement that his government would seek to be 'tough on crime and tough on the causes of crime' (1997 Labour Party Manifesto). The current debate about the causes of, and ways of tackling, this problem embraces a number of fields of study including law, policing, politics, moral philosophy, psychology, sociology, biology, architectural design, *welfare* economics and statistics. Much of the academic literature on the topic is discipline-focused and therefore takes place within a particular discursive paradigm. Many argue, however, that the multi-disciplinary nature of the problem also points to the need for effective remedies to involve a multi-agency approach.

Tilley (2005) suggests that clear thinking about the topic involves finding ways of classifying different forms of prevention methods. By referencing a number of contemporary authors, it is possible to identify a variety of conceptual classifications within the literature. A well-established classification is that originally proffered by Brantingham and Faust (1976) that distinguishes between 'primary', 'secondary' and 'tertiary' prevention, referring respectively to preventing an act occurring in the first place, discouraging those who might become involved from doing so and dealing with those who are already exhibiting anti-social behaviour. Cross-cutting these conceptual categories, the Home Office points to various preventive 'mechanisms' (Tilley *et al.*, 2004) that include 'situational', 'social', 'individual treatment' and 'policing/ criminal justice' mechanisms.

Housing practitioners and other professionally involved agents, such as architects, planners and the police, tend to consider the issue by making reference to causal factors that are overtly operational in character. The professional practice literature highlights factors such as poor physical designing of properties and estates, ineffective landlord and tenant relations, a lack of community engagement and deficient inter-agency collaboration.

implications for practice

- A prominent theme amongst both academic and practice commentators is the need for speedy intervention. An idea that has been particularly influential has become known as the 'broken windows' approach. This came into prominence in 1982 with the publication of a journal article by Wilson and Kelling. With its use of 'broken windows' as a metaphor, the argument here is that a failure to respond quickly to a series of minor misdemeanours signals a lack of community concern that can have a cumulative affect that eventually leads to physical deterioration and rising crime rates. Critics of the 'broken widows' approach argue that it fails to take full account of all the underlying structural characteristics of a neighbourhood such as a low level of employment, social alienation, a high level of household debt and poor community cohesion.

- The Crime and Disorder Act 1998 (Sections 5–7) established local 'community safety partnerships' (CSPs), sometimes called 'crime reduction partnerships', with a view to creating a framework for effective inter-agency approaches to deal with the local issues in this field. CSPs are made up of representatives from the 'responsible authorities' including the police, local authorities, fire and rescue authorities, the probation service and health and housing agencies. The responsible authorities work together to protect their local communities from crime and to help people feel safer. They work out how to deal with local issues associated with anti-social behaviour, as well as drug and alcohol misuse and reoffending. They annually assess local crime priorities and consult partners and the local community about how to deal with them.

- Under the provisions of the Anti-Social Behaviour, Crime and Policing Act (2014), the police, local authorities and housing associations have been given new powers to tackle anti-social behaviour and make neighbourhoods safer. The legislation seeks to achieve this by introducing simpler, more effective powers that provide better protection for victims and communities. It introduces the idea of a 'community trigger' that will operate to empower victims and communities to have a greater say in how agencies respond to complaints of anti-social behaviour and out-of-court sanctions for offenders.

- The new legislation has remodelled the existing system of civil injunctions designed to clamp down on anti-social behaviour. Since their introduction in 1998, Anti-Social Behaviour Orders (ASBOs) have been both a prominent and a controversial feature of the policing/criminal justice mechanisms for dealing with serious nuisance offences committed by adults and children over ten years of age. ASBOs have now been replaced with new civil injunctions. Under this arrangement, if anti-social behaviour occurs near a property, or affects the housing management functions of the landlord, the court may grant an injunction to prevent nuisance or annoyance (IPNA) against a person aged ten or over. The new rules have been criticized by the Children's Commissioner and other commentators, because they could be used to widen the definition of anti-social behaviour by reducing the burden of proof. The concern is that this might promote intolerance of youth by shifting the definition to include low-level unruliness and that in so doing everyday activities, such as skateboarding and ball games, might be outlawed in certain locations.

- Although the justice system focuses on restraining and deterrence approaches to the problem, the police have been in the forefront of advocating spatial planning and design principles to help improve community safety and reduce the fear of crime. This work is rooted in 1980s' Home Office research led by Alice Coleman and, prior to that, American ideas developed in the 1970s by Oscar Newman and others. This has resulted in the *development* of a set of principles entitled 'Secure by Design' that can be consulted by those seeking guidance on how to improve security on estates and areas that are vulnerable to opportunistic criminal and anti-social behaviour. This guidance highlights the need for natural surveillance and designing roads and footpaths so they are overlooked. In such ways, the design of housing layouts can make a major contribution both to the prevention of crime and reducing the fear of crime. These design features include secure vehicle parking, adequate lighting of communal areas, fostering a sense of ownership of the local environment, control of access to individual and common curtilages, defensible space and landscape design supporting natural surveillance and safety.

KEY TEXTS

- Burney, E. (2009) *Making People Behave: Anti-social Behaviour, Politics and Policy* (Devon: Willan Publishing)
- Coleman, A. (1985) *Utopia on Trial: Vision and Reality in Planned Housing* (London: Hilary Shipman Ltd). Revised edition now available
- Newman, O. (1973) *Defensible Space: People and Design in the Violent City* (London: Architectural Press)
- See supplement to *Inside Housing* October 2014 for an outline of the provisions of the Crime and Policing Act (2014) as they apply to housing practice
- Tilley, N. (ed.) (2005) *Handbook of Crime Prevention and Community Safety* (Devon: Willan Publishing)
- Housing Quality Network. http://hqnetwork.co.uk/
- The Community Safety Journal/Safer Communities
- http://www.securedbydesign.com/pdfs/SBD-principles.pdf
- https://www.gov.uk/asbo
- https://www.gov.uk/browse/housing/noise-neighbours
- www.crimereduction.gov.uk

asset management

SEE ALSO accounts; business planning; capital and revenue; finance; quality; risk and uncertainty; value; welfare

assets
The word 'asset' has its origins in the Old French use 'asez' (enough). By the fourteenth century, the phrase 'have assets' was used to indicate that a person owned property that was sufficient to meet his or her debts and other financial liabilities. It maintains this use in modern legal and accounting parlance where it is used to refer to all the physical and financial resources available to meet personal or corporate debt.

'Tangible assets' are those property and other real assets that the organization needs in order to run its affairs. They take physical forms such as buildings, machinery and land in use. In a retail chain, for example, the main tangible assets will be the stock of shops and associated offices. In a university they will include things such as teaching rooms, laboratories, common rooms, offices and so on. In a housing organization, they will include things such as its stock of houses, offices, fleet of vehicles, equipment and so on. The anticipated net yield derived from the ownership of a tangible asset in a given accounting period is called the Expected Net Return (ENR). Where the tangible asset is a dwelling, the ENR may be calculated as:

Rent + other revenues derived from operating the asset (e.g. revenue grants) + capital appreciation – operating costs (including depreciation).

For accounting purposes, tangible assets have to be distinguished from investment assets. Accounting conventions require tangible assets to be depreciated through time (unlike investment and financial assets) to ensure that proper account is taken of their long-run refurbishment and replacement needs.

'Investment assets' comprise money reserves and any land bank that the enterprise might possess. 'Financial assets' include financial instruments such as stocks, bonds, bank deposits and the like. For a social landlord, its future net rents can also be regarded as part of its financial assets. The present *value* of those future net rents provide a measure of the organization's ability to service debt.

asset management
In the context of housing administration, 'asset management' generally refers to the practices and processes involved in producing, acquiring, maintaining and disposing of the organization's tangible assets. As with any area of business activity, sound asset management has both a strategic and an operational dimension. Strategic housing asset management is concerned with more than a programme of repairs and improvements. It seeks to provide a policy framework within which to make decisions about retaining, maintaining, improving, developing and selling properties. In its widest conception, it looks to how the tangible assets can best be used to help deliver the organization's mission and vision. In particular, the asset management policy seeks to ensure that the current and future stock of assets is of the right type, in the right location and meets current and future standards and aspirations.

The professional practice and academic literatures include a good deal of comment about the distinction between 'response' and 'planned' maintenance and how an appropriate mix of both needs to be integrated into asset management activities. Some housing analysts distinguish between 'primary' and 'secondary' maintenance as a way of discussing how they are dealt with and paid for. Primary maintenance comprises all works that are necessary to keep the dwelling safe and 'fit for purpose'.

implications for practice
- Net Present Value calculations are normally used when assessing the financial performance of individual properties and groups of property types and locations.
- An issue facing many landlords is the lack of 'fit' between household needs and the current stock (e.g. shortage of certain types of dwelling). This problem has been exacerbated by recent *welfare* reforms such as the so-called 'bedroom tax' that has increased the demand for smaller *dwellings*.
- Tenant satisfaction surveys indicate that the responsiveness and effectiveness of a landlord's repairs and maintenance service is at, or close to, the top of most tenants' concerns.

- Because property managers are dealing with valuable physical assets, it is important that when making a major decision (such as whether to renew a run down building through redevelopment or through rehabilitation), they confront the 'time–cost dilemma' (Garnett, 2000). The time–cost dilemma arises because buildings are durable assets and money has a 'time value'. This poses a dilemma for those making decisions about how much to invest in any building project.

This notion focuses on two fundamental, 'opportunity cost' questions.

- Should the building(s) in question be renewed to a high standard or a low standard or something in between?
- Is it worthwhile spending more now on the renewal in order to save costs later on?

Renewing buildings is expensive and there will always be pressure to cut costs and do the job 'cheaply'. However, when put into a longer time frame (e.g. over the economic life of the building, or the term of the loan taken out to pay for the works), it may be possible to demonstrate that raising the specification will save money in the long run. These savings might take the form of reduced repair bills or improved energy efficiency, or less time spent on dealing with complaints and so on. Furthermore, spending more 'upfront' may bring about important intangible benefits such as increased tenant satisfaction or an improved image for the organization. The possibility of achieving these future cost savings and intangible benefits poses a dilemma for the decision-makers. This 'time–cost dilemma' poses the two crucial questions mentioned earlier that might be reformulated thus: Should we increase our spending NOW in order to gain cost savings and other benefits in the FUTURE or should we do the job 'adequately' but more cheaply and thereby conserve our CURRENT reserves and/or minimize FUTURE loan service charges?

Although stock maintenance and improvement is a key issue for all landlords, specific operational issues and priorities will vary widely from landlord to landlord. At any one time, a particular provider might be confronted with challenging problems relating to things such as sub-standard non-traditional units (e.g. 'Cornish' PRC, Unity PRC, Reema PRC), under-utilization of communal facilities in its sheltered housing schemes, difficult-to-let high-rise units, asbestos in early post-war dwellings, stock location problems (stock in the wrong place), a backlog of repairs and improvement works, skilled staff shortages and contractor problems. Such a list (which is indicative only) substantiates the need for both a well thought-out strategic approach and a high level of skilled operational management. In short, asset management is at the very heart of effective housing management.

KEY TEXTS
- Garnett (1994) *To Redevelop or Rehabilitate? A CBA Approach to Decision-making* (Bristol: UWE). Republished as *The Needleman Rule* (2015) by Leaping Frog Publications at: http://leapingfrogpublications. co.uk/housing-society
- For a fuller discussion on types of maintenance, see the RICS and CIH websites.

audit

SEE ALSO accountability; accounts; continuous improvement; governance; risk and uncertainty; value for money

The word 'audit' comes from the Latin 'audire' 'to hear' and has been used since the early fifteenth century to refer to the process of officially examining financial *accounts*, a procedure that was originally an oral activity.

Much contemporary auditing practice is founded on the good *governance* principles laid out in the Turnbull Report (1999). These emphasize the need for effective control systems, such as internal audits, that give a priority to risk identification and amelioration. Official audits are expected to be systematic, thorough and carried out by professionally qualified firms or individuals. Internal and external audits have somewhat different functions.

'External auditors' are independent of the organization and are primarily concerned with ensuring that financial statements and other number-based accounts of the organization's performance present a correct representation of the financial position for the period under review. As a result, external auditors will focus on recorded information relating to revenues, expenses and liabilities. They will also examine and comment on the effectiveness of control procedures that impact on these areas.

'Internal auditors' work within an organization and report to its senior staff and audit committee and/or directors. They help to design the company's organizing systems and comment on specific risk management policies. They also ensure that all policies implemented for risk management are operating effectively. The work of the internal auditor tends to be continuous and based both on the internal control systems of the business and its *quality* assurance processes.

implications for practice
- The main function of any audit is to create, develop and maintain management and monitoring systems that assure probity.
- Internal audits should also 'add value' to the organization's operations by encouraging and guiding *continuous improvement* plans and enhancing *value for money* by critiquing managerial and administrative processes and procedures.
- In housing organizations, the internal audit aids the drafting of 'annual efficiency statements' and other regulatory/compliance documentation.
- Audits provide senior management and the board or governing committee with an independent and objective opinion about the adequacy of the organization's control arrangements, risk management practices and governance protocols and procedures. This opinion forms part of the framework of assurances that the board and its audit committee receives and should be used to inform the annual Statement on Internal Control.

KEY TEXTS
- Garnett, D. (2015) *What Is Audit? An Introduction to Auditing in Housing Organisations.* http://www.leapingfrogpublications.co.uk/housing-society
- National Housing Federation (2014a) *Understanding Assurances: A Guide for Housing Association Board Members*

- National Housing Federation (2014b) *Countering Fraud: A Guide for Housing Association Board Members*
- Smith and Williamson (2014) *Finance Demystified: A Guide for Housing Association Board Members and Non-finance Executives* (London: NHF)

b

business planning

SEE ALSO accountability; continuous improvement; culture; perform-ance monitoring; regulation; social returns; value; value for money

Broadly speaking, a business plan is a proposal for achieving some-thing. Because such documents are written with a variety of audi-ences in mind, housing organizations normally create a number of versions, each written in a different style and each incorporating different amounts of information and levels of analysis.

Tenants and leaseholders, boards of management, lending institutions, grant providers and the various regulators all expect a *social housing* provider to operate in a coherent, responsible and 'business-like' manner. These stakeholders require evidence of performance-based objectives, results-orientated outputs and finan-cial viability. These three business markers are commonplace in the private sector that has developed a battery of tools and techniques to use in seeking to achieve them. The problem is that traditional business tools do not always sit comfortably in an externally regu-lated public interest setting in which the primary objectives and outputs are social rather than commercial. This means that private sector business planning techniques have to be adapted so that the housing enterprise can take proper account of the fact that it has wider *community* responsibilities as well as financial goals.

The key version of the business plan will be that operated by the organization's management teams, whose focus will be on the rela-tionship between strategic objectives and the operational practices that move the business towards the achievement of those objectives. Business planning is an active process and a business plan is not an end in itself: it is a provisional framework for action. When the focus is on activity, attention is moved from 'product' to 'process' – from the idea of a static plan to the idea of a dynamic planning process. This means that an effective 'plan' will bring together a collection of documents pointing to action.

Long-term strategic goals are normally designed around mission statements. These statements tend to be written in a language that is more aspirational than technical. They usually incorporate an analysis of the organization's underlying values (that gives its activities a moral orientation) and a description of its operational *culture* (that gives its actions an ethical orientation). As well as providing a moral and ethical orientation for action, mission statements should succinctly summarize the business's overriding purpose. The corporate strategy is then grounded in this publicly declared mission. The strategic plan typically identifies four planning levels that can be represented by the acronym MOST:

Mission   **O**bjectives   **S**trategy   **T**actics

Objectives are specific goals that need to be achieved in order to fulfil the mission: they constitute the various priorities, projects and activities that naturally flow from the mission. Strategy describes how the objectives will be achieved, and in so doing it specifies key policy directions and identifies the real and financial resources needed. Usually there are a variety of approaches to delivering policies and acquiring and using resources. The organization therefore also needs to consider its tactics. Tactics determine what the business does on a day-to-day basis to achieve its objectives. Tactics determine immediate actions.

In order to progress the strategy, the organization will need to translate it into a more detailed corporate or company plan that sets out operational objectives and tangible targets for the medium term. In turn, to achieve these corporate objectives and hit these targets, the various sections and departments within the organization will need to devise detailed action plans of their own to guide their immediate and short-term programmes of activity. This means that the overall business planning process involves a number of linked documented plans that cascade down from the strategic to the operational level (see Figure 1).

implications for practice
- The business plan is the highest level document. It sets and establishes the key business assumptions and earmarks the

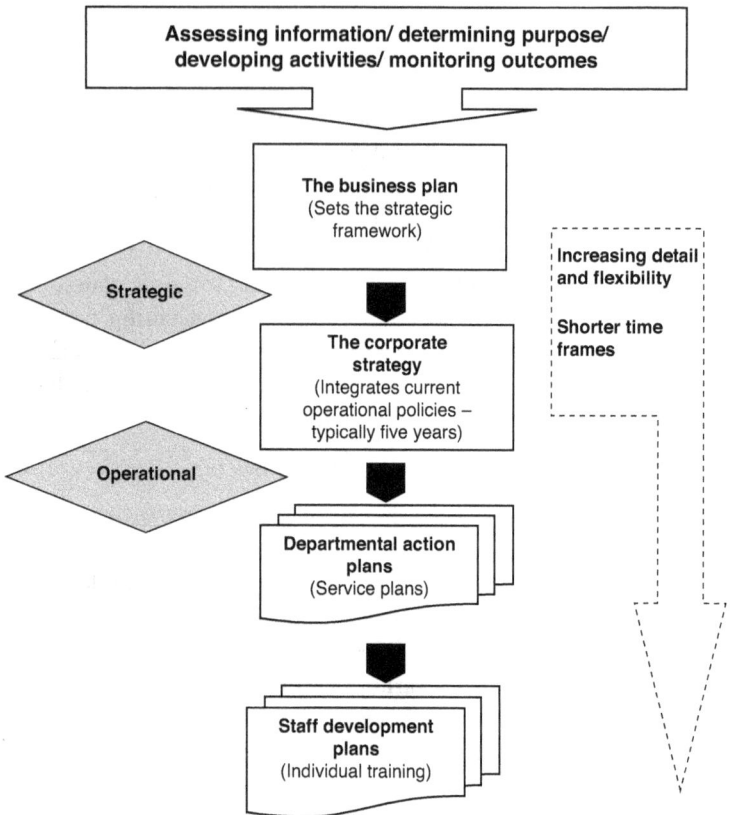

FIGURE I *The overall business planning process*
Source: Based on Garnett and Perry (2005).

budgetary provisions of the organization in the broadest
terms. Business plans have to be financially viable. This
is just as true of regulated social businesses as it is of free
enterprise commercial businesses. Typically, the business
plan looks forward for 30 years and sets the overall prudential
guidelines within which the business has to operate in order to
demonstrate its ability to cover its long-run costs and repay any
major long-term loan liabilities.

• Inevitably, a business plan contains a lot of details. However, the
general purpose of business planning can be summarized by
reference to four key activities:

1. 'Assessing' the organization's current position with regard to its performance, resources and business environment.
2. 'Determining' its priorities and objectives for various planning periods (the long-, intermediate- and short-term).
3. 'Developing' action plans and using its resources to achieve these time-specific aims.
4. 'Monitoring' performance against the plan on a regular basis and feeding back what has been learnt.

These four key aspects of business planning functions permeate the overall planning process.

KEY TEXTS

- Hill, C. W. L. and Jones, G. R. (2001) *Strategic Management*. Latest edition (Boston: Houghton Mifflin, Means Business, Inc.)
- Public versions of housing business plans are accessible on the websites of local authorities, ALMOs and housing associations
- There are a number of popular guides aimed at the small business community; for example, Adams, R. (2003) *The Successful Business Plan*. 4th edn (Palo Alto: The Planning Shop)

c

capital and revenue

SEE ALSO accounts; asset management; cost of housing; dwellings; finance; risk and uncertainty; social returns; value for money

capital

The word 'capital' stems from the Latin 'capitalis' 'relating to the head', and its use in English is traceable back to the early thirteenth century. From the sixteenth and seventeenth centuries it was applied to crimes that headed the list of offences (e.g. murder and treason). On the same basis it was applied to the head city of a country, the most important ships in the navy and to upper case letters that head a sentence. The financial sense (1620s) is from the Latin 'capitale' 'stock/property' (neutral of 'capitalis'). In indicating the wealth of an individual or group, it originally referred to moveable property (as in 'chattels') such as slaves or cattle. By the late eighteenth century, and with the emergence of the Industrial Revolution, its meaning had shifted and had come to refer specifically to the forms of non-moveable wealth that are employed in the processes of production. In this more modern sense a distinction is made between 'fixed capital' that is long-lasting and re-useable and 'circulating capital' that is constantly used up and replenished during production. Capital assets in the form of land and buildings are sometimes referred to as 'real estate'.

'Money capital' refers to the stock of money that is used to acquire real, physical and tangible assets. 'Capital expenditure' refers to the money that is expended on the acquisition or substantial improvement of real assets. The acquired assets are sometimes referred to as 'fixed capital formation'. Fixed capital formation is composed of assets of a relatively permanent nature and, in a housing context, can be thought of largely as anything that increases the quantity or *quality* of the stock of buildings. Such capital is referred to as 'fixed', not because it is immoveable, but because the money capital has become locked into the bricks and mortar and is therefore no longer available to be used immediately. If the organization decides to use its asset wealth on some other project it may have to unlock ('unfix') it so that liquid funds once more become available for use. This is why when a real asset is sold it is said to have been 'liquidated'. In extreme cases, an organization may have to liquidate its real assets in order to settle its debts. 'Liquid capital' refers to cash or other assets that are readily convertible into cash.

The process of planning and evaluating proposals for investment in real capital assets is called 'capital budgeting'. It entails the use of 'opportunity costing' techniques that are designed to ensure that the available money capital is being put to its best possible use. These techniques are necessary because *accounts* are designed to record the past rather than appraise the future. Capital investment is typically facilitated by either committing the organization's accumulated savings to the construction, acquisition or improvement of an asset or by borrowing funds to do so. Surplus revenues and/or grants are sometimes also available for investment purposes.

'Capital expenditure' includes payments made to lawyers, surveyors and other professionals in connection with the purchase of land and existing buildings as well as all the material, labour and other costs incurred in the erection of new buildings. Money spent on converting or improving, as against maintaining and repairing, the existing stock of *dwellings* results in more or better quality housing being available and is therefore regarded as capital expenditure in the same way as money spent on constructing new units is so regarded.

'Capital income' is income that comes from the ownership of capital assets, such as interest received, dividends or any sort of capital gain. It can be thought of as a return on accumulated wealth rather than revenues from providing goods and services. The phrase may also be used to mean any revenue that is used for capital expenditures, although in this sense it is less commonly used.

The money received from selling fixed assets (such as land, buildings, vehicles, plant and equipment) is known as a 'capital receipt'. The government may also specify by *regulation* what constitutes a capital receipt: for example, if a local authority lends money to a third party for capital expenditure, repayment of the amount borrowed must be treated as a capital receipt.

There are recognized 'best practice' restrictions on how a capital receipt should be used. Broadly, sound financial management principles indicate that the money should only be used to repay debt or to pay for new fixed assets. The money may also be invested, pending use in one of these two ways. The extent of government prescription regarding how capital receipts may be used has varied greatly over the years. In particular, governments have, at different times, placed restrictions on how the receipts from council house sales can be utilized, including a requirement that a proportion be clawed back into a central or regional pool. However, in line with 'localism' principles, recent administrations have been inclined to encourage long-term *business planning* by allowing more flexibility in how local authorities and other housing agencies employ their capital receipts so long as they follow the accepted principles of sound financial management.

depreciation

Depreciation measures the reduction in the *value* of an asset with the passage of time, due, in particular, to wear and tear. In the past, social landlords often argued that regular maintenance and periodic refurbishment of their housing properties have the effect of maintaining values thereby eliminating the need to provide for depreciation. With the shift in emphasis towards resource accounting, the Financial Reporting Council no longer accepts this reasoning (see *accounts*). For accounting purposes, *social housing* properties are regarded as 'tangible fixed assets' rather than 'investment assets' (see 'capital income', p. 27). As such, they are primarily valued for their economic usefulness rather than for their potential to appreciate in exchange value. Good accounting practice requires all tangible fixed assets to be depreciated to reflect the consumption of their economic benefit. This requires the social landlords to charge a depreciable amount for their housing properties to the income and expenditure account on a systematic basis over their useful economic lives, which is defined as the period over which the organization expects to derive economic benefits from the asset. A traditionally built new dwelling is normally assumed to have an economic life of 60–80 years (its physical life may well be in excess of this).

A depreciation payment is intended to charge the revenue account with the cost of using the asset, that is, by the amount consumed in providing the service. It includes wear and tear and the effects of obsolescence (resulting from changes in fashion, technology, etc.). It is assumed that each year the effective economic life of the tangible asset is reduced, and it is the value of this 'reduction in useful life' that has to be paid for out of current revenue.

The 'normal' approach to calculating depreciation is the current value of the asset minus its residual value, allocated over the remaining useful economic life of the asset. Because land is not depreciated, the residual value will normally be the land value. Housing regulators tend to argue that the depreciation method should be simple and transparent.

impairment

If conditions change causing a reduction in the recoverable amount of a fixed asset below its carrying value in the balance sheet, this is called 'impairment'. The notion of impairment has to be distinguished from that of depreciation. With the passage of time, factors other than condition obsolescence (e.g. wear and tear) can come into play that can 'impair' the value of a property. In other words, events or changed circumstances may cause the value of the assets to decline at a faster rate than that allowed for by the depreciation methodology. This is a problem because good accounting practice requires the landlord to ensure that properties are not shown in the books at an amount exceeding their exchange value (called the 'recoverable amount'). For this reason, social landlords are required to address the issue of impairment of housing properties in addition to depreciation. The 'recoverable amount' is defined as the higher of their net realizable value and value in use.

The landlord should instigate an impairment review where there is an indication that carrying values may not be recoverable. Examples of events or changed circumstances that might prompt an impairment review include a change in demand for social housing in the area with consequential high void rates and transfer requests. Significant adverse changes in the statutory or regulatory environment might also impact on asset values in the balance sheet.

revenue

The use of the term 'revenue' meaning 'return' (from the Latin 'revenire') in the context of income from property or possessions is long-established. 'Revenue expenditure' is defined as expenditure that is incurred in acquiring consumable and other non-permanent goods and services. This type of spending can be referred to as 'current' or 'consumption expenditure' and is sometimes termed 'running costs' or 'costs-in-use'. In a housing context, it refers to those recurring payments on general administration, loan interest and debt redemption together with those payments made for maintaining, repairing and managing the housing stock. In other words, housing revenue expenditure comprises all outgoings incurred as part of the day-to-day provision of housing services together with that incurred in maintaining the real capital assets in a habitable state. Because the costs of servicing loans taken out to purchase capital items are regarded as part of revenue expenditure, capital expenditure decisions can have significant revenue consequences. 'Revenue income' pays for revenue expenditure. In a housing context, revenue income is derived from rents, service charges, and/ or other trading or employment earnings together with any available investment income or revenue subsidy entitlement. In extreme cases, when a household or agency is unable to pay its recurring revenue costs, creditors may require it to generate the money by liquidating some of its assets.

the relationship between capital and revenue expenditure

The difference between capital and revenue is a theoretical one and, in practice, accounting procedures and conventions sometimes blur the distinction. What gets counted as capital or revenue may, for example, be determined by what funds are available. This has to be kept in mind when considering how various institutions actually classify their expenditure: for example, capital works may be financed from revenue. It is also worth re-emphasizing the point made earlier that capital expenditure decisions will carry with them future revenue commitments, and this is particularly true when money is borrowed because the debt has to be serviced and repaid out of future revenue incomes.

implications for practice

- Compared with revenue spending, capital investment often commits relatively large amounts of money for relatively long periods of time. Furthermore, such decisions tend to be difficult or impossible to reverse once the funds have been committed and the investment project begun (see *risk and uncertainty*).
- In common with other *welfare* agencies, housing organizations need to take account of a wide range of non-financial factors when making capital budgeting decisions (see *social returns*). Housing investment produces valued social returns that are reflected in the findings of tenant satisfaction surveys and in reduced levels of urban disutility such as unemployment, disease and *anti-social behaviour*.

KEY TEXTS

- Smith and Williamson (2014) *Finance Demystified: A Guide for Housing Association Board Members and Non-finance Executives* (London: NHF)
- Woods, F. (2009) *Book-Keeping and Accounts* (Financial Times/ Pitman)

care and support

SEE ALSO choice; low income households; merit goods and services; partnerships; regulation; subsidies; welfare

In professional *welfare* provision, a distinction is usually drawn between the notions of 'care' and 'support'. Care provision tends to be more intensively interventionist and individually focused than in support arrangements. With respect to both, there now tends to be a focus on early intervention and working with (rather than for) people in ways that recognize that, in most cases, the individual is the expert in his or her own life.

Since the growth of the housing association movement in the mid-1960s, social landlords have concentrated a significant proportion of their resources on the *development* of specialist housing for those who require help in order to be able to sustain their tenancy and maintain a dignified and reasonably independent way of life. Such housing schemes provide integral support services to a wide range of vulnerable people, including the elderly, those with mental health problems, ex-offenders, the young 'at risk', the homeless, victims of domestic violence and those recovering from drug addiction.

Until the late 1990s, there was a degree of confusion about the extent to which service charges for such housing-related support could be met by housing benefit payments. In August 1997 a crisis was precipitated by a series of high-profile court cases that disqualified nearly all support charges from being covered by housing benefit. In response, the government introduced a new funding system in 2003 known as 'Supporting People' (SP). This programme created a 'single pot' approach to the provision of housing-related support by merging six separate funding streams into one. This was intended to allow county and unitary local authorities to plan and commission services in ways that were more integrated and cost effective.

Supporting People (SP) built on the earlier 'Care in the Community' programme (1989) and reflected a further acceptance of the efficacy of subjecting the planning of welfare policies to interdisciplinary analysis and the delivery of support services to interagency working. It provides housing-related support to help vulnerable people to live as independently as possible in the *community*. This could be in their own homes or in hostels, sheltered housing or other specialized supported housing. It provides complementary support for people who may also need personal or medical care (SP only funds housing support). This can be part of a package that, as well as reducing isolation and enhancing mobility and general safety, offers help with debt counselling, life-skills training, form filling, advice on paying bills and the provision of emergency alarms.

As part of its ongoing welfare reform agenda, in 2009, the government withdrew the requirement for authorities to ring-fence SP funding and since that date it has been cut significantly. This has presented *social housing* providers with a policy dilemma. With increasing longevity, the proportion of older people in the population is rising, bringing consequential increases in the demand for residential care and support facilities. At the same time the future of revenue funding for such provision is becoming increasingly uncertain and insecure. Reductions in SP funding have led many social landlords to review their strategic approaches to the delivery of housing-related support services. Many have become concerned with taking on risks associated with long-term employment contracts in a system in which revenue funding is diminishing and becoming uncertain. Some now restrict support to sheltered housing (see below), some have sought partnering arrangements to keep a service in place, some have set up volunteer 'befriending' groups to replace previous professional support, some have incorporated housing-related care into their core commitments and some have withdrawn completely.

In addition to funding cuts, extra risk is being put on providers through the introduction of 'payment by results' by which some funding support is conditional on defined outcomes related to such measures as reduced hospital admissions. Some fear that the funding cuts may result in fewer housing providers bidding to run care and support services with the possible consequence of greater burdens falling on GPs, accident and emergency units, the ambulance service and the police. One of the problems of evaluating this form of support is that the costs are front-loaded and explicit while the benefits are spread over time, are intangible and difficult to quantify in monetary terms.

types of supported housing

Some specialist schemes are long term, designed for people who need support to live independently, others are short term, designed to help people acquire the emotional and practical skills needed to move on into more mainstream housing. The range includes homes (often grouped) that are specifically designed for, and allocated to, particular clients who require specialized facilities and various forms of help to remain physically secure and independent. The Care Standards Act 2000 established standards for residential care accommodation and design.

'Sheltered housing' is a term used to describe a form of supported housing for *rent* or sale that is normally aimed at the 'active elderly'. It typically constitutes self-contained, purpose-built flats, houses or bungalows with their own front doors, kitchens and bathrooms. They offer safe, independent living for single people or couples and usually provide a limited amount of extra help if and when needed. This help focuses on physical security and general well-being, caretaking and property management. The manager or other staff will normally provide a 'befriending' function for residents and act as a link to other (non-housing) services, including the health, personal care, and emergency services and residents' families. Emergency alarm systems are a common feature in such schemes. A manager or a warden may live within the scheme, but increasingly, they operate peripatetically.

'Extra care housing' is sometimes referred to as 'very sheltered housing'. It is social or private housing that has been modified to suit people with long-term conditions or disabilities that make living in their own home difficult, but who do not want to move into a residential care home. Extra care housing includes converted properties and purpose-built accommodation such as retirement villages, apartments and bungalows. They can be large-scale schemes with several hundred properties. Some housing units may be for sale, others to rent and some are a mixture of both through shared ownership arrangements. Extra care housing can be run by housing associations and charities, local authorities or private sector providers. Most residents are older people, but this type of housing is becoming popular with people with disabilities regardless of their age. It is usually seen as a long-term housing solution, but certain developments offer rehabilitation and intermediate care options for residents, and some specialize in care for people with dementia.

'Care homes' (also known as residential care) provide accommodation, nursing and personal care to a wide range of adults, including older people and others with a range of disabilities. They can vary considerably in size, facilities and environment but they share an emphasis on providing appropriate accommodation for those with physical or mental incapacity and who are deemed to be experiencing long-term vulnerability. Care homes can be run directly by local authorities or by private companies or individuals.

'Community care services' is the term given to a range of support that is arranged and provided by local authority social services departments mainly to adults who have been formally assessed and found to have specific care needs because of age or disability. The term 'social service department' here includes 'social work departments' in Scotland and the Health and Social Services Trust in Northern

Ireland and relevant departments of the Welsh Government and Assembly. Although this support can involve help with gaining access to a care home, much of it is directed to the provision of the kind of support designed to allow individuals to remain in their own homes. Typical examples of care provided include help with bathing and washing, getting up, dressing and going to bed, shopping and managing *finances* (where there are capacity issues), home help tasks such as cleaning and cooking, adaptations to enhance mobility and safety such as stair lifts, ramps and hand rails, meals delivered to the home or provided at day care centres or lunch clubs and recreational, cultural and occupational activities. Funds for these sorts of activities are under strain but, in theory at least, they could involve several visits a day or even 24-hour care where necessary.

Fundamental changes to the structure of the NHS were implemented in April 2013 under the provisions of the Health and Social Care Act 2012 (England only). Strategic health authorities and primary care trusts were replaced by the NHS Commissioning Board and around 200 clinical commissioning groups (CCGs). Capital grant powers were transferred from primary care trusts to CCGs, which have a statutory duty to consider the integration of health-related services. The collaborative arrangements were reformulated by the legislation and established health and well-being boards as a forum where key leaders from the health and care systems work together to improve the health and well-being of their local populations and reduce health inequalities. Health and well-being board members collaborate to understand their local communities' needs, agree on priorities and encourage commissioners to work in a more joined-up way and facilitate coordinated arrangements between the NHS and local councils.

In the last quarter of the twentieth century, the phrases 'joined up thinking' and 'joined up government' began to appear in official and popular commentaries on central policy-making in general and social policy-making in particular. Most academic and professional commentators argue that there remains a lack of proper integration in the field of 'care and support' and that the coordination of housing, health and well-being facilities remains a 'work in progress'.

implications for practice
- In May 2013, the government introduced the Care and Support Bill to Parliament. The new legislation (2014) proposes 'a single modern law for adult care and support' to replace the 'existing outdated and complex legislation'. It aims to reform social care to ensure that the system effectively reflects the needs of service users whilst supporting their caregivers and families.
- This new system should promote integration between care and support, health and housing. The legislation states that 'the provision of housing accommodation is a health-related service' and its definition of 'well-being' includes 'suitability of living accommodation'.
- The 2014 legislation extends the list of partners with which LAs have a duty to cooperate to include housing associations.

KEY TEXTS
- Mullins, D. and Murie, A. (2006) *Housing Policy in the UK* (Basingstoke: Palgrave Macmillan), Chapter 11
- Central and local government websites; for example, http://www.local.gov.uk/health/-/journal_content/56/10180/3510973/ARTICLE#sthash.3ekQQgLw.dpuf; http://www.adviceguide.org.uk/wales/relationships_w/relationships_looking_after_people_E/community_care.htm; http://www.ofsted.gov.uk/inspection-reports/find-inspection-report

choice

SEE ALSO **affordability; allocations; culture; housing market; nudge theory; participation; quality; value**

Since the late twentieth century, the word 'choice' has constantly appeared in policy statements regarding the provision of *welfare* services in the United Kingdom. In the context of service provision and consumption, the notion of 'choice' is closely tied to market theory and implicitly advocates the efficacy of 'consumer sovereignty'. Advocates of this policy approach argue that service users are well-positioned to understand their own needs and preferences and by expressing their choices within the welfare system, appropriate priorities will be delivered. The argument is underpinned by academic work in the field of 'public choice theory' (Niskanen,

1971) and is sometimes categorized under the heading 'new public management'. It is supported by politico-economic arguments of right-leaning think tanks such as the Adam Smith Institute. Critics of this attitudinal shift in emphasis argue that it uncritically accepts the assumed benefits of a 'consumer society' and allows policy-makers to avoid public concerns about the contribution of central funding support and the role of experts in identifying future needs and in defining what counts as 'service quality'. Concern is also expressed about how a consumerist approach might affect the distribution of vital services in ways that would disadvantage vulnerable groups and inarticulate individuals. Some of these arguments against the 'marketization' of welfare services are underpinned by the academic work of welfare theorists such as Richard Titmuss and left-leaning think tanks such as the Institute for Public Policy Research.

Referencing Peters and Waterman's research (1982), Mullins and Murie (2006) suggest that 'new public management' ideas have their roots in the US business philosophy that successful firms should 'stick close to the customer', and that this proposition has, in recent years, had a significant influence on the nature of British public service provision. The term 'choice' is currently being used in *social housing* agencies and local government to describe a number of discretely different approaches to provision, namely:

- 'individual choice' in which the user elects between options, for example, which provider (hospital, school, landlord, etc.), which kitchen cupboard design to fit as part of an internal house refurbishment, when to receive the service and so on;
- 'personalization' that involves giving a more personalized service, by tailoring it to the individual user's needs, for example, designing an individual curriculum for a particular student or adapting a home to accommodate disability and so on;
- 'collective choice' that involves the delegation of decision-making powers and/or devolving budgets to an identifiable group of users or user representatives;
- 'collective influence ("voice")' where users have an opportunity to participate in decision-making, for example, discussions on parish plans, tenant scrutiny panels and so on.

For many years the housing regulators have reinforced this shift in management emphasis by expressly incorporating phrases relating to a user focus when reporting on agency appraisal methodologies. On a broader housing policy canvas, two areas in which the idea of enhancing choice has recently had a significant effect has been the introduction of 'choice-based lettings' (see *allocations*) and the government's 'localism agenda' (see *affordability*).

The issues of 'tenure choice' and 'tenure neutrality' feature strongly in the academic literature and have long been areas of interest to economists (e.g. Mills, 1990) who have sought to build decision models analysing how rational choices are made about whether to *rent* or to buy. These usually focus on a comparison of the present *value* of net cash outflows associated with each *tenure*. Such models might be criticized for the narrowness of their focus and their lack of ability to take account of people's behavioural dispositions. In real life, such decisions will be determined by a subtle and complicated interaction between an enormous range of ever-changing factors such as tax status, age, state of health, beliefs about future market trends, personal circumstances, attitudes to risk and so on.

Tenure choice is crucially influenced by personal circumstances such as job security, familial relationships and health. These factors could change over time, pointing to the desirability of tenure neutrality (i.e. in terms of tax treatment) and flexibility. Some housing associations are now exploring the possibility of developing a 'flexible tenure' approach for some residents that will allow easier entries and exits to different tenure arrangements as personal circumstances change. This has proved to be a difficult policy to implement because historically each tenure has been grounded in its own specific funding regime and administrative arrangements.

It is important to be aware that the question of 'choice and public policy' should not be regarded as a simple 'right–left' ideological debate about the appropriate balance between individualism and collectivism, empowerment and control or local power and central authority. Its prominence in the policy and practice literatures is a reflection of continuing wider and more general concerns about the nature of citizenship and the role of the state and bureaucracies in a modern liberal democracy.

KEY TEXTS
- Marsh, A. and Mullins, D. (eds) (1998) *Housing and Public Policy: Citizenship, Choice and Control* (Buckingham and Philadelphia, PA: Open University Press)
- Mullins, D. and Murie, A. (2006) *Housing Policy in the UK* (Basingstoke: Palgrave Macmillan)

community

SEE ALSO choice; development; diversity; partnerships; social enterprise; social returns

A study of the popular and academic literature in the fields of geography, human ecology, politics and organizational analysis indicates that 'community' has become one of those words that is widely used without having a universally agreed meaning. The word is derived from the old French communité (Latin 'communitas') and referred to a *quality* of fellowship that embraced common interests and relations. In the medieval period, it began to extend its application from a noun of quality to a concrete noun of place denoting a location that contains a 'body of fellow townsmen' (see 'OED'). In the twentieth century, influential urban sociologists and human ecologists associated with the Chicago School of thinkers highlighted this notion of 'community' by focusing on those definitions that emphasized the word's spatial connotations (Park and Burgess, 1925). During this period, however, in the academic literature, the original relational (as against spatial) meaning of 'community' persisted so that the term has now come to acquire meanings that relate to both people and places.

The emergence of electronic social networking has given added emphasis to the need to distinguish between a community that is a fixed location and one that is an association of interests. To overcome any ambiguity associated with the word, planning and housing professionals often refer to 'neighbourhoods', 'districts', 'areas' or 'locations' when explicitly referencing place.

The 'people–place' aspects of community are prominent in the government's localism agenda. The legislation recognizes the need for community involvement to be coordinated and local authorities are charged with a leadership role over the process. This is, however, not intended to be traditional, top-down leadership, but an approach that involves councillors and officers, using their resources to engage local people and organizations in creating a community partnership of shared commitment. Part I of the Local Government Act 2000 enshrines in law the role of community leadership, giving councils new powers to promote the well-being of their areas. It provides a legal framework to support and strengthen this role and reduces a number of planning barriers and statutory obstacles that might inhibit their ability to work with others to promote the economic, social and environmental well-being of their areas.

The government's commitment to localism was given popular expression around the notion of the 'Big Society'. Research by Ipsos Mori indicates a degree of ambivalence about the idea. Although more people seem to support it than to oppose it, the majority of respondents believe its driving rationale is to allow the government to cut back on public spending on services. It would appear that individuals simultaneously hold contradictory views about community involvement. As a general idea it is applauded while at the same time, most people do not want to take any responsibility for service provision themselves. There is also a strong belief that basic services should be the same everywhere and there is much disapproval of what has become known as the 'postcode lottery'.

implications for practice
- One aspect of the localism agenda looks to *social housing* agencies and other not-for-profit organizations to take over neighbourhood services from local authorities in ways that will develop responsive and resilient communities. The National Housing Federation argues that this new environment provides housing associations with opportunities to develop the reach of their businesses and extend their community contributions into new areas beyond the provision of homes and traditional housing services (see *diversity*).
- Under Part I of the Local Government Act 2000, local authorities in England and Wales have to produce a community strategy to promote the social, economic and environmental well-being of their areas and achieve 'sustainable communities'. The other regional administrations have indicated similar expectations about community involvement in neighbourhood planning.

- It is now intended that local communities will be able to use neighbourhood planning to influence the granting of full or outline planning permissions in areas where they most want to see new homes and businesses, making it easier and quicker for *development* to go ahead. Some commentators have argued that it may have the opposite effect. Automatic public resistance to new development is sometimes referred to as 'NIMBYism' – 'Not In My Back Yard'. (Total resistance to local development proposals is sometimes referred to as 'NOTE' – 'Not Over There Either' or 'NTNA' – 'Not There Not Anywhere'.)

KEY TEXTS

- Aldrich, H. (2004) *Organizations Evolving* (London: Sage Publications) Chapter 11, for a survey of the academic literature on the two main meanings of community
- Department for Communities and Local Government (2012) *A Plain English Guide to the Localism Act, November 2011*
- Lee, P. (2010) 'Competitiveness and Social Exclusion: The Importance of Place and Rescaling in Housing and Regeneration Policies' in P. Malpass and R. Rowlands (eds), *Housing, Markets and Policy* (Abingdon: Routledge)
- National Housing Federation (2012a) *Localism Act 2011: Housing and Planning, A Guide for Housing Associations*
- National Housing Federation (2013a) *Government: Localism and Communities Agenda.* www.housing.org.uk
- National Housing Federation (2013b) *Deciding Your Direction.* www.housing.org.uk
- Rowlands, R. (2010) 'Sustainable Communities: Housing, Dogma and the Opportunities Missed' in P. Malpass and R. Rowlands (eds) *Housing, Markets and Policy* (Abingdon: Routledge)
- www.housing.org.uk/investingincommunities

continuous improvement

SEE ALSO **culture; performance monitoring; quality; social returns; value for money; welfare**

Anyone working in the public and voluntary sectors will be familiar with the phrase 'continuous improvement'. It is a term in constant use by regulators and *quality* inspectors and it is an idea that underpins government's policy commitments to achieve *value for money*

(VFM) from those economic activities that receive support from the public purse. Continuous improvement is often referred to by the Japanese word 'Kaizen'. Kaizen means 'change for the better' and covers all processes in an organization. It involves making continual small improvements to a process rather than big changes at irregular intervals. This requires close monitoring and control, changes to the uses of manpower, machinery, processes, materials and money to improve business efficiency in all its senses.

It is perhaps self-evident that a key objective of government policy is to provide 'quality' services. But it was not always the case. Before the middle of the nineteenth century there was a conscious policy to provide poor quality *welfare* support based on poorly funded outdoor relief and the dreaded workhouses. This was partly because the costs of paying to help the destitute fell on the parishes and the middle class ratepayers in those parishes did not want to pay for expensive facilities. It was also partly a response to the philosophy of 'self-help' (made famous by Samuel Smiles) and the distinction made between the 'deserving' and 'undeserving' poor. Many argued that good quality welfare services would encourage people to remain idle and indolent, whilst minimal outdoor relief and harsh workhouse conditions would encourage people to look after themselves and not rely on the parish.

The experiences of two world wars had a dramatic effect on national attitudes towards welfare provision. The twentieth century saw the gradual emergence of a modern 'welfare state' much of which focused on national, rather than parish, concerns about social security, health, education and housing. Many of the new types of service were used extensively by those who were not destitute (including the middle and better-off working classes) and, from the start, there was an expectation that our schools, medical services and council housing should be provided in ways that demonstrated both professional management and quality outputs.

With an established welfare state philosophy coupled with the now emerging notion of *social returns*, not only do contemporary British governments seek quality outputs from public investment, but they also expect that those providing the services plan for 'continuous improvements' over time.

The notion of 'continuous improvement' has its roots in welfare economic theory and, in particular, the ideas of the Italian philosopher and writer Vilfredo Pareto (1848–1923).

a pareto optimum and a pareto improvement

Pareto posed the following philosophical question: 'Suppose, albeit unrealistically, that we could alter our policies or practices in such a way that at least one person's welfare would be improved without damaging the welfare of anyone else: what would this mean?' Not surprisingly, he argued that in such a hypothetical situation there would be a clear gain in total perceived welfare (so long as any 'losers' are adequately compensated). By extending the logic of this argument, welfare economists have attempted to conceive what would be the theoretically 'best' arrangement in a given situation. That is, they have attempted to define that arrangement that would, in theory, constitute the situation of maximum total welfare. The logic runs as follows:

> If we compare two situations, and in the second at least one person is better off than in the first and no one is worse off, then the second situation must be superior to the first. It also follows that the first situation is *sub-optimal* because it can be improved.

The logic goes on to suggest that the best of all arrangements, the 'optimal' situation, must be one in which, no one can be made any better off without making someone else worse off. Such a 'best possible' arrangement is known as a 'Pareto optimum' and obviously represents a hypothetical situation in which the maximum total welfare is achieved.

The notion of the Pareto optimum is extremely theoretical. Although it is philosophical, the idea does provide a hypothetical 'bench mark' against which we can conceive sub-optimal arrangements and consider policies designed to better them. When considering a particular decision in terms of this approach, we should ask the general question, 'Will the change in policy or practice move us towards a Pareto optimum?' If the answer is 'yes', then the change will represent what is known as a 'Pareto improvement', and will, on the face of it, be a sound decision in welfare economic terms.

A problem with this analysis is that it is too theoretical to be of much direct practical use. It is logically sound but begs all sorts of practical questions. Not the least of these is, 'How do we decide whether or not the change will lead to a Pareto improvement?' The technique of cost–benefit analysis (CBA) was developed in order to tackle such a question.

The pursuit of continuous improvement implies that managers can distinguish between, and have procedures in place for monitoring efficiency, effectiveness and user experiences. It also implies that the organization's practices are carried out in a fair and equitable manner. It assumes that the organizational *culture* is one in which strategies and operational practices embrace consultations with stakeholders, bare comparison to other similar organizations, and are exposed to competitive forces where appropriate. Above all, it requires that current arrangements are constantly challenged and justified.

Figure 2 demonstrates the circular, joined-up nature of the process.

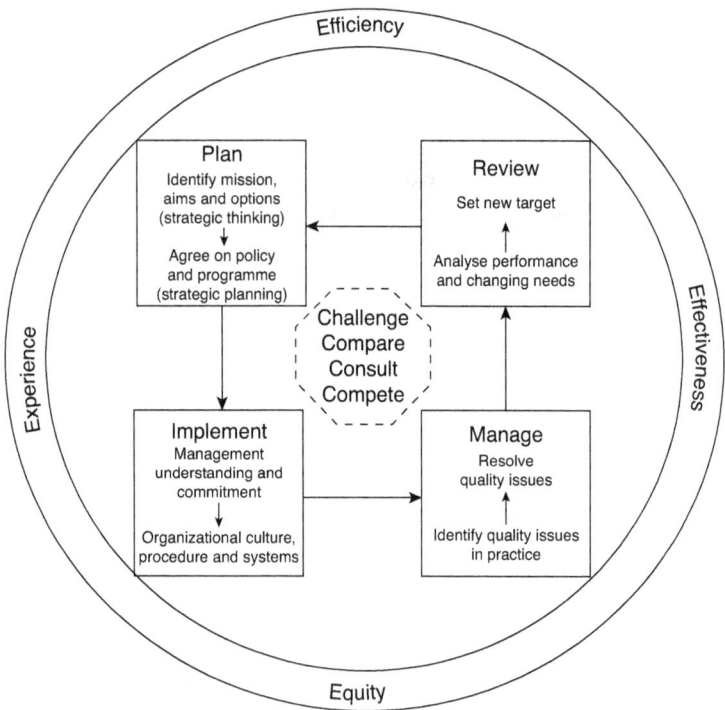

FIGURE 2   *The idea of continuous improvement*

Organizations that have a full commitment to continuous improvement will have established arrangements to monitor and manage its pursuit.

implications for practice

- In the pursuit of value for money, social landlords are required to demonstrate 'continuous improvement' (a move towards 'optimality') in the delivery of their services.
- Inspectors sometimes note that this notion is not properly understood by the boards, executives and staff of the organizations they visit. The point is usually made that the pursuit of continuous improvement requires those leading and managing the organization to have a clear concept of what the optimum position would look like and have in place processes and procedures that come together to create a coherent method for moving towards it.

KEY TEXTS

- In both the academic and practice literatures, this topic is often subsumed under discussions about value for money or management accounting. Management texts tend to cover it as an aspect of *total quality management* (TQM) and *value chain analysis*. See, for example, Drury, C. (2001) *Management Accounting for Business Decisions* (Stamford: Thomson)
- Johnson, G. (1988) 'Rethinking Incrementalism', *Strategic Management Journal*, 9: pp. 75–91
- See also the publications of the Chartered Quality Institute. http://www.thecqi.org/Knowledge-Hub/Resources/Factsheets/Continual-improvement/

cost of housing

SEE ALSO **housing market; regulation; subsidies; value**

In popular speech, the words 'cost' and 'price' are interchangeable. This was always the case until the nineteenth century when economic thinkers began to make subtle distinctions in their meaning. Writers on the 'labour theory of value' began to distinguish between 'cost' as the 'quantity of labour required to produce' something, and 'price' as the 'quantity of labour that its possessor will take in exchange' for it (John Ruskin, 1894, Chapter 1).

In economics 'cost' and 'price' are now treated as two distinct concepts. Market theorists regard 'costs' as the 'costs of production' that have to be expended to make a good or service available for sale and 'price' as the 'exchange value' that has to be paid by the final consumer to acquire it. The difference between cost and price constitutes the profit or surplus revenue for the producer/supplier. Most social landlords are 'not-for-profit' organizations and they charge rents that are normally below the market price. Historically, the gap between cost and price has been met by some form of subsidy (see *subsidies*).

'Cost effectiveness' involves achieving the least cost to produce a defined outcome (see *value for money*).

KEY TEXT

- Golland, A. and Blake, R. (eds) (2004) *Housing Development: Theory, Process and Practice* (London: Routledge)

culture

SEE ALSO **business planning; diversity; social enterprise; sustainability**

Raymond Williams suggests that 'culture' is one of the two or three most complicated words in the English language. This is largely because it has come to be used in different ways in several distinct disciplines. As early as the sixteenth century its use was extended from a noun of process that referred specifically to the tending of agricultural products, to apply to personal education and *development*. By the seventeenth century the notion of the 'cultivated mind' was no longer a metaphor for an educated person, but had become an established idea in its own right.

In 1869 the association of culture with education, artistic endeavour and literary criticism was greatly enhanced by the publication of Matthew Arnold's influential essays on 'Culture and Anarchy'. As an educationalist, Arnold's concerns were to tackle ignorance and counteract what he saw as the dangers of philistinism. However, over time, particularly in the twentieth century, his somewhat idealistic notion of culture as 'the best that has been known and thought in the world' came to be interpreted as 'high culture' that carried elitist overtones. In response, social thinkers such as John Ruskin and William Morris began to develop a broader notion of culture that related to the common life of the people.

Edward B. Tylor, a contemporary of Arnold's, was at the forefront of developing an anthropological theory of culture that can be thought of as providing a broader understanding of the term that regarded it, not so much as a 'force for good' for which an educated elite strive, but as the 'whole way of life' of an identifiable, coherent *community*. This view, which is now well established, was further developed in the twentieth century by social theorists (notably Stuart Hall), and more particularly, by anthropologists such as Margaret Mead and Gregory Bateson.

Once established as an independent category, the anthropological notion of culture was soon extended from Tylor's application to 'primitive communities' to any form of coherent grouping. During the twentieth century it has been used to provide an identity to nation states, regions, localities, religions, sects, clubs and a wide variety of organizations, including businesses.

business culture

The idea that an organization has a culture particular to itself clearly stems from the world's anthropological application. In his essay 'Notes towards the Definition of Culture' (1962), T. S. Eliot makes the point that a proper understanding of an organization's culture is complicated by the fact that groups are composed of individuals. This means that inevitably there will be subtle and complex interactions of cultural attitudes between the dispositions of these individuals and the overarching cultures of which they are a part. Furthermore, the organizational culture will itself be embedded in the culture of the societal groupings with which it is associated, including society at large. Any understanding of how 'culture' relates to, and impacts upon, a particular organization like a business needs to take account of Eliot's three levels of analysis.

Following Eliot's observation, the point could be made that because housing is multi-faceted, housing agencies comprise individuals from a wide range of professional backgrounds and that the education, training and experiences of these individuals will inevitably be part of the mix of an organization's culture. In addition to their individual dispositions, accountants, tenant liaison officers, plumbers and IT technicians are likely to have discretely different opinions and attitudes about what counts as 'good practice' that stem, in part at least, from assumptions taken from their different professional cultures.

In the academic literature, 'business culture' is sometimes referred to as 'institutional culture'. In the late twentieth century, a number of social theorists sought to explain the complexity of interactions embedded in organizations by referencing ideas taken from structuralist philosophy. As a result, many academic commentators now analyse institutional cultures by seeking to articulate the dichotomy between the 'formal' constraining power of social structure and the 'informal' effects of cumulative individual actions – what is sometimes referred to as the 'structure and agency dichotomy'.

In terms of more everyday language and analysis, it can be said that a particular institutional culture comprises the declared and accepted values and norms that govern the behaviour of those who work for, or engage with, the organization. It guides and informs the ways in which they interact with each other, their clients and other stakeholders outside the organization. In this way, the organizational culture sets the structural and moral contexts within which the mission and its associated values and goals might be pursued. The word 'might' in this context is important as the publication of a mission statement is no guarantee of actual institutional values and behaviours. It can be argued that most organizations have an overt (public) culture and a hidden (internal) culture. It is sometimes said that an organization's true culture determines what it does when no one is looking.

Charles Handy (1985) popularized a method of analysing organizational culture that links operations to that of structure. Following Handy, the cultural categories of organizations described below might be distinguished.

'Power culture' concentrates authority in a few hands. Control flows from the centre like a web. Power cultures have few rules and limited bureaucracy. They are capable of making swift decisions. Housing organizations tend to have relatively shallow management structures and have an established tradition of empowering residents to participate in *governance* and decision-making.

'Role culture' gives people clearly delegated authorities within a defined structure. Because housing management is a multi-faceted activity, operations such as development, *rent* collection, voids management, property maintenance, tenant and community liaison and so on are normally carried out by identifiable teams that have their own targets, processes and reporting systems. This can lead to the problem of what is sometimes referred to as 'silo management' in which operations are insulated from each other in ways that inhibit the ability of the organization to produce an effective 'joined-up' response to a problem. In recent years, housing regulators have sought to ensure that housing organizations do not display the features of 'silo management'. In particular they have been keen to ensure that tenants and other stakeholders who contact the organization with a complaint or issue are not passed around from team to team and that inter-team responsibilities are coordinated.

'Task culture' creates teams to solve particular problems and carry out specific tasks. Here, power and authority are derived from expertise. These cultures often feature the multiple reporting lines of a matrix structure. Because housing management involves the application of a wide range of professional skills, a high proportion of staff is qualified in specific areas such as accountancy, building technology, sociology, law, surveying and so on, and this produces a diffusion of authority.

'Person culture' exists where key individuals dominate the organization and its decision-making processes. Some professional partnerships can operate as person cultures particularly when each partner brings a peculiar expertise and clientele to the firm. It is generally accepted that it would be difficult for a social landlord to survive and prosper under this sort of culture since the concept of a socially orientated, people-centred organization suggests that a group of like-minded individuals pursue the organizational goals. A strong person culture can inhibit a corporate commitment to shared learning and research.

'Learning culture' is actively sought by many organizations that appreciate the value of research and open approaches to the analysis of mistakes. In recent years, a number of housing agencies have invested in whole-organization training programmes designed to change the corporate culture by equipping staff at all levels with the intrinsic motivation and capability to work as a team and in which individual team members are able to reflect on their role in the organization and also learn from their own and their colleagues' mistakes and successes. This approach to culture change and development was famously articulated by Donald Schon (1983) and his influential notion of 'reflective practice'. The Chartered Institute of Housing declares a commitment to cultivating 'reflective practice' and requires a consideration of its meaning and application in any professional housing course that it validates.

The culture of a successful organization is constantly evolving to accommodate changing business circumstances. Furthermore, such organizations tend also to be aware that a strong cultural identity can have dangers as well as advantages. It may stifle dissent and inhibit innovation and new ways of thinking.

KEY TEXTS

- Aldrich, H. (2004) *Organizations Evolving* (London: Sage Publications)
- Deal, T. E. and Kennedy, A. A. (1982) *Corporate Cultures: The Rites and Rituals of Corporate Life* (Harmondsworth: Penguin Books)
- Handy, C. B. (1985) *Understanding Organizations* (Harmondsworth: Penguin Books)
- Johnson, G., Scholes, K. and Whittington, R. (2011) *Exploring Corporate Strategy: Texts and Cases.* 9th edn (Harlow: Prentice Hall)
- Parker, M. (2000) *Organisational Culture and Identity* (London: Sage Publications)
- Schein, E. H. (2004) *Organizational Culture and Leadership* (San Francisco: Jossey-Bass)

d

development

SEE ALSO affordability; asset management; business planning; capital
and revenue; community; finance; homelessness; housing law;
need and demand; nudge theory; partnerships; risk and uncertainty;
sustainability; value

The word 'development' originally meant unfolding or unwrapping
and was applied to the process of unfurling a standard in battle.
The poet and cultural historian Jack Lindsay (1962) argued that
the modern concept of 'development' emerged in the eighteenth
century with the appearance of biology as a science, when it began
to be used to refer to the growth of living organisms. In contemporary society the term is constantly applied to describe forward
advances and the process of growth in all sorts of areas. Its specific
application to land and landed property was established during the
nineteenth century when its more general meaning of 'advancement through progressive stages' (1836) began to be applied to
building contracts and commentaries on urbanization. It was
only in the early twentieth century that the notion was extended to
describe 'a state of economic advancement'.

Planning legislation sets the control framework within which
land and property development takes place. In recent times, succes-
sive governments have issued numerous policy statements, technical circulars and guidance notes that together constitute a virtual
library of regulating documentation. By the second decade of the
twenty-first century it was being argued that this was inhibiting
development, stifling economic growth and limiting democratic
involvement in local planning and decision-making. Part VI of the
Localism Act 2011 reformed the system with a view to making it
simpler, clearer, less bureaucratic and more open to democratic
involvement (see *affordability*).

local development strategies

Although strategies are largely shaped by local housing needs and aspirations, these are, to some extent, influenced by national expectations that are set by central organizations such as the Homes and Communities Agency (HCA), Northern Ireland's Department of Social Development (DSDNI), the Housing Strategy and Equality Branch of the Welsh Assembly Government and the Scottish Government.

All the national agencies endorse the role of local authorities (LAs) as leaders in shaping and encouraging appropriate local housing strategies. They expect LAs to work with all the members of the local *community* and with other statutory, private, community and voluntary bodies to create a shared development vision for their communities that incorporates an assessment of local housing needs and supply capacities in all *tenures* (see *need and demand*). A survey of LA websites reveals a diverse range of strategies within the broad objectives of tackling *homelessness* and stimulating socio-economic development through the provision of decent affordable homes. Strategies for increasing the supply of homes operate in the context of the local planning framework and local action plans.

Local authorities are no longer the main providers of *social housing* and since the 1980s, many of those who have retained a landlord function have not had the ability to build new houses to meet the known demand for affordable homes in their districts. With the introduction of 'self-financing' in 2012 (see *finance*) this inhibition is gradually weakening as they are now able to use surpluses within the housing revenue account (HRA) for their own housing plans rather than have them diverted to central government.

development risk

Risk is an integral aspect of all capital projects and manifests itself in a variety of ways at different stages in a project's life cycle. History teaches us that construction projects are difficult to plan in terms of risk management and that outturns often demonstrate problems with cost and time overruns. Construction issues have caused serious problems to a number of housing associations, and they constitute one of the most common reasons for an association to be taken into administration or taken over by another agency. Even minor miscalculations associated with development projects can bring about problems such as a loss of reputation, a drain on reserves, failure to acquire future grant support, legal action, loss of staff morale and distortions in the business plan. To avoid such problems development officers tend to take a great deal of care over the nature and content of the contract. Contract risks are defined as the risks that stem from the procurement process. Contract risk constitutes a significant element of overall project risk. Among other things, the contract apportions risk between the parties.

Procurement processes provide different routes to the creation, improvement or renewal of tangible capital assets; each route carries a different risk profile. The main *choice* is between the following: traditional (design-led) procurement route; design and build; management fee; private finance initiative (PFI) – build/ operate/transfer and self-build.

housing renewal

There exists an extensive terminology relating to aspects of housing renewal. This includes terms such as 'rehabilitation', 'refurbish-ment', 'enhancement', 'modernization', 'major repair', 'improve-ment', 're-improvement' and 'tenure diversification'. Some of these terms are derived from official funding mechanisms rather than from the academic literature. The existence of such a collec-tion of terms can lead to confusion. This means that the concept of 'housing renewal' is not one that lends itself to precise or clear definition. What can be said is that it goes beyond maintenance or repair, and implies more than improvement, modernization or renewal of building components. It means returning *dwellings* to 'fitness for purpose', which may involve repair, refurbishment, demolition and rebuilding, or diversification of tenure, or any combination of all four.

To cut through this semantic confusion, we can say that housing renewal broadly takes two generalized forms (or a mixture of both):

1. 'Refurbishment' can apply to individual properties or to whole estates. It goes beyond major improvements and the replacement of defunct or obsolete building components. It implies the complete renovation of properties and typically involves a noticeable change in appearance, an upgrading of functional *quality*, and an enhancement of desirability, *rent*-earning potential

and capital *value*. When applied to residential estates it implies an improvement in the reputation and popularity of such estates. Key aspects can include higher security standards, improved amenities, modernized interiors, repaired exteriors and investment in the surrounding environment. It may also involve some conversion work.

2. 'Redevelopment' involves site clearance followed by rebuilding to modern standards. Redevelopment allows for the site or estate to be transformed in terms of building mix, design and quality.

Housing renewal is likely to enhance the 'use value' of the asset. In turn, the enhanced use value can result in increased 'capital and exchange values' (see *value*).

Housing renewal can have many aims, including economic regeneration, social inclusion, crime reduction, reduced truancy rates and the maintenance or enhancement of the environmental character of the area. However its overt objective is to return dwellings to fitness for purpose once more by raising currently poor levels of performance and amenity to acceptable standards. Housing renewal, however, cannot be treated in isolation: reference should be made to the wider background of policy emphasis that is now placed on planned economic regeneration to tackle the causes rather than the symptoms of decline. This means that housing renewal should be thought of as more than a physical process.

implications for practice
- The new National Planning Framework was introduced in 2012 to simplify and speed up the operation of the planning consent process by, for example, requiring local authorities to have in place a five-year, land supply plan.
- Recent planning reforms should not be seen in isolation from other measures that are designed to encourage local economic development such as the New Home Bonus (see *nudge theory*), Local Enterprise Partnerships and other government-sponsored agencies such as Scottish Enterprise and Highlands and Islands Enterprise (see *partnerships*).
- Development projects are complex and technical: so complex, in fact, that a number of things are almost certain to 'go wrong' during the development period. It has been estimated that

the typical £12 million construction project comprises some 400,000 separate 'decisions' (Adamson, 2001). For instance, if 99.9 per cent of these decisions can be judged to be 'correct' – this will result in 400 'errors'. If 80 per cent of these 'errors' are picked up, this will leave 80 'errors' undetected. Assuming that 20 per cent of these are 'serious', this will mean that 16 'serious errors' will have occurred. These should be the basis of risk management for the project.

- Whichever procurement route is chosen, a poorly conceived contract can impose avoidable costs and contract failure can trigger penalty clauses. This having been said, the nature of risk will vary with different types of procurement route. Project managers normally seek to cover these possible risks by translating them into a contract 'cost' measured in financial terms. This cost then has to be accepted (paid for as a contingency) or shifted (paid for as insurance or some other premium). Risk analysis within the construction industry has led to the following broad estimation of contingency figures: (a) 6–9 per cent of scheme cost for new build; (b) 15 per cent of scheme cost for refurbishment (Adamson, 2001).

KEY TEXTS

- Blewitt, J. (2010) *Understanding Sustainable Development* (London: Earthscan)
- Bramley, G., Munro, M. and Pawson, H. (2004) *Key Issues in Housing: Policies and Markets in 21st-Century Britain* (Basingstoke: Palgrave Macmillan), Chapter 6
- Evans, A. (2009) 'Development should Benefit Local Communities' in B. Pattison and J. Vine (eds), *Perspectives on the Future of Housing: A Collection of Viewpoints on the UK Housing System* (Coalville: Building and Social Housing Foundation)
- Laying the Foundations: A Housing Strategy for England
- Oxley, M. (2004) *Economics, Planning and Housing* (Basingstoke: Palgrave Macmillan)
- Winch, G. M. (2010) *Managing Construction Projects* (Oxford: Wiley-Blackwell)
- http://www.wlga.gov.uk (Welsh Local Government Association)
- Housingstrategy&equalitiesbranch@wales.gsi.gov.uk
- http://www.scotland.gov.uk/

• https://www.gov.uk/government/uploads/system/uploads/attachment_
  data/file/7532/2033676.pdf

diversity

SEE ALSO **allocations; care and support; choice; culture; equity; private renting; regulation; risk and uncertainty; social enterprise; welfare**

In general speech, 'diversity' is a word that has had neutral, negative and distinctly positive applications. The 'quality of being diverse' (from the Old French 'diversité') indicates, in a neutral way, 'difference' or 'distinctiveness'. History teaches us that in most societies 'differences from the norm' can be regarded with suspicion or even fear, and that difference can be seen as odd, unwelcomed or perverse (from the Latin 'diversitatem' contrariness, contradiction, disagreement – now obsolete). Diversity as a virtue in a nation is an idea that emerged with the rise of modern democracies in the 1790s. It was used to indicate a political philosophy of civil order and balance in which no one faction or 'rank' should be allowed to use democratic processes to arrogate all power unto itself. In this positive sense it points to, and predates, its modern meaning of protecting the rights and interests of minorities. Its contemporary (positive) focus on minority interests is quite recent and only became a major area of research and academic comment in the late 1980s and as an expressed feature of social (including housing) policy in the late 1990s.

In housing, the notion of 'diversity' is used to signify two broad aspects of landlordism. The first is concerned with questions of social pluralism ('the management of diversity'), and the second with broadening the scope of activity beyond the traditional or 'core' business ('diversification').

diversity management

Much of the wider debate about managing diversity focuses on the international, national and regional dimensions rather than the local or internal business dimensions. That is, it is concerned with immigration and its associated issues such as assimilation, quotas, employment, rights to benefits, access to services, area identity and so on (e.g. Nicola Ross in 'Giddens, 2003').

Early housing management concerns focused on the question of social diversification on estates. Private developers have argued that the existence of social tenures inhibits their ability to market private house sales. In contrast, sociologists have pointed to an array of social problems that can arise when there is a lack of diverse *tenure* arrangements on an estate. In the 1960s and 1970s the allocation policies of some councils were criticized for isolating so-called diffi-cult tenants on 'dump estates'. The issue of tenure diversity and its relationship to the *quality* of life in a locality remains a topic of discussion today (see 'Kearns and Mason, 2007').

Much of the business management literature on diversity stems from the field of occupational psychology and concen-trates on employment issues and the notion of 'equal opportu-nities'. In recent years some institutional analysts have argued that this focus is somewhat negative and reactive, and that effec-tive organizations take a more positive and proactive approach to employment diversity by moving from 'equalizing oppor-tunities' to 'affirming diversity' (Thomas, 1990). Kandola and Fullerton (1994) put forward a working definition of 'diversity management' that consists of visible and non-visible differences that will include factors such as gender, age, social background, race, disability, personality and work-style. The proposition they advance is that this 'mosaic of difference' is in itself an asset that, if managed intelligently, will create a business environment in which everybody feels valued, where their talents are being fully used and in which, as a result, organizational goals will be more readily met. Although poorly managed diverse organizations can become incoherent and display fragmented (or even discordant) messages, well-managed diversity can encourage innovation. As Walter Lippmann once famously said, 'Where all think alike, no one thinks very much.'

The Equality Act 2010 provides legal protection from discrimina-tion both in the workplace and in wider society. It replaced previous anti-discrimination laws with a single Act, making the law easier to understand and strengthening protection in some situations. It sets out the different ways in which it is unlawful to treat someone. It covers disability, equal pay and age discrimination.

Section 153 of the Act enables the Welsh and Scottish minis-ters to impose specific duties on certain public bodies through secondary legislation. Before the Act came into force there were several pieces of legislation to cover discrimination, notably the Sex Discrimination Act 1975, the Race Relations Act 1976 and the Disability Discrimination Act 1995.

diversification

Companies diversify for a variety of reasons. In some cases, it is part of a growth and efficiency policy designed to reduce unit costs of production. These advantages might occur when a company expands its business into areas that are at different points on the same production path, such as when a manufacturer owns its supplier and/or distributor. This form of 'vertical integration' can allow for a greater degree of quality control, reduce transportation expenses, speed up turnaround times and bring about tax advantages. Some housing agencies have sought the advantages of vertical integration by setting up their own in-house surveying and building and repairs teams and many incorporate design and *development* expertise into their establishments. However, such advantages are not automatically achieved and sometimes it is more effective for an organization to rely on the expertise and economies of scale of other providers rather than be vertically integrated.

Falling grant rates have provided a stimulus to some social landlords who have ambitions to maintain their development programmes to generate new revenue streams. These new sources of revenue can be utilized to cross-subsidize their *social housing* activities. Building on their existing strengths, some associations have now set up commercial profit-seeking companies in fields such as facilities management and private property lettings.

The changing nature of subsidy support, coupled with recent developments around tenure restructuring (e.g. the requirement to provide 'affordable' homes let at up to 80 per cent of market rent) have led some social housing agencies to consider diversifying horizontally rather than vertically. That is, they have diversified around the traditional core business of a social landlord. 'Horizontal integration' occurs when a firm expands its operations at the same point of production. This might be regarded more as 'growth' than 'diversification'. It can be achieved through internal growth or external merger or some form of legal partnering agreement. Some social landlords earn fees by managing homes built or owned by private

landlords or another social agency. Some have purchased properties outright from an existing landlord. Others have used private
sector renting to cross-subsidize affordable housing programmes.

Because business diversification carries financial and reputational dangers, it is a growth strategy that needs to be based on
market research and careful analysis that considers its exposure to
new risks and the organization's capacity to operate effectively in
the wider field. The process of diversification can also require subtle
adjustments to the corporate *culture* that need to be understood and
agreed prior to its introduction.

implications for practice

- Although an increasing number of housing associations are
  moving into market renting, for most that do, it represents
  a relatively small part of their turnover and asset base.
  Associations may also take part in the HCA's Private Rented
  Sector Initiative (PRSI) that involves working with local
  authorities and private sector businesses in ways that attract
  large-scale institutional investment into the rented housing
  sector.
- The expansion of core expertise that results from vertical
  integration can provide opportunities to market goods and
  services to existing customers or reach out to new markets. This
  can increase revenues and extend a brand reputation into other
  markets.
- Many associations provide accommodation tailored to the needs
  of older people (see *care and support*) and some have diversified
  their investment profiles by developing homes for sale in this
  market. This is largely a response to research (e.g. Henley
  Business School) that indicates that the number of households
  aged over 65 is increasing and will constitute about 60 per cent
  by 2033. Where there is a local demand, some associations are
  now considering investing in areas that are more tangential to
  their traditional business activities such as holiday homes and
  specialist accommodation for students or nurses.
- Regulators are now advising that most 'non-core' activities (i.e.
  everything except social housing) should be carried out by a
  separate entity and be 'ring-fenced' from social housing so that
  if the non-core activity fails, the social housing will not be put at

risk. It also suggests that every social housing provider above a certain size should prepare a 'living will' setting out how, if the business fails as a whole, its affairs will be wound up in a way that protects its social housing assets.

KEY TEXTS
- Kandola, R. and Fullerton, J. (1994) *Diversity in Action: Managing the Mosaic* (London: Chartered Institute of Personal Development)
- Kearns, A. and Mason, P. (2007) 'Mixed Tenure Communities and Neighbourhood Quality', *Housing Studies* 22 (5): pp. 661–691
- https://www.gov.uk/equality-act-2010-guidance

dwellings

SEE ALSO **proprietary interests; social returns; tenure**

To dwell is to linger, ponder or pause. By the fourteenth century, the verb was commonly used to describe the act of staying put and then, by extension, the word 'dwelling' was used to refer to the place or building in which a person resided.

The terms 'housing', 'houses' and 'house' are sometimes used generically to cover all types of residential unit. However, they can be used more specifically to describe a particular class of domestic property; in this way houses are sometimes distinguished from bungalows, maisonettes, flats and so on. To overcome this potential confusion, government and other official publications use the term 'housing' to describe habitation in general or the stock of accommodation in a defined area and have established the convention of using the term 'dwelling' to describe an individual unit of accommodation.

Within this convention, the term 'dwelling' is taken to mean any building or part of a building used as a unit of habitation that has its own separate entrance. To be a 'self-contained' dwelling it must afford the occupier access to the outside world without having to invade some other household's private living space. If a dwelling is shared by more than one household it is said to be in 'multiple occupation'.

A dwelling can be in a number of physical forms and, in the United Kingdom, these are generally classified as houses (detached, semi-detached or terraced), bungalows, maisonettes, flats, high or low rise, or mobile homes, sometimes called park homes. Dwellings in multiple occupation can include bedsits, old people's homes, student residences, homeless persons' hostels and hotels.

the socio-economic nature of a dwelling

It can be said that a dwelling is at one and the same time a consumer commodity, private investment and a social good. These primary characteristics exist simultaneously in all dwellings irrespective of *tenure* and affects the ways in which people think about and behave towards particular dwellings (see *proprietary interests*). It has also had a profound effect on how the authorities have treated dwellings for tax purposes.

KEY TEXT

- https://www.gov.uk/government/statistical-data-sets/live-tables-on-dwelling-stock-including-vacants

e

equity

SEE ALSO allocations; business planning; capital and revenue; community; diversity; fuel poverty; housing law; low cost home ownership; low income households; mortgages; proprietary interests; sustainability; value; value for money; welfare

Equity is a word, like *community* or *welfare*, that began by signifying a general social condition and then, over time, developed more specific senses while still retaining its original meaning. The first meaning of equity in English was a direct translation from the original Old French 'equité', a word whose Latin root means 'even', 'just' and 'equal'. It could refer to the *quality* of being impartial, reasonable and fair, and contemporary social service providers are expected to operate in ways that demonstrate an 'equitable' incidence of the costs of provision and management (burdens) and an equitable distribution of the outputs (benefits).

It was not until the late sixteenth century that a new, more specific, meaning emerged that placed equity in the arena of law where it provided remedies other than those covered by the common law. Perhaps because many of the usages of equity involved legal disputes over rights and claims of ownership, by the turn of the twentieth century, the word started being used in the field of *finance* to mean a stock, share or other security representing an ownership interest. At this point terms such as 'home equity', 'equity loan' and 'equity release' became common finance terms.

equity in land and property

When related to landed property, the term 'equity' refers to that part of the property's market *value* after the deduction of any charges against it. On a mortgaged property it represents that part of the *value* that is 'owned' by the occupier as against the mortgage provider.

negative equity

When house prices fall for a prolonged period there is a danger that the market value of a dwelling drops below the value of the mortgage debt. When this occurs the owner-occupier is said to be in 'negative equity'.

equity release

When house prices rise for a prolonged period there are a number of ways in which all or part of the equity can be unlocked and spent on general consumption. As the market value of an occupier's dwelling increases over time it may be possible to borrow against the equity growth. Equity release loans are often used to finance home improvements. Many households unlock part of their accumulated housing equity later in life by 'trading down'. This typically involves selling the family home and then purchasing a smaller, and less valuable, retirement property. Equity can also be unlocked when the occupier dies and his or her estate is inherited by people who then sell the fixed asset with a view to acquiring liquid assets (see *capital and revenue*). In addition, commercial equity release schemes became popular in the early 1980s when house prices were rising rapidly. The buoyant nature of the *housing market* in the late 1990s and early 2000s encouraged many people to unlock the liquid wealth tied up in their homes.

shared equity

This term is used to describe schemes in which individuals can, under a *leasehold* agreement, buy part of a property with the aid of a loan from a third party, such as the government, a private developer or a social landlord, with the remaining part of the property being owned by the third party (see *low cost home ownership*).

equity loans

This term is used to describe government-backed schemes designed to help would-be homeowners who have difficulty in accumulating funds for a mortgage deposit (see *mortgages* and *low cost home ownership*).

equity, ethics and social justice

As well as referring to legally enforceable interests in land and property, 'equity' is also a term that is applied to the nature of rules and to modes of behaviour. An important distinction exists between 'formal' and 'procedural' fairness. A rule can be judged to be 'formally' fair or unfair in itself and, quite separately, how it is applied or administered may or may not be fair or proper. To behave 'equitably' is to act in ways that are judged to be 'fair'. We might say that ethics is 'fairness in action'.

Over the years, much has been written about the distinction between 'inequality' and 'unfairness'. We self-evidently (and inevitably) live in an unequal society and socio-political comment has tended to focus on whether or not inequalities are 'justified' rather than whether they should exist at all. As in other areas of welfare provision, housing policy questions have paid particular attention to the pursuit of equality of 'opportunity' and 'treatment'. Key aspects of these questions have been formed into principles of application and some have been codified in manuals of 'best practice' and in equal opportunities legislation and other statutes such as the 1995 Disability Discrimination Act and the Equality Act 2010.

equity and distributional justice

Over the years there has been a good deal of academic, professional and popular debate about what counts as a fair or equitable distribution of welfare burdens and benefits. Housing-related policies can have significant distributional consequences. The welfare reform agenda of 2012–2015 that introduced the universal credit system and the so-called bedroom tax (see *welfare*) attracted much support from those who saw the changes as a 'fairer' use of scarce welfare resources. Others criticized the reforms as 'unfair' penalizing poor and vulnerable individuals and households. Recent aspects of national energy policy have also been described as 'unjust' by organizations such as the Joseph Rowntree Foundation (JRF) and the Centre for Sustainable Energy (CSE) (see *low income households*).

equity and value for money

John Rawls has argued that, 'Justice is the first virtue of social institutions, as truth is of systems of thought' (1972, p. 3). In the 1990s the Labour Government moved away from 'compulsory competitive tendering' as a way of seeking *value for money* (VFM) in the public sector to one of 'best value analysis'. Simply put, this meant that public service organizations should no longer rely on crude short-term market testing to demonstrate VFM outcomes. 'Best value' principles required investment decisions to take account of a wider spectrum of factors and to take a long-term view of expected costs and benefits when planning their spending programmes. This meant that along with 'efficiency', 'effectiveness' and 'positive user experience', *equity* was now regarded as a fundamental overarching goal of housing management (see Figure 6, p. 204).

Economic and financial decisions change situations: they have an impact. As a result, some people are made better off and some are made worse off. The positive and negative outcomes of such decisions (the 'marginal social costs and benefits') are distributed differentially to different interest groups. When spending patterns change, 'best value' principles require agencies to be clear about who is going to gain and who is going to pay or lose out in some other way.

Assessing the impact of financial decisions again brings up questions of time and inter-generational justice. Costs and benefits associated with housing decisions come on stream at different times so it is possible for one generation of tenants or occupiers to enjoy or pay for the spending decisions made at some other time. This can be illustrated by reference to the issue of paying for major repairs. If future repairs are paid for by means of a sinking fund, then the burden will fall on current *rent* payers. If, on the other hand, they are paid for by a loan taken out at the time of the works, then future loan charges will displace the cost burden onto the rents of future tenants.

KEY TEXTS
- Garnett, D. and Perry, J. (2005) *Housing Finance* (Coventry: Chartered Institute of Housing and The Housing Studies Association)
- Lund, B. (2011) *Understanding Housing Policy* (Bristol: The Polity Press), Chapter 10

f

finance

SEE ALSO accounts; asset management; business planning; capital and revenue; community; cost of housing; development; private renting; proprietary interests; risk and uncertainty; social enterprise; social returns; subsidies; value for money

The term 'finance' stems from the Latin 'finis' indicating the ending of a monetary debt, fine or tax liability; in English usage it was gradually extended to embrace money management in general (eighteenth century). Housing finance can be thought of as a system of money and credit that operates to enable all types of residential property to be produced, managed, acquired, maintained, repaired, renewed and exchanged. A key distinction is usually made between finance that is used for *capital and revenue* purposes and finance that is used to augment incomes (see *capital and revenue, low income households* and *subsidies*).

One way of conceptualizing the nature and scope of 'housing finance' is to regard it as a mechanism for linking money inputs (sources of finance) to money outputs (expenditure). Treating housing finance as a system of bridging money inputs and outputs is useful on two counts. First, it highlights the functions to which the finance is eventually put and thereby acts as a reminder that raising and spending money are not ends in themselves: that is, it underlines the point that financial arrangements exist to facilitate proprietary plans and public policies. Second, it provides a simple, conceptual framework and vocabulary that can be used to discuss the financial arrangements associated with all types of housing in all types of *tenure*.

revenue financing
Every local authority with 50 or more council houses is required to keep a separate, ring-fenced Housing Revenue Account, which

is a landlord trading account detailing income and expenditure relating to its housing stock. In line with the principles of 'resource accounting' (see *capital and revenue*), this arrangement ensures that there is no cross-subsidy between council tenants and council taxpayers.

In April 2012 the government ended the previous housing revenue account subsidy system that redistributed resources between authorities in line with a needs formula and replaced it with a new arrangement called 'self-financing' that is assumed to be more in line with the principles of resource accounting. Following the localism legislation (2011), councils, just like housing associations, can now keep their rental income and use it to manage their housing affairs. The objectives of this reform are to give each council the resources, incentives and flexibility it needs to manage its own housing stock for the long term and to improve service *quality* and efficiency. It is also intended to give tenants the information they need to hold their landlord to account by creating a clear relationship between the *rent* a municipal landlord collects and the services it provides.

As with council housing, the main sources of revenue income for housing associations are rents, service charges and any earnings from invested reserves. It is many years since associations have received government revenue support grants to help meet the day-to-day costs of being a landlord.

In recent years the state has used the benefit system to redirect its fiscal support away from landlords and towards residents (e.g. council tax and housing benefit).

capital financing

Housing capital expenditure is typically financed by borrowing and/or by the use of accumulated savings (reserves). It is often financed through the reinvestment of capital receipts from asset sales. Revenue income, grants, contributions from regional *development* funds and gifts can supplement such sources.

Private debt finance going into housing supply has historically come from two main sources – conventional corporate loans provided by banks and other financial institutions, and bond finance (either publicly listed or privately placed). Until recently, in the housing association sector, banks made long-term finance (up to 30 years) available at competitive rates. For those associations whose balance sheets were modestly geared, this conventional corporate debt was the most cost-effective way of borrowing money to fund growth, development and the acquisition of new homes. In recent years long-term debt finance has become more difficult to acquire and its costs have risen significantly. Banks are coming under considerable regulatory pressure and are being encouraged to match the lifetime of their assets with their liabilities and this has resulted in a shift in the profile of their lending away from long-term loans towards short- or medium-term finance of five to seven years. Where long-term corporate debt remains available, lenders may demand an ability to re-price at intervals above five years and for many associations this represents a financial risk that they are unwilling to take. Refinancing introduces a degree of uncertainty that makes long-term planning more problematic. There is now evidence that the funding of affordable housing is moving towards a divided position with the banks providing short-term finance (which could be on an individual project basis) and the capital markets and wider institutional investors becoming an important source of long-term funding.

Bond finance is already established as an important element of housing association finance. There appears to be a good appetite for this provision from the market. Some £4.4 billion was invested in *social housing* via public and private placement bond issues in 2012, bringing the total for the sector to £12 billion by the end of that year (Macauley, 2013). The Housing Finance Corporation (HFC) can act as a conduit for the sector, enabling smaller- and medium-sized associations to access the markets in an indirect way by aggregating their individual funding requirements to an amount that is acceptable to the market.

The nature of an ALMO means that the delivery of its capital funding plans will require the involvement of its parent authority. Its sources of capital funding are similar to those of a council housing department. Local authorities can borrow funds from the capital markets at preferential rates via the Public Works Loans Board. Through this mechanism capital finance can be passed on, usually with an added margin, to an authority's ALMO. As an arm's length organization, an ALMO's financial *accounts* are ring-fenced and, in line with resource accounting principles, it will have its own capital reserve account (sometimes called the 'affordable housing reserve'). Capital receipts from the disposal of assets associated with HRA are paid into this reserve where they are then available for future reinvestment.

community funding

Community projects and not-for-profit community enterprises can be funded by charging for services, receiving grants and donations or by creating debt. Most social housing agencies see themselves as being more than just a landlord and often include support for community projects or community organizations as part of their mission and vision. This support can take the form of direct funding to community groups from the agency itself or in providing advice and support in their bids for Lottery and other grant applications.

Some legal structures allow a social business to raise funds through the issue of community shares and/or bonds. With the support of organizations, such as the Community Shares Unit, Big Society Capital, Locality and the Co-operative UK, a social investment market is gradually emerging that is creating a new asset class focusing on community ventures run by industrial and provident/community benefit societies. Community shares are a new way of raising investment capital from communities. In 2014 the government introduced tax concessions to encourage the development of this sector.

regional funding

The devolved nature of the United Kingdom means that central government support for economic growth and development varies between the national regions. Much of this support aims at developing markets rather than building homes or improving regional infrastructures. There is, however, a growing awareness that sustainable economic growth is crucially dependent on the provision of adequate and appropriate housing and infrastructure investment. Periodically, European regional funds are channelled through the United Kingdom's regional governments, assemblies and national regional development agencies such as Scottish Enterprise and England's Local Enterprise Partnerships.

implications for practice
- Capital market finance is no longer limited to the larger associations issuing in their own names. There is also a move to

private placements that enable small bond debt to be placed with individual investors. Until recently, associations would need to seek upwards of £50 million per transaction to access capital markets on their own, but now figures can be as low as £10 million.

- Capital market investors are often not so much concerned with a landlord having an officially high letter score with credit rating agencies, as being able to demonstrate sound financial and *asset management* policies, together with the appointment and retention of high-quality managers and board members.
- For the 2014–2020 funding period, the European Regional Development Fund (ERDF), the European Social Fund (ESF) and part of the European Agricultural Fund for Rural Development (EAFRD) will be brought together into an EU Structural and Investment Funds Growth Programme. The top priorities of this Programme are innovation, support for small enterprises, low carbon emissions, the cultivation of skills and employment and social inclusion.

KEY TEXTS

- For information on regional policy, see websites for Local Enterprise Partnerships, Scottish Enterprise, the Welsh Government and the Northern Ireland Development Strategy
- Garnett, D. and Perry, J. (2005) *Housing Finance* (Coventry: Chartered Institute of Housing and The Housing Studies Association)
- King, P. (2009) *Understanding Housing Finance: Meeting Needs and Making Choices* (London and New York: Routledge)
- Mullins, D. and Murie, A. (2006) *Housing Policy in the UK* (Basingstoke: Palgrave Macmillan), Chapter 8
- Smith Institute (2011) *Making the Most of HRA Reform* (London: Price Waterhouse Coopers). www.psrc.pwc.com
- Smith and Williamson (2014) *Finance Demystified: A Guide for Housing Association Board Members and Non-finance Executives* (London: NHF)

fuel poverty

SEE ALSO **equity; low income households; merit goods and services; sustainability; value for money**

The government has legally binding targets to ensure that no households are in fuel poverty by 2016 and to reduce carbon emissions up to 80 per cent by 2050. As with any social issue requiring govern-ment intervention, an official definition of the problem is necessary if public monies are to be directed to its alleviation in ways that can be seen to be coherent, consistent and fair. For many years any household that had spent more than 10 per cent of its disposable income on energy consumption was defined as being 'fuel poor'. In 2012/2013 the debate surrounding the drafting of the energy bill brought about a different definition that is now incorporated into the new legislation. People in fuel poverty are now defined as those whose fuel costs are above average and whose residual income after fuel costs is below the poverty line (see *low income households*). The change in definition reduced the official number of fuel poor in 2014 from 3.2 million to 2.4 million.

Data published by the Office for National Statistics (ONS) and the National Records of Scotland (NRS) indicate that although the long-term trend of excess winter mortality is downwards, there are still about 30,000 'excess winter deaths' in England and Wales alone, with some further 2,500 in Scotland. The seasonal increase in winter mortality is defined as the difference between the number of deaths in the four-month winter period (December to March) and the average number of deaths in the two four-month periods that precede and follow winter. There is no single cause for the addi-tional deaths and only few are the result of acute hypothermia. Most result from respiratory or circulatory diseases such as pneumonia, coronary heart disease and stroke. In a typical year only a small proportion of the deaths have influenza recorded as the underlying cause. Although it is not possible to quantify the contribution that cold and damp living conditions make to these mortalities, it is clearly implicated to some significant extent.

Although fuel poverty is a matter of 'life and death' for some, it is a matter of real concern to many. The inability to heat a home adequately means that many people's lives are diminished in all sorts of ways. Some poorer households are confronted with difficult income management decisions characterized by the phrase 'heat or eat?' It is known that some older people are frightened to use their heating systems for fear of the resultant bills and some retreat to bed at unsociable times just to keep warm.

It is estimated that by 2020 current policies will have the effect of reducing the financial burden on households. The benefit will, however, not be evenly spread. The top 10 per cent of earners are expected to benefit by 14 per cent reduction to average bills while the bottom 10 per cent by about 7 per cent.

A report published in March 2013 by the Centre for Sustainable Energy (CSE) on behalf of the Joseph Rowntree Foundation focused on the 'triple injustice' that current energy policies place on low income households. The report stressed the need to meet climate change targets (some 27 per cent of UK CO_2 emissions come from *dwellings*) but called for a fairer approach to how policies impact on poorer households. Using the government's own assessments of policy costs and impacts, the CSE's analysis found that low income households (i) benefit least from energy policies; (ii) pay a proportionately higher share of the policy costs and (iii) produce proportionately the least emissions. The lowest income group is expected to spend 10.5 per cent of income on energy bills and the richest only 1.3 per cent and, even if the policies are fully successful, there will still be nearly three million fuel poor in 2020. The mean annual household emission of the top 10 per cent earners is about three times that of the bottom 10 per cent. In terms of vehicle emissions, the top 10 per cent earners are generating more than seven times the amount of the bottom 10 per cent.

KEY TEXTS

- Hills, J. (2012) *Getting the Measure of Fuel Poverty.* Final Report of the Fuel Poverty Review, CASE Report 72 March 2012
- Joseph Rowntree Foundation (2013) *Distribution of Carbon Emissions in the UK: Implications for Domestic Energy Policy*
- https://www.gov.uk/government/publications/final-report-of-the-fuel-poverty-review

g

governance

SEE ALSO audit; business planning; continuous improvement; culture; participation; regulation

Simply put, 'governance' is defined as the processes and arrangements that determine how authoritative decisions are made, implemented and monitored. It can be used in a number of contexts such as corporate governance, international governance, national governance and local governance. In terms of strict dictionary definitions, there is no real difference in meaning between the term 'governance' and the term 'government'. Both words are derived from the Greek Κυβερνήτης ('kyvernites') and the Latin 'gubernator' meaning 'steersman', 'pilot' or 'rudder'. From this original maritime application, the terms eventually came to describe the established authority in an organization or society that guides, regulates and controls things in general.

Although historically the terms 'government' and 'governance' are interchangeable, in recent times policy analysts often use them differently to distinguish between the processes by which an organization or society operates ('governance') and the constitutional authority that is set up to approve and steer these processes and systems ('government'). This distinction allows for a difference to be drawn between 'top-down' government (power over) and 'bottom-up' governance (power to). Whilst 'governance' is a 'process' often involving a number of legitimized groups and arrangements, 'a government' is a single 'authority' with specifically constituted powers and duties that give it the right to legislate and make rules which others are required to follow. In participative organizations such as *social housing* agencies, the term 'government' tends to be used to refer to the exercise of ultimate authority by an executive group working under the guidance and ultimate control of a board of directors/trustees. The term 'governance' is used to refer to a process that embraces a variety of extended influences that exist in determining how things get done. Government is achieved by establishing properly constituted executive authority. Governance is achieved by the involvement of a network of interests in the strategic and operational decision-making processes. Both government and governance (and the relationship between the two) should operate in the context of rules of procedure delineating limits of authority and lines of responsibility.

The Independent Commission on Good Governance in Public Services Chaired by Sir Alan Langlands (2005) reflects the high profile that this topic now possesses. More than 450,000 people contribute as governors of public services, including school governors, members of NHS boards, local strategic partnerships, police and probation boards, community safety and children's partnerships, housing associations, ALMOs, learning and skills councils and universities.

Langlands's principles of good governance

Governors/directors have heavy responsibilities in times of rapid change and high expectations from their service users and other stakeholders. The Commission drafted a set of six principles for governing public services. These six principles constitute the proposed 'standard':

1. Focus on the organization's purpose and on outcomes for citizens and service users.
2. Engage stakeholders and make *accountability* real.
3. Perform effectively in clearly defined functions and roles.
4. Promote values for the whole organization and behave ethically.
5. Develop the capacity and capability of the governing body to be effective.
6. Take informed, transparent decisions and manage *risk and uncertainty*.

In local authority housing departments, tenants play no part in the direct government of affairs. This 'top-down' aspect of management authority lies with the elected members and the professional housing managers who implement decisions made by councillors.

Council tenants, however, can exercise a good deal of 'bottom-up' influence by getting involved in a variety of governance arrangements such as tenants' consultative committees and forums. In most arms-length management organisations (ALMOs) and housing associations, tenants are involved in both the organization's wider governance (through tenants' forums, working parties, etc.) and the organization's direct government (as board members). In the case of tenant management organizations (TMOs), tenants are the dominant players in both the government and governance functions.

principles of 'good governance' in housing organizations

The pursuit of 'good governance' is not simply concerned with the nature and scope of management arrangements, rules and procedures: it is also concerned with 'how they are used' in developing and delivering the service. Good governance provides the overarching administrative and ethical framework within which the housing agency pursues its mission and vision (see *business planning*). Because different social landlords have different objectives there can be no one, simple definition of 'good governance' covering the sector. However, there is general agreement about what constitutes the nature and scope of the processes and procedures that need to be in place in order for the business to be (and to be seen to be) run effectively, efficiently and with due regard to propriety. Well-governed housing organizations display a genuine concern for the interests of current and future stakeholders. More specifically, the term refers to the following aspects of the relationship between the organization, those who own or fund it and those it serves and employs: transparency, effectiveness, openness, responsiveness, accountability, the rule of law and the acceptance of *diversity* and pluralism. In most societies there is also a consensus that organizations that have social and *welfare* objectives and are supported by public monies should embrace practices that explicitly benefit poor and excluded groups.

The object of 'good' governance in the housing field is to establish appropriate interactions between the governmental authority (e.g. board of management or council committee) and the wider network of participant stakeholders who have a legitimate interest in how the organization runs its affairs (e.g. tenants' consultative

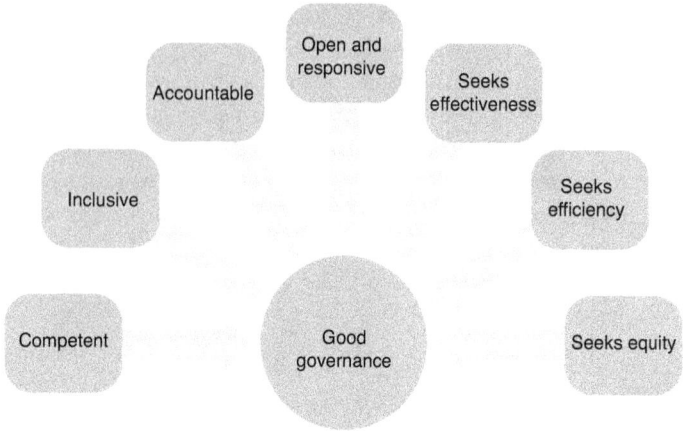

FIGURE 3   *The principles of good governance*

committees). This means that good governance has a 'relational' dimension. There is general agreement that a well-run organization will continuously explore how the interactions between those participating in the processes of governance might be changed in ways that foster better outcomes. It is also recognized that well-governed organizations are clear how the opinions of service users will be incorporated into discussions about what counts as a 'better outcome' (i.e. improved service). This means that the balance between 'top-down' and 'bottom-up' forces must be considered to be appropriate by stakeholders, funders and the regulators.

KEY TEXTS
- The Langlands Report (2005) *Report of the Independent Commission on Good Governance in Public Services* (London: OPM/CIPFA)
- Lowe, S. (2004) *Housing Policy Analysis: British Housing in Cultural and Comparative Context* (Basingstoke: Palgrave Macmillan)
- National Housing Federation (2010) *Excellence in Governance: Compliance Checklist*
- National Housing Federation (2012b) *Code of Conduct: With Good Practice for Members*

h

home ownership

SEE ALSO affordability; culture; equity; housing law; leasehold; low cost home ownership; low income households; mortgages; proprietary interests; sustainability; tenure

During the twentieth century, owner-occupation developed from being a restricted way of holding residential property that catered largely for the housing needs of the upper echelons of society into the nation's predominant *tenure* arrangement. This growth has been particularly prominent over the past 35 years. During the 1980s, following the Thatcher government's introduction of the 'right to buy' (RTB) and other *low cost home ownership* (LCHO) initiatives, the proportion of households that owned their own homes rose from about a half to two-thirds. By 2002 the ownership proportion peaked at just under 70 per cent. In the early years of the twenty-first century, despite historically low mortgage interest rates and relatively stable prices, the growth of home ownership slowed and the proportion fell back to less than 65 per cent by 2014 (see *tenure*). The slow-down in large part can be explained by the economic recession and the difficulties of mortgage availability following the financial crisis that preceded it. In response to the slow-down, David Cameron's Coalition Government introduced a variety of new initiatives to help stimulate owner-occupation (see *low cost home ownership*).

the concept of 'ownership'
Both lawyers and economists make the point that a house is not 'owned' in the same way that consumer durables such as cameras and refrigerators are 'owned' (see *proprietary interests*). In purchasing a dwelling the owner-occupier does not so much gain absolute possession of the building and the land, as acquire a bundle of legally enforceable freehold or *leasehold* rights relating to

their use and disposal. This is an important point because it underlines the fact that others may also 'own' legal rights or interests in the same property, such as tenancy rights or rights of easement. Such legal interests have a market *value* of their own and their existence can therefore affect the exchange value of the freehold or leasehold.

The fullest individual, legal ownership of real property is called 'fee simple'. Fee simple is associated with freehold rights and it is the form of ownership that most people think of in relation to owner-occupation (see *tenure*). Subject to any underlying rights of the Crown, third-party tenancy, leasehold or easement interests, and any mortgage encumbrances, planning laws and health codes, the fee simple holder has the nearest thing possible to absolute ownership rights. These rights can be left to the owner's heirs forever or until such time as they dispose of the property. Long leases are normally regarded as a form of home ownership (see *leasehold*).

the imagery and culture of ownership

During the second half of the twentieth century, the aspiration to own one's own home, and thereby become part of the 'property-owning democracy', was actively encouraged both by the rhetoric that accompanied government housing policy and by the commercial advertising that was part of the rapidly expanding property and mortgage markets. In addition, as home ownership became more accessible to a wider section of society, the advantages of owning one's own home were increasingly pointed to in the popular media.

For many commentators, the case for expanding owner-occupation is grounded in the presuppositions of market ideology. In so far as it embraces demand-led market mechanisms that operate to fulfil domestic desires in ways that enhance life chances, the tenure can be said to encapsulate the values of a free-enterprise *culture*. In the minds of those who are ideologically predisposed towards owner-occupation, its growth is also seen to foster individuality and personal responsibility. In terms of this view, home ownership is assumed to be 'good' for the individual, enhancing self-fulfilment, personal independence and financial security, and also 'good' for the wider *community*, by spreading capital wealth and thereby cultivating 'responsible' attitudes towards property in particular and society's socio-economic structures in general.

By the 1980s the popular discourse on home ownership was characterized by pronouncements that carried a distinct cultural symbolism of responsibility and self-fulfilment. This helped to create a political climate in which the government could argue that it had a 'moral duty' to make home ownership more widely available. That as many people as possible should be encouraged to own their own homes was presented as 'common sense'. This compares with what we might term a 'rational' explanation of the growth of the tenure. This non-ideological explanation accepts that the advantages of home ownership can be tangible but argues that they are not intrinsic in the tenure. That is, it argues that they do not naturally occur in all places when a certain stage of socio-economic *development* is reached, but rather that they are largely the consequence of financial, fiscal, legal and other arrangements that are specific in terms of time and space.

Although attitudes to home ownership were modified by the sharp downturn in the property market that occurred after 1989, in Britain a powerful ideological advocacy of owner-occupation still exists. Politicians, mortgage providers and the press still commonly employ such housing imagery as 'castles' (of security) and 'ladders' (of mobility), and many commentators still point to the 'moral' imperative of most people becoming homeowners in line with their 'natural' desires and interests.

the dual nature of the owner-occupier's proprietary economic interests

Owners have both 'consumption' and 'investment' interests vested in the *dwellings* they occupy. To the owner-occupier the dwelling possesses both the characteristics of a home and a financial asset. The dual nature of the occupier's economic interests in the property has, over the years, led to much debate about how this tenure should be treated with respect to taxation liability and subsidy support. This dual interest also has to be borne in mind when analysing questions relating to the *affordability* and *sustainability* of the tenure (see *proprietary interests*).

KEY TEXTS

- Lowe, S. (2004) *Housing Policy Analysis: British Housing in Cultural and Comparative Context* (Basingstoke: Palgrave Macmillan)
- Lowe, S. (2011) *The Housing Debate* (Bristol: The Policy Press, University of Bristol), Chapter 1
- 'The political and cultural significance of home-ownership' Appendix 1 to Chapter 6, in Garnett, D. and Perry, J. (2005) *Housing Finance*: (Coventry: Chartered Institute of Housing and The Housing Studies Association)
- Statistics regarding home ownership are readily accessible on government sites, for example, http://www.ons.gov.uk/ons/rel/census/2011-census/detailed-characteristics-on-housing-for-local-authorities-in-england-and-wales/short-story-on-detailed-characteristics.html
- Williams, P. (2010) 'Home Ownership – Where Now?' in P. Malpass and R. Rowlands (eds), *Housing, Markets and Policy* (Abingdon: Routledge)

homelessness

SEE ALSO allocations; low income households; merit goods and services; need and demand; private renting; tenure

Homelessness represents the most acute form of housing need. Official definitions vary from country to country and among different entities or institutions within a country. They also vary over time. Stuart Lowe (2011, p. 18) makes the point that the personal circumstances of those who are in the most acute housing need (i.e. with nowhere to shelter or sleep) are constantly changing with people moving in and out of the category on a week-by-week basis. He suggests that homelessness should be seen as a volatile flow of highly vulnerable people rather than as a fixed *tenure* group.

The simple dictionary definition of homelessness as 'the condition of people with nowhere to live' masks a whole range of socio-legal complexities that have a long and chequered history. Homeless individuals typically are people who are not able to acquire or maintain constant, safe, secure, habitable accommodation. The most extreme form of homelessness involves the inability to have access to a safe and adequate place to sleep. The term will usually also include anyone whose normal night-time residence is an emergency or domestic violence shelter or a short-stay hostel. In practice, the notion of homelessness is usually extended to include more than just so-called rough sleepers. Households who are physically housed but whose accommodation is regarded as overcrowded, insanitary, unsafe or in some other way unsatisfactory are included in official definitions of the category. This means that the classification boundary between the homeless and those in general housing need can be unclear.

Official definitions of homelessness are important because, for many years, local authorities have had a statutory duty to help the 'unintentionally homeless' as defined by the 1996 Homelessness Act. Under subsequent legislation (Homelessness Act 2002), local authority waiting lists were opened to a wide category of applicants and this led to a criticism that people were registering who had no real chance of acquiring a social tenancy. Waiting lists were also seen as poor measures of homelessness because they were seldom up to date and many people remained registered after they had found accommodation in the private sector – and some in 'legitimate need' failed to register, judging it to be a waste of time.

implications for practice
- The duties of local authorities (LAs) were amended by the provisions of the Localism Act 2011 (Sections 147–149). Every authority must still have in place an *allocations* scheme that identifies priorities and ensures that 'reasonable preference' is given to people with urgent housing needs. Central government also continues to fund support and advice to prevent homelessness and rough sleeping and reduce the reliance on using unsuitable 'bed and breakfast' accommodation.
- The 2011 legislation allows LAs to discharge their statutory duty to secure housing for homeless households with an offer of 'suitable' accommodation in the private rented sector (PRS) for a fixed period. Under the previous rules, people who became homeless were able to refuse offers of accommodation in the private rented sector, and insist that they should be housed in temporary accommodation until a long-term social home was made available. Critics of the new arrangements (e.g. the NHF) are concerned about the ability of LAs to secure suitable accommodation in the private rented sector.

KEY TEXTS

- Lowe, S. (2011) *Housing Policy Analysis: British Housing in Cultural and Comparative Context* (Basingstoke: Palgrave Macmillan)
- Lund, B. (2011) *Understanding Housing Policy* (Bristol: The Policy Press)
- National Housing Federation (2012a) *Localism Act 2011: Housing and Planning, A Guide for Housing Associations*
- Wilcox, S. (2009) 'Where Are We Now?' in B. Pattison and J. Vine (eds), *Perspectives on the Future of Housing: A Collection of Viewpoints on the UK Housing System* (Coalville: Building and Social Housing Foundation)
- http://www.scotland.gov.uk/Topics/Built-Environment/Housing/homeless
- http://www.housingadviceni.org/homelessness
- LA and DCLG websites.

housing law

SEE ALSO affordability; anti-social behaviour; care and support; community; development; equity; governance; homelessness; leasehold; low cost home ownership; planning gain; proprietary interests; regulation; subsidies; tenancy agreements

Legal rights, duties and remedies permeate housing practice. Much of the context of how this occurs is pointed to in other entries. In its narrowest sense, the term 'housing law' refers to legislation that has its primary focus on the enforceable rights and remedies associated with residential property interests (i.e. Housing Acts of Parliament). It also applies to other legislation that contains sections that make specific reference to residential property rights, interests and duties (e.g. legislation relating to benefit rights, planning, *development* and localism). Housing practice is also subjected to a wide range of general legislation in areas such as employment, taxation and equal opportunities. As with other organizations, housing agencies are subjected to the law of tort, particularly as it applies in areas such as negligence, nuisance and privacy. In addition to statute law and common law, much of the work of housing practitioners is directed and constrained by specialist contract law in areas such as construction, landlord and tenant and procurement.

KEY TEXTS

- Arden, A. and Dymond, A. (2012) *Manual of Housing Law*. 9th edn (London: Sweet and Maxwell)
- Each month, Shelter's team of legal experts research all the latest news and developments in housing law and policy, and then condense it into an easy-to-read, downloadable bulletin for housing practitioners and advice workers, for free.
- Reeves, P. (2014) *Affordable and Social Housing: Policy and Practice* (New York: Routledge)
- There are a number of housing law websites designed to provide a user-friendly guide through different aspects of UK housing law. See: http://www.housinglaw.org.uk/index.htm
- http://england.shelter.org.uk/professional_resources/shelters_housing_law_update

housing market

SEE ALSO **accountability; equity; home ownership; merit goods and services; need and demand; subsidies; welfare**

In 1907, referring back to the early writers on economics, Irvin Fisher, the famous American theorist and social campaigner, remarked that it appeared that if you caught a parrot and taught it to say 'supply and demand' you would have created an 'excellent economist'. In making this knowingly cynical witticism, Fisher was suggesting that crude market economic theory sought to explain movements in prices, wages, rents, interest and profits with the glib proposition that 'it's all a matter of market forces'. The parrot analogy (some trace a similar reference back further to the nineteenth-century historian Thomas Carlyle) indicates the powerful influence market theory has had on political as well as economic thinking. In many respects markets embrace both mechanistic and ideological ideas.

the market as mechanism

In its simplest mechanistic conception, a market can be thought of as a place where buyers and sellers meet to do business. It has long been recognized that trading markets can exist outside of a fixed location and it is therefore possible to talk about the stock market, the labour market, the property market and so on.

What all these trading markets have in common is that they bring together the forces of 'supply and demand'. The market mechanism is sometimes referred to as the 'price mechanism' because the interplay of supply and demand in a freely competitive market is assumed to produce an 'equilibrium market price' that balances what producers are prepared to accept with what consumers are prepared to pay.

Compared with many markets, the housing market lacks coherence because *dwellings* are strongly differentiated by six classifications: 'tenure', 'location', 'type', 'size', 'condition' and 'time'. This means that unless two units of accommodation share similar across-the-board characteristics, they cannot be said to be in the same market. For example, if there are two physically identical houses available in the same street today but one is for *rent* and the other is for sale, despite their physical and locational similarities, they cannot properly be said to be in the same market even if they are available on the same day. Similarly, if two identically designed, well-maintained houses are going to be advertised at different months of the year, they cannot be said to be in the same market. If one is in Glasgow and the other is in Exeter they cannot be said to be in the same market. Indeed, if one is in Princes Street Edinburgh and the other is in Ferniehill Road Edinburgh, they cannot be said to be in the same market. For all these reasons, the notion of there being a single, unified housing market is of limited use and indeed, when looking at statistics (such as annual increases in house prices or construction rates), such a notion may be positively unhelpful. As any estate agent knows, it is usually more sensible to think of housing supply and demand as operating in coherent 'sub-markets'. For a discretely coherent housing sub-market to exist, there has to be what we can term a 'coincidence of categories'. So, for example, although it is difficult to identify 'the' housing market as such, we can clearly say that 'a' market does exist for identical newly built, currently available, owner-occupier, three-bedroomed bungalows close to the sea in Christchurch Dorset.

Much housing legislation has been driven by two competing political views about society's social and economic objectives. Since the nineteenth century, the *regulation* of housing has always involved political arguments about the requisite roles of market forces and the state. Although a little simplistic, we might say that these debates demonstrate two different ideological positions competing to justify and direct housing policies.

market failure: a role for the state

Adam Smith postulated that, under competitive conditions, market forces act (invisibly) to ensure that successful producers create products and services that people need or want and can afford. This famous postulation assumed the existence of what economists now refer to as 'the conditions of perfect completion'. It is also assumed that no state regulation exists covering such things as minimum building standards. It is argued that under these 'perfect' conditions the forces of supply and demand will ensure that producers are unable to charge 'excessive' prices and that it is in their interests to produce the quantity and *quality* of goods and services that consumers want, given their budgetary constraints.

If unfettered free-enterprise market arrangements were seen to achieve the housing policy objectives society demands, there would be no calls for government intervention in the housing system. In large part, it is the failure of market forces to deliver these objectives that has brought about state involvement in this field. This 'failure' of the market has been recognized by historians, market theorists and social policy analysts.

In reality, housing markets are far from competitive because individual housing units are heavily differentiated in terms of the six classifications mentioned earlier. Market competitiveness is weakened further by the fact that house-building is a highly capital intensive activity that requires specific skills of a technical, craft and professional nature. These factors act as barriers that make it difficult for new suppliers to enter the market to compete. Because housing is a highly complex commodity (both technically and legally) most would-be consumers lack the sort of 'perfect knowledge' needed to make fully rational *choices* between market alternatives. Indeed, this lack of 'market knowledge' is the primary reason for the existence of exchange professionals such as surveyors, mortgage advisors, estate agents and conveyance lawyers. Competition is also inhibited by the fact that dwelling units are immobile and spatially separated. Because buildings are geographically fixed, a surplus in one area cannot be used to alleviate a shortage in some other area. Similarly, a surplus of large detached family houses in an area cannot be readily used to alleviate a shortage of bed-sits for students in the same district. Competition is inhibited also by the way in which the housing system is fragmented by a variety of tenure arrangements. All of these factors reduce the possibility of achieving the 'coincidence of categories' necessary for a coherent competitive market to exist.

One other problematic issue pointed to by economists is the so-called inelastic ways in which housing market forces respond to society's needs and changes in wider market conditions. The ability and willingness of the building industry to respond to the current challenge of responding to housing shortages will depend, to a large extent, on the general long-run performance of the economy. New house sales depend on transaction rates in the housing market and, in turn, these tend to increase in times of economic growth and decrease in times of economic slow-down.

Even if there is continued economic growth and a consequential general sustained demand for owner-occupied housing, the construction industry's response to any such increase may be inhibited by a variety of specific factors that reduce what economists refer to as the 'price elasticity of housing supply', which measures the responsiveness of producers to a given increase in price. If prices rise by a certain percentage, and supply adjusts more than proportionately, the response is said to be 'elastic'. Conversely, if the output response is less than proportionate to the increase in price, it is said to be 'inelastic'. In 2003, Kate Barker, a member of the Bank of England Monetary Policy Committee that sets interest rates, was commissioned to produce a report identifying the main barriers to the production of more new housing. This investigated, among other things, why the supply of new housing is price inelastic. The report indicated that, in the future, the price elasticity of supply will be affected by variables such as the capacity of the construction industry, shortages of land, the slow and unwieldy nature of the planning consent system and the planning restrictions themselves, including political constraints on the use of greenfield sites.

Most economists argue that housing markets are multifaceted, unusually complex and 'imperfectly competitive', and for all these reasons it cannot be relied upon to work automatically in the interests of consumers. In addition to the housing market's technical failure to approximate to the conditions of 'perfect competition', it can be said to fail to meet society's housing objectives in another important respect: namely, it has too restrictive a view of what counts as 'housing need'.

Social theorists argue that market arrangements fail to take proper account of the housing needs of low income and other vulnerable households. Market theory equates need with the notion of effective demand. In so doing, it is said to recognize only those needs that are expressed in the market place. 'Effective demand' is defined as a want or need backed by cash. This means that under market arrangements needs can only be made 'effective' by purchasing the required goods or services from a market provider at a price set by the forces of supply and demand. Under such arrangements those without sufficient purchasing power are unable to make their wants and needs effective. The much-lauded freedom of *choice* denoted by the market notion of 'consumer sovereignty' is restricted to those with sufficient income to pay the market price. Thus, in a free market economy everybody is free to sleep under a railway arch but only those with sufficient money can purchase a warm, dry room for the night.

Over time, to any one household, a particular type of housing can become more or less affordable. This will depend on comparative changes between the price of occupation of the dwelling in question (e.g. rent or mortgage repayment) and the disposable income of the household in question. Social analysts point out that we can only rely on the operation of market forces to accommodate the interests of *low income households* if it can be demonstrated that the comparative price and income changes are such that good quality housing is becoming more rather than less affordable to this group.

Some market advocates argue that the market will provide for low income groups through a process of 'filtering'. This argument says that over time dwellings tend to decline in *value* and thus become accessible to people on lower incomes. Social analysts, however, point out that the effectiveness of 'trading up' or 'filtering' as a means of raising housing standards hinges on the speed of value-decline relative to quality-decline:

If the value of the standing stock depreciates so rapidly that even low-income households can afford units which are still above the quality standards of social adequacy, the private market is a satisfactory instrument of public policy. (Lowry, 1960, p. 364)

Twentieth-century policy-makers have sought to identify broader definitions of housing need than that provided by the market concept of effective demand (see *need and demand*).

KEY TEXTS

- Challis, P. (2009) 'What Role for the Public Sector?' in B. Pattison and J. Vine (eds), *Perspectives on the Future of Housing: A Collection of Viewpoints on the UK Housing System* (Coalville: Building and Social Housing Foundation)
- Elphicke, N. and House, K. (2015) *From Statutory Provider to Housing Enabler: Review into the Local Authority Role in Housing Supply.* The Elphicke House Report (London: DCLG/HMSO)
- For an extended version of this entry see 'housing and society'
- King, P. (2009) *Understanding Housing Finance: Meeting Needs and Making Choices* (London and New York: Routledge), Chapter 3
- Lowe, S. (2011) *The Housing Debate* (Bristol: The Policy Press, University of Bristol), Chapter 1
- Oxley, M. (2004) *Economics, Planning and Housing* (Basingstoke: Palgrave Macmillan)

i

inclusion and exclusion

SEE ALSO equity; governance; low income households; participation

In housing and other areas of social service provision, the notion of 'inclusion' has come to have positive approbatory connotations and is often sought for as an element of public and social policy. Conversely, the notion of 'exclusion' has come to have pejorative connotations and is often presented as an unwanted outcome of some provisional arrangements. It is interesting to note that in its original application (late sixteenth century), inclusion was a neutral descriptive noun meaning 'a shutting in' (from the Latin 'inclūs') and carried no judgemental undertones.

The strictest antonym of inclusion is 'non-inclusion' which is a term that still tends to be used when a simple, non-critical description of the state of not being 'shut in' is required. Since the second half of the twentieth century and the foundation of the modern *welfare* state and its associated services, the word 'exclusion' has come to carry strong negative connotations that are variously associated with synonyms such as 'debarment', 'expulsion', 'omission', 'rejection' or a 'lack' (of articulacy, influence, power or resources).

social exclusion and inclusion

The notion of 'social exclusion' emerged in political rhetoric in the 1970s when ministers in Jacques Chirac's government related it to how certain groups in French society were 'shut out' of the national social security system of that time (Silver, 1995). Much of the literature on social exclusion understandably ties the concept into the wider debate about the nature of 'poverty' (see *low income households*). The term 'poverty' is used to describe the bottom end of low income and is generally used to identify those individuals or households who are denied an income sufficient for their material needs.

When this denies them opportunities to take part in activities that are an accepted part of society's daily life they are often described as being 'socially excluded'. In this way the notion of 'poverty' has been extended from the material into social, cultural and political life so that someone can be seen to be impoverished in ways other than simply experiencing a lack of resources.

In 1997 the government set up the Social Exclusion Unit (SEU) as part of the Prime Minister's Office. In 2006 its work was merged with the Prime Minister's Strategy Unit. Its purpose was to improve government action in order to bring about a reduction in social exclusion by creating 'joined-up solutions to joined-up problems'. Social exclusion typically occurs when people or areas suffer from a combination of linked problems such as unemployment and reduced mobility, low incomes, limited skills, low educational achievement, high drug use, poor general health and high incidences of depression and anxiety. Some commentators (the Social Exclusion Unit) have argued that other consequences of social exclusion might include higher than average incidences of family breakdown, school truancies and teenage pregnancies. The notion of 'personal social inclusion' refers to the individual's ability to participate fully in normal social activities or engage in political and civic life. The term is often used to describe the process of combating social exclusion. The need for a joined-up policy approach is precisely because the lack of inclusion is typically the result of personal issues other than income deficiency. It can be the result of some combination of factors such as disability, discrimination, lack of knowledge and education and lack of confidence. It may also, in part, be the result of locational factors such as a lack of employment opportunities, physical deprivation, high incidences of crime and disorder, rural isolation and so on. Poor *quality* housing is seen to be both an indicator of, and a contributor to, social exclusion.

digital inclusion
It is thought that 4.1 million of the 8.7 million adults who have never been online live in *social housing* (National Housing Federation). There is currently a great deal of effort being made by social landlords to help residents gain or improve their access to the internet. Research by the NHF and other housing organizations

point to the following consequences of a household having no, or only limited, access to the digital world:

- Home access to a computer and the internet can improve children's educational performances. If the 1.6 million children who live in families which do not use the internet had connectivity at home, it could boost their total lifetime earnings by over £10 billion (NHF).
- It is estimated that between 75 per cent and 90 per cent of jobs require at least some computer usage. Being online also gives people more opportunities to search and apply for jobs.
- Offline households are missing out on estimated savings of £560 per year from shopping and paying bills online.
- The proposed introduction of universal credit replacing a number of previously existing benefit entitlements (including Housing Benefit and Job Seeker's Allowance) will eventually require claimants to apply online.

KEY TEXTS

- Aldrich, H., Kenway, P., MacInnes, T. and Parekh, A. (2012) *Monitoring Poverty and Social Exclusion 2012* (York: Joseph Rowntree Foundation)
- Balchin, P. and Rhoden, M. (2002) *Housing Policy: An Introduction* (New York: Routledge), Chapter 14
- 'Digital by Default report': This report was produced by Housing Technology, with Race Online 2012 and sponsored by Family Mosaic, RCT Homes and Richmond Housing. It includes case studies of how housing associations are working to provide their tenants with online access and gives many examples of digital inclusion projects. http://www.ukonlinecentres.com/
- Lee, P. (2010) 'Competitiveness and Social Exclusion: The Importance of Place and Rescaling in Housing and Regeneration Policies' in P. Malpass and R. Rowlands (eds), *Housing, Markets and Policy* (Abingdon: Routledge)
- Lowe, S. (2004) *Housing Policy Analysis: British Housing in Cultural and Comparative Context* (Basingstoke: Palgrave Macmillan), Chapter 5
- http://www.gseu.org.uk
- http://www.housing.org.uk/policy/investing-in-communities/federation-support-for-community-investment/digital-inclusion/

1

leasehold

SEE ALSO equity; home ownership; housing law; proprietary interests; tenancy agreements; tenure

Leasehold is an agreement whereby a 'buyer' (sometimes called a 'tenant', 'leaseholder' or 'lessee') acquires the right to use the landed property for a specific period in return for a land *rent* to the 'fee simple' owner (the 'lessor' or 'freeholder'). At the end of the period or 'term' of the lease (that can be up to 999 years), all the property rights revert to the party that holds title in 'fee simple'. Under a lease agreement, the lessor's interest in the property will be longer than the term of the lease. An arrangement providing an equal term would comprise a conveyance or assignment rather than a lease.

Leasehold is a long-established way of owning property in the United Kingdom and several million residential properties are held on long leases (two-thirds being flats). The contract creates a 'leasehold estate' that can be thought of as a personal property interest. In addition to a purchase price, the agreement sometimes requires the leaseholder to pay a periodic ground rent to the freehold landlord. A 'lease option' is an arrangement whereby the lessee has the right to purchase the freehold either during the lease term or at its end. A 'long lease' is one that is in excess of 21 years. In practical terms, long leaseholders can be thought of as a class of owner-occupier. The term 'owner-occupier' carries no legal weight and long leaseholders usually consider themselves to be owners – indeed, they are considered as such by virtually everyone else, including the government. They are, however, subjected to *regulation* by other parties (i.e. lessors) who can influence their expenditure, their ability to sell the house or flat and its market *value*. Ultimately, these other parties can also influence the right of the occupier to remain in the home they have 'bought'. The lack of occupiers' management rights and *tenure* security has been a long-standing cause of complaint amongst leaseholders, and the issue of leasehold reform became a major political issue during the second half of the twentieth century.

leasehold reform

Leasehold relationships are grounded in ancient laws that many regard to be anachronistic. In particular, it is felt to be inappropriate in modern times for a landlord, who only has a limited *equity* stake in a property, to be in a position to manipulate the law in ways that restrict the *proprietary interests* that owner-occupiers have vested in their homes.

The law of landlord and tenant contains within it the influence of the common law and, particularly, the 'laissez-faire' philosophy that dominated the law of contract and the law of property in the nineteenth century. With the emergence of new attitudes towards consumer protection, equity and natural justice in the twentieth century, there was a growing recognition that common law principles assuming equal bargaining power between parties may cause unfairness. Consequently, reformers emphasized the need to assess residential tenancy laws in terms of the protection they provided to residents. This eventually led to changes in leasehold law. These changes were brought in by the provisions of the Leasehold Reform Act (1967) and then extended and amended by the Commonhold and Leasehold Reform Act 2002 (as amended 2014).

'Commonhold' is a new way of owning property in multi-occupancy buildings and offers an alternative to the traditional leasehold arrangements. It was introduced through the 2002 Act and allows for multi-occupancy buildings to be divided into units with freehold rights and shared ownership of common areas and services. Commonhold can be applied to residential and commercial buildings. However, in practice, it is more likely to be used in flatted residential *developments*. As well as enhancing the rights of occupiers in the ways in which they can use and manage their homes, commonhold also provides those owning the new property interest with a form of long-term economic security.

Commonhold is far from established, with few major housing developments adopting it as a tenure arrangement. Most flats are leasehold, and leasehold is still the typical legal form for houses bought through shared ownership (see *low cost home ownership*).

In addition to the introduction of commonhold, the 2002 Act made important amendments to previous legislation. A long-standing area of concern had centred on how *value* changes should be borne or enjoyed by the parties. The so-called marriage value is based on a calculation that links together the freehold and the lease-hold interests. It is a complicated calculation made up of the rise in property prices and the declining value of the lease. Over time the marriage value will tend to increase thereby generating an element of 'profit'. In some cases this value increase, or 'profit', can be considerable, amounting to tens, or even hundreds of thousands of pounds. Surveyors often disagree about the valuation, and tenants can challenge the landlord's claim at a tribunal. Some argue that the complicated nature of the calculation and difficulties of challenging the landlord's figure give the freeholder an unfair advantage in the negotiation. The new legislation extended the jurisdiction of lease-hold valuation tribunals in an attempt to address the issue of estab-lishing a fair distribution of the effects of value changes. The Act also provided for a range of enhanced rights for the tenants – notably the 'Right to Manage' for long leaseholders was established.

An important feature of leasehold is that tenants have 'exclu-sive possession' rights which give them the authority to exclude all other people, including the landlords or their agents, from entering the leased property (apart from periodic visits allowed for in the lease agreement and agreed at the time by the leaseholder, to check the state of repair and general condition of the land or buildings).

licenses

Licenses are different from leases. An agreement that does not include the right to exclusive possession would call for a 'license'. In property law, a license grants permission to enter or use the property of another without breaching the laws of trespass or theft. There are three broad license categories: bare licenses, contractual licenses and licenses coupled with an interest. A 'bare license' is a non-contractual arrangement that applies when it can be reason-ably assumed that entry to a property will not constitute trespass. It applies where the permission to enter is implied and covers occasions such as delivering post, entering a shop as a customer or sales representative, calling on someone as a neighbour or for some legitimate social or commercial purpose. A 'contractual license' provides for an expressed occupying purpose in exchange for some consideration. Ticket holders, for example, have the right to enter sports grounds or concert venues to attend events for which they have paid an entry fee. Some councils and social landlords grant permission to use part of their land as allotments or for some other agreed purpose. A 'license tied to an interest' exists when a person has the right to enter a property to take possession of something that is located there (e.g. an automobile or household appliance) to which they have a legally enforceable right (e.g. after default on a loan or purchase agreement).

KEY TEXTS

- Robinson, P. (2003) *Leasehold Management: A Good Practice Guide* (Coalville: Chartered Institute of Housing, National Housing Federation and The Housing Corporation)
- HM Government (2014) *Practice Guide 27: The Leasehold Reform Legislation*. https://www.gov.uk/government/publications/the-leasehold-reform-legislation
- https://www.gov.uk/leasehold-property

low cost home ownership

SEE ALSO equity; home ownership; housing market; leasehold; low income households; mortgages; need and demand; tenure

In recent years all the main political parties have declared a commitment to assist those on the *affordability* margins of owner-occupation to gain access to the *tenure*. Recent governments have pursued this commitment by establishing a variety of 'low cost home ownership' (LCHO) initiatives.

Although there is a good deal of academic and political argument about the efficacy of specific proposals, there now exists a consensus that LCHO policies should embrace two general commitments. They are as follows:

1. To make it easier to gain access to the tenure ('becoming' an owner–occupier).

2. To help sustain the tenure for those who have gained access ('being' an owner–occupier).

The former of these commitments is better established than the latter.

becoming an owner–occupier: help to gain access to the sector
Since the phasing out of mortgage income tax relief (MITR) in 2000, the statutory 'Right to Buy' (and subsequently the separate 'Right to Acquire') has been by far the largest *home ownership* initiative. This has enabled many tenants to buy their homes.

The right to buy provisions were the centrepiece of the Housing Act 1980 and the Tenants' Rights etc. (Scotland) Act 1980. Although previous legislation had granted local authorities discretionary powers to sell, in practice few transfers occurred so the statutory obligation to offer for sale was an important change in emphasis. The new legislation established the principle that a secure tenant opting to purchase is entitled to a discount on the market *value* of the property, and that this discount should be dependent on the previous length of the tenancy. The *regulations* require a minimum residency period and they put a ceiling on the total amount of discount that can be granted to a purchaser. To qualify, the property must be self-contained and be the applicant's only or main residence and the tenancy must have been held for a minimum qualifying period. Joint applications with people who share the tenancy or who live in the property may be allowed under certain circumstances. If the home was previously owned by a local authority and was then sold to another landlord (such as a housing association) while the applicant was living in it, he or she may still have the right to buy. This is called 'Preserved Right to Buy'.

The 'Right to Acquire' (RTA) was introduced in the Housing Act 1996, and gives eligible tenants of housing associations and other registered social landlords a statutory right to buy their homes at a discount, depending on the local authority area in which the property is located. The scheme only applies to properties built or purchased with public funds or transferred from a local authority after 1 April 1997. As with the RTB provisions, eligible properties must be self-contained and be the sole or main residence of the applicant and joint applications can be made under certain circumstances. The discounts are usually less generous than under the RTB and are fixed within a band. The primary legislation allowed local authorities to apply for some properties in their districts to be excluded (by specific statutory instruments) so long as they met certain criteria. This has resulted in some homes in some areas being exempt from the RTA. Typically these exempt properties are in rural settlements or in the form of sheltered accommodation for the elderly.

shared ownership and shared equity schemes

Apart from RTB, shared ownership and shared *equity* are the two main types of low cost home ownership (LCHO) scheme supported by the government. These schemes are available to a wide range of households wishing to buy a property but who cannot afford to pay the full market price. Although they are similar, 'shared ownership' and 'shared equity' schemes tend to have somewhat different structural features.

With 'shared equity', individuals can, under a *leasehold* agreement, buy part of a property with the aid of a loan from a third party such as the government, a private developer or a social landlord (with the remaining part of the property being owned by the third party). Under such an arrangement no *rent* is paid. When the property is sold, the government or other third party who owns the 'sleeping' stake will be entitled to receive their share of the *value* (*equity*) of the property at the time of sale.

'Shared ownership' is a leasehold arrangement that involves the landlord selling the occupier an ownership stake or 'share' in the property and then charging an appropriate rent on the residual. In determining the size of the stake (typically 25–75 per cent) and the rental charge (typically 1–3 per cent of the residual value) a balance is sought between affordability (for the occupier) and financial viability (for the other party – usually a social landlord).

Like shared equity, the principle of shared ownership is that it allows households who aspire to owner-occupation to gain a rung on the 'housing ladder' by owning a proportion of the property's equity. As and when they can afford to do so, the occupier will have the option to acquire a larger share. In this way they may, over time, 'staircase' to full ownership. The occupier usually becomes responsible for the repairs and maintenance of the property. If the occupier owns 100 per cent of the home and wishes to sell, the housing agency has a 21-year 'first refusal' right. Where less than 100 per cent is owned by the occupier, the landlord has the right to find a buyer for it.

In recent years access to house purchase *finance* has constituted a significant barrier to those wishing to enter the tenure as first-time buyers. In response, UK national governments have, at different times, set up a variety of LCHO arrangements aimed at helping people who wish to purchase a home but cannot do so without financial assistance. These tend to be temporary measures and have been marketed under a number of titles such as 'NewBuy', 'HomeBuy' and 'Help to Buy'. Details of these and similar financial support schemes in Wales, Scotland and Northern Ireland are constantly under review and current information on them is readily accessible on central and local government websites.

A feature of these schemes is that they are time-limited and have been introduced, in part, as a governmental response to economic stagnation. They have been steered through Parliament on the basis that, as well as helping home ownership, they create a stimulus to the construction industry and thereby help to 'jump-start' economic recovery. Critics have made the point that these types of demand-side assistance are easy to introduce but politically difficult to abandon and there are concerns that they may be extended and create long-term distortions in the property market. LCHO initiatives of this kind are further criticized by some economists for stimulating market demand without enhancing supply. Market theory points to the danger of the *housing market* over-heating and bringing about another 'housing bubble' in which financial aid from the tax-payer is simply 'burned off' by rising house prices.

being an owner-occupier: sustaining the 'marginal' owner

Because of the dualistic nature of the owner-occupier's *proprietary interest* it is possible to consider affordability in this sector by referencing two key ratios. First, because owners have a long-run 'investment interest' in their *dwellings*, affordability in this sector is sometimes discussed in terms of the ratio between the 'nominal' and the 'real' costs of borrowing and investing. This approach enables analysts (e.g. Wilcox, 1996) to make the point that capital apprecia-tion and house-price inflation can work to the long-term financial advantage of owners so that, over time, the acquisition costs can become more and more affordable. If, over a given period, interest rates are, say, 6 per cent, and over the same period, the asset's exchange value has appreciated by the same amount of 6 per cent, then, although the 'nominal' cost of the loan, or the opportunity cost of the money capital withdrawn from savings to purchase the property, is 6 per cent, the 'real' capital cost is zero. By focusing on the real cost of capital, it is possible to argue that, over the longer period (e.g. since the 1930s) the cost of acquiring owner-occupied housing assets has fallen.

Because owners have a continuing 'consumption interest' in their dwellings, affordability in this sector is sometimes discussed in terms of the ratio between the household's disposable income and its occupancy costs. For new entrants to the tenure, mort-gage repayment costs often constitute a high proportion of these outgoings. This means that existing owners can experience a relatively high 'real income effect' when mortgage interest rates go up or down. The real income effect measures how much the household's disposable monthly income changes as a result of an alteration in interest charges. An apparently 'small' change in interest rates can bring about a significant real income effect on some households. In other words, it can alter the household's disposable income by a significantly greater proportion than the interest rate change.

For most of the twentieth century, state support for existing home owners operated through the fiscal system in the form of mort-gage income tax relief (MITR). During the 1990s, this support was phased out and came to an end in 2000. For many owning house-holds, the servicing of outstanding mortgage debt remains the most expensive aspect of home ownership. This financial burden has a regional as well as a social dimension. In 2013, as part of its series 'Wealth in Great Britain', the Office for National Statistics (ONS) released numbers measuring how much British households owe on their *mortgages*. This revealed that, perhaps surprisingly, fewer than two in five households have property debt. By 2015, more than 50 per cent of home owners will be 'mortgage-free' households with a home that they own outright. Many of these will be older people who took a mortgage out in the 1960s, 1970s and 1980s.

In addition to financial problems, many marginal owner-occupiers also need technical help and advice if they are to cope with the problems of managing their property assets. Home Improvement Agencies (HIAs) are small, locally based not-for-profit organizations. They help home owners and private sector tenants who are older, disabled or on low income to repair, improve, maintain or adapt their homes. They provide people-centred, cost-effective assistance, and help to tackle poor or unsuitable housing, enabling residents to remain in their own home, safe, secure, warm and independent. They are sometimes referred to as 'Care and Repair agencies', 'Staying Put schemes' or 'handyperson services'. They are usually managed by housing associations or local authorities and some operate as charitable organizations.

KEY TEXTS

- Jones, C. (2010) 'The Right to Buy' in P. Malpass and R. Rowlands (eds), *Housing, Markets and Policy* (Abingdon: Routledge)
- NSO Main Report (2006/2008 and 2008/2010) *The Burden of Property Debt in Great Britain*. www.ons.gov.uk/ons/
- There is an extensive academic literature on the history and philosophy of LCHO. See for example: Garnett, D. and Perry, J. (2005) *Housing Finance* (Coventry: Chartered Institute of Housing and The Housing Studies Association), Chapter 6; Lowe, S. (2004) *Housing Policy Analysis: British Housing in Cultural and Comparative Context* (Basingstoke: Palgrave Macmillan), Chapter 7; Mullins, D. and Murie, A. (2006) *Housing Policy in the UK* (Basingstoke: Palgrave Macmillan), Chapter 5
- http://www.helptobuy.org.uk
- https://www.gov.uk/affordable-home-ownership-schemes/overview
- https://www.gov.uk/affordable-home-ownership-schemes/help-to-buy-equity-loans
- http://www.helptobuy.org.uk/
- http://www.thisismoney.co.uk/money/mortgageshome/article-2398896/How-Help-Buy-works-worth-considering-NewBuy-instead.html#ixzz2sivtyV7E
- http://wales.gov.uk/topics/?lang=en
- http://www.scotland.gov.uk/Topics/Built-Environment/Housing/investment/grants/hso/

low income households

SEE ALSO affordability; fuel poverty; inclusion and exclusion; low cost home ownership; merit goods and services; nudge theory; subsidies; sustainability

It might be argued that the term 'low income households' is a modern euphemism for the old, well-established notion of 'the poor'. Indeed, there is an element of truth in this proposition. In contemporary society, labelling a person or a household as 'poor' is seen to be stigmatizing and agencies such as *social housing* providers, who subscribe to the principles of 'social mobility' and 'inclusion', are keen to avoid negative stereotyping that puts people in a fixed and degrading social category. The notion of 'low income households' is a vague relative concept and the category can be regarded as part of a wider income continuum in which some people can be expected to migrate gradually to a 'higher' income status. By contrast, historically, 'poverty' has tended to be seen as a fairly fixed socio-economic category that locks people into a sort of 'trap' from which it is difficult or impossible to escape – hence the well-known fatalistic phrase 'the poor are always with us'.

When government support for those on limited incomes is provided, it is necessary to establish the cost to the public purse and to identify potential beneficiaries. This requires the creation of clear and measurable qualifying benchmarks. In this way the benefits system is bound to maintain the notion that 'poverty' persists and that within the general category 'low income' we can identify particular households that are in specifically defined financial distress. Sometimes an attempt is made to avoid a strong poverty categorization (e.g. Gordon Brown's 'tax credits' sought to associate the poor with the universal system of taxation). Sometimes the notion of 'poverty' is inferred without being officially proclaimed (e.g. by using such terms as 'benefit' or 'entitlement'). And sometimes the notion of 'poverty' is expressed in a focused, as against general, way – as in the idea of *fuel poverty*.

Definitions of 'poverty' are culturally determined which means that what counts as 'poverty' varies between periods and places. In the current academic and practice literatures, there are three broad definitions of poverty in common usage in the United Kingdom: 'absolute poverty', 'relative poverty' and 'social exclusion'. Absolute poverty is seen as the lack of sufficient resources with which to maintain an acceptable standard of living. Relative poverty is identified by comparing an individual's income with the average (usually the median) for the population. Those surviving on less than 60 per cent of the national median wage are generally regarded as being in poverty. Social exclusion is a relatively new term that is increasingly used to widen the notion of poverty to include other socio-economic factors than just income. It is used to describe what happens when individuals or areas suffer from a combination of linked problems such as unemployment, poor educational attainment and skills, poor housing, high crime environments, bad health and family breakdown. From a household perspective, this widens the definition of poverty to embrace both low income and the sorts of social, political and cultural 'impoverishments' that come from living in deprived areas (see *inclusion and exclusion*).

In the twenty-first century, the most commonly used way to measure poverty is by relating it to incomes. A person is most usually considered 'poor' if his or her income falls below some minimum level assumed to be necessary to meet basic needs. This minimum level is often referred to as 'the poverty line'. International poverty lines vary and each country uses boundaries that are appropriate to its level of *development* and societal norms and values. By this income measure, some 20–25 per cent of the United Kingdom's population could be regarded as being in poverty throughout the early years of the twenty-first century.

A recent Joseph Rowntree Foundation report sought to define the poverty line more precisely so that it can be used more effectively to develop policies and target resources appropriately (Aldrich *et al.*, 2012). The JRF definition is based on net household income, adjusted for family size and after housing costs have been deducted. Assessing government (Department for Work and Pensions (DWP)) figures, the report's authors found that the working adults without dependent children were the most likely group to be living in poverty and that child poverty was the lowest for 25 years. It can be said that those in poverty today are noticeably different from 25 years ago. While the proportion of working-age adults without children had risen by more than one-third since the early 1990s, the proportion of pensioners in poverty had halved. The number of people in low-paid employment was rising in 2012, pointing to the probability of an intensification of this changed configuration. In terms of *tenure* distribution, poverty was no longer concentrated in the social rented sector: the number of very low income households in the private rented sector had become as high as that for the social rented sector (having doubled between 2000 and 2012). More recent data from the Institute of Fiscal Studies, the Trussell Trust and the BBC indicate that in Britain in 2013/2014 some 13 million people were living below the poverty line, 400 food banks were helping to feed some 347,000 people of which about 127,000 were children, and the UK domestic debt figure had reached £1.43 trillion, with some 9 million people struggling with significant debt problems (creating large profits in excess of £2 billion for so called pay day lending firms).

Historically, poverty has been associated with unemployment. Since the Second World War, the main approach governments have taken to dealing with long-term 'structural' poverty has been to encourage economic growth and job creation. The Hills Report (2007) advocated that social and affordable housing should be more aligned with employment incentives and social mobility. In recent years, there has been a good deal of debate about the perceived issue of 'low', rather than 'no' income from employment. All the main political parties emphasize the key relationship between poverty and employment and much official policy has been directed to encouraging and actively helping people into paid jobs. Recent examples of this policy approach include the 'Flexible New Deal' and the Northern Ireland's 'Steps to Work' programmes, the 'Working Families Tax Credit' arrangements and the establishment of a 'minimum wage'.

Policies for tackling poverty are made in many areas of government. With devolution, this is even more complex as responsibilities are now split between central, devolved and local government. The private, voluntary and charitable sectors also play a role in researching and implementing solutions.

Many people argue that improving the long-term prospects of low-income groups can only be achieved through education and training and that increased spending in these areas should be seen as an 'investment' in Britain's future productivity rather than as a 'cost' to the public purse.

specific fiscal measures: housing benefit, council tax support and the introduction of universal credit

'Housing benefit' and 'council tax support' have, in recent years, been the two key housing-related fiscal mechanisms for aiding low income households.

'Housing benefit' was originally introduced in 1988 as a weekly means-tested assistance to low income households to help them pay their *rent*. It is a housing-tied social security payment that takes the form of a 'rebate' to council tenants and an 'allowance' to housing association and private tenants. It is administered by those local authorities that have responsibilities for providing housing services (i.e. district, metropolitan, London borough and unitary councils.) Most of the cost, however, is met by central government via the Department for Work and Pensions (DWP).

The benefit provides a supplement to real income that is related to the claimant's actual or notional housing costs. Rebates to council tenants are deducted from the rent bill while allowances to private tenants are normally made by payments that can be paid to the tenant or directly to the landlord (the decision is normally the tenant's). Until recently housing associations were paid directly by the benefit authority (i.e. the local authority). Since 2014 the benefit is normally paid to tenants and the associations can now no longer deal with one agency but have to have in place a much more complicated and expensive administrative process for receiving the payments indirectly from their tenants. In certain circumstances (typically persistent default) the benefit payments can still be paid directly to the landlord, and tenants can still choose this option if they so wish.

Although, broadly speaking, the size of the rent determines the level of support, this can be reduced if either the rent or the accommodation is deemed to be 'excessive'. The principle of the scheme is that claimants, who receive other prescribed benefits or who have very low incomes, are entitled (with certain exceptions) to rebates or payments towards the amount of their eligible rent. Claimants in this category may also be entitled to a rebate of up to 100 per cent of their council tax so long as their homes are classed in specifically prescribed council tax bands.

In the case of those claiming benefit whose incomes are higher than that allowing full rent coverage, a means-tested formula, referred to as a 'taper', is used to determine the actual extent of benefit entitlement. The taper reduces the maximum benefit payable by a fixed percentage for every £1 of additional income over the prescribed income level. Detailed calculations of housing benefit entitlement can be complex because the system is continually being changed and deals with people in a wide variety of circumstances and with more than one tenure. For example, since 2008, new private sector benefit claimants receive housing benefit under revised, more restrictive rules called the 'local housing allowance', that were intended to encourage those entitled to benefit to seek out cheaper accommodation.

For some years the cost of providing housing benefit has been a hot political issue. Since its inception the cost to the Treasury has continually risen and by 2013–2014 it totalled £23.8 billion, or almost 30 per cent of the entire *welfare* budget. Particularly in times of recession, housing benefit has taken a great deal of the strain of the state's welfare agenda. Given the size of the commitment, the Treasury has shown an interest in finding ways of reducing, or at least capping, its commitment to the housing benefit bill. This has proved to be difficult because entitlement is largely governed by procedural rules that cannot be bypassed without some form of legislative intervention. At different times ministers have considered adjusting the entitlement rules to exclude some categories of potential claimants or reduce their entitlement rights (e.g. younger claimants). Such proposed changes are always politically charged and are highly controversial.

Arguably the most controversial change in recent times has been the use of the housing benefit system to try to tackle the 'under-occupation' of social housing. The 'under-occupancy charge', commonly referred to as the 'bedroom tax', was introduced in April 2013. Under this *regulation*, if a claimant is judged to be under-occupying the home, his or her entitlement to housing benefit is reduced by 14 per cent for one bedroom and 25 per cent for two or more bedrooms above an assumed requirement.

'Council Tax Support' (CTS) started on 1 April 2013. It replaced Council Tax Benefit (CTB) in England and Wales. In Scotland the devolved Parliament used its devolved powers to replace the CTB with its own Council Tax Reduction Scheme. The new arrangements are broadly designed to allow local councils to design their own support schemes while providing legal protection for vulnerable households.

universal credit

Universal credit (UC) represents a major reform of the whole benefits system. It takes the form of a single untaxed monthly payment given to people of working age when their income falls below a certain level. It is means-tested which means that, as well as income, savings and some kinds of property will be included in any assessment of entitlement. Over time UC is planned to replace a raft of existing benefits and tax credits. It is to be administered by Jobcentre Plus who will ensure that applicants meet various conditions, including a 'claimant commitment', which is a document that requires the person to be prepared for work, seek work or better paid employment, or work more hours. This is intended to reflect one of the key principles behind UC, namely that people who are able to work must look for work and those who can better themselves should seek to do so.

As a major reform, UC is rationalizing a hugely complex range of existing benefit arrangements and its introduction is being rolled out gradually. From April 2013 it was piloted in a small number of areas and this exercise identified a number of technical and administrative problems that need to be addressed before its final enactments. As so often with major policy changes, 'the devil may be in the detail – but the imps are in the implementation'.

implications for practice
- Universal credit (UC) will eventually replace the following benefits and tax credits: Housing Benefit; Income Support; Income-based Jobseeker's Allowance; Income-related Employment and Support Allowance; Child Tax Credit and Working Tax Credit. The same sanctions are currently being trialled under Jobseekers' Allowance (since October 2012).

KEY TEXTS
- Aldrich, H., Kenway, P., MacInnes, T. and Parekh, A. (2012) *Monitoring Poverty and Social Exclusion 2012* (York: Joseph Rowntree Foundation)
- Hills, J. (2007) *Ends and Means: The Future Roles of Social Housing in England* (The Hills Report, CASE Report 34, February 2007) (HCA: The Hills Report)

- Phelps, L. (2009) 'Prevention is Better than Cure' in B. Pattison and J. Vine (eds), *Perspectives on the Future of Housing: A Collection of Viewpoints on the UK Housing System* (Coalville: Building and Social Housing Foundation)
- Price Waterhouse Coopers (2011) *Hard Times, New Choices: A New Deal for Housing Associations*
- http://www.citizensadvice.org.uk/
- https://www.gov.uk/government/topics/housing
- http://www.cse.org.uk/
- http://www.ons.gov.uk/ons/rel/was/wealth-in-great-britain-wave-2/the-burden-of-household-debt-in-great-britain/index.html

m

merit goods and services

SEE ALSO affordability; equity; housing market; low income
households; need and demand; subsidies

Economists have developed the concept of 'merit' to help explain
why the state may intervene to provide certain goods and services
directly, or to redistribute disposable incomes so as to increase the
consumption of certain goods and services provided by the market.
It is argued that some things are so meritorious (central to a civi-
lized life or to the general national interest) that, even if an unregu-
lated free market system 'could' provide them, the state 'should'
nevertheless involve itself to ensure that a sufficient quantity of an
appropriate *quality* at an affordable price is, in fact, provided. In
contemporary Britain, for example, there is a general consensus
that education, medical treatment, legal remedies and shelter are
so crucial to the maintenance of a worthwhile life and an effective
economy, that all citizens, including those with little means, should
have access to a minimum level of schooling, health care, legal
advice/representation and accommodation. Without state involvement there is no doubt that the market would provide facilities in
these areas, but the problem is that such provision might not be
sufficient to meet all needs, or be of an appropriate standard or type,
or be in the right place, or be of a price that all in need could afford.
In other words, without state involvement, it is likely that there
would be a degree of 'under-consumption' of these merit goods
and services: under-consumption, that is, in comparison with that
which society regards as being necessary and appropriate for the
needs of a modern, advanced economy.

Housing at the level (size, quality, etc.) that most people in Britain
enjoy today cannot be regarded as a 'merit good'. However, over the
years the state has set certain levels of housing consumption that

it regards to be the minimum necessary for a 'decent' life (given individual household circumstances), and it is this minimum that represents the 'merit need' that qualifies for subsidy support for those who are unable to pay for it.

the difference between a 'merit good' and a 'public good'

Pure public goods and services are those things that are provided collectively by the state because individuals operating in a market cannot sensibly pay for them. In other words, by their very nature, their consumption is indivisible: in providing them for one they become available to all. Good examples would be national defence, sewers and street lighting. Some goods and services 'could' be marketed to individuals but society may decide that such an arrangement would be administratively cumbersome or in some other way inconvenient or inappropriate. These are referred to as 'quasi-public goods and services' and might include roads, a police and fire service and education. The extent to which quasi-public goods and services are financed or administered by the state will to some extent depend upon the political ideology of the government in power.

Dwellings (whether rented or owned) and housing services (such as advice, repairs, maintenance and improvements) are capable of being supplied on an individual basis and therefore do not display the features of pure public goods and services. This means that whether they are provided by the state or by the price system will be a matter of political judgement.

KEY TEXTS
- Garnett, D. and Perry, J (2005) *Housing Finance* (Coventry: Chartered Institute of Housing and The Housing Studies Association)
- King, P. (2009) *Understanding Housing Finance: Meeting Needs and Making Choices* (London and New York: Routledge)
- Oxley, M. (2004) *Economics, Planning and Housing* (Basingstoke: Palgrave Macmillan)

mortgages

SEE ALSO **finance; home ownership; low cost home ownership**

Houses that are not inherited or bought outright are usually acquired by means of a loan. Where the property itself is used as a security for the repayment, the loan is referred to as a 'mortgage'. A mortgage is a form of loan that is secured by pledging a piece of real estate as collateral. The word 'mortgage' is made up of the two French words – 'mort' meaning dead and 'gage' meaning pledge. This is because the pledged estate becomes 'dead' or entirely forfeited to the lender if the borrower defaults on the agreed terms.

Some people get confused about the use of the terms 'mortgagor' and 'mortgagee'. What has to be remembered is that it is the householder who makes over the title to the house as security for the loan and is therefore classed as a 'mortgagor' (just as someone who makes available employment is an employer). Conversely, it is the lender who receives the title and is therefore classed as a 'mortgagee' (just as someone who receives employment from someone else is an employee). Because with mortgage arrangements the property is pledged as security, the mortgagee retains the title deeds as collateral until the loan is repaid. However, the buyer occupies the property as if it were already his or her own. One of the reasons that conveyancing is such a convoluted business involving the employment of legal advisers is that until the twentieth century, property transactions were largely restricted to the landed classes and involved the transfer or break-up of complex estates.

types of mortgage

Mortgages are made up of two basic elements: the outstanding debt or 'principal' and the 'interest' charges. How these two elements are treated depends on the type of mortgage agreement entered into.

Mortgage types are largely distinguished by reference to how the interest is calculated (variable, fixed, tracking an index, etc.) and how the loan is to be serviced (straightforward repayments, tied to an endowment policy, pension/savings-linked, etc.). At any one time there are a variety of mortgage loans available, and which is best for a particular borrower depends on his or her financial situation and long-term plans. The two primary categories are the 'repayment or annuity' method and the 'interest only' method. A standard repayment mortgage gradually pays off the capital over the loan period (referred to as the 'term') so that the outstanding debt diminishes year by year (hence 'annuity'). With an interest only loan, the capital is repaid in one go at the end of the term. The mortgage market is highly competitive and, within these two broad categories, building societies and banks continually vary the range of loans on offer.

An annuity mortgage is the most straightforward type of house purchase loan. Such a mortgage agreement involves the borrower making periodic payments (usually monthly) to the lender, partly of interest on the outstanding loan and partly of capital to repay the outstanding principal. In the early years, most of the monthly payment goes to paying off the interest, but as the outstanding loan is gradually repaid the interest element reduces and eventually the major part of the payment is used to repay the principal. The actual monthly payment will depend on the size of the loan, the length of the repayment period and the prevailing rate of interest. The typical arrangement involves a level payment schedule that requires the repayment of a fixed monthly sum that only varies with changes in the rate of interest. In Britain the mortgage term is usually no longer than 30 years.

Interest only mortgages require the borrower to repay, or 'amortize', the capital at the end of the term. This form of loan has grown in popularity in recent years, particularly amongst buy-to-let investors and first-time buyers. This is because they are cheaper to service month by month than a repayment mortgage. However, some experts are concerned that many people taking out such loans have not given enough thought to how they will repay the capital.

By 2014, some 10 per cent of household with interest only loans (some 30 per cent of all mortgagors) were saving nothing and many others were not saving enough to complete their loan agreement. From April 2014, new rules set by the Financial Conduct Authority (FCA) require lenders to check that borrowers have a credible plan to repay the capital. This involves monitoring the risk of default by, among other things, considering the debt's loan:value ratio and giving advice on the mortgagor's repayment strategy. The mortgagor, however, is ultimately responsible for ensuring that funds are available to pay off the debt at the end of the term. A well-established approach is to take out an 'endowment policy' that is arranged by the mortgage lender. This involves the borrower paying two separate payments each month: interest directly to the lender together with a premium to an insurance/investment company. These premiums generate a fund that is designed to repay the principal on maturity (with or without 'profits'). In this way, it is planned that the capital will be repaid at the end of the term using the proceeds of the matured policy. The endowment policy is deposited with the lending institution throughout the duration of the mortgage term. As well as being a mortgage-tied investment, an endowment also generates life assurance protection for the purchaser and may include a savings (i.e. 'with profits') element. There are various types of endowment mortgage, all with built-in life cover but with somewhat differing arrangements and potential benefits or drawbacks. Endowment mortgage terms are typically for 20–25 years.

Compared with repayment mortgages, endowment policies are less flexible. In the case of a repayment mortgage the borrower can normally lengthen or shorten the term of the loan to suit changing circumstances. By contrast, an endowment mortgage is a long-term contract (including automatic life assurance) and once the agreement is made, the parties are normally committed to it for the full term. If the policy is cashed in early, the mortgagor may not get back all the premiums paid. All endowment policies are 'portable' and the policyholders are able to take the policies with them when they move house.

If the investment performs badly, the mortgagor could face a shortfall on her or his loan at the end of the repayment period. In the 1980s and early 1990s endowments were popular and heavily marketed by lenders. However, many people were not told of the real investment risk. This was subsequently regarded as 'misselling' and lenders eventually faced large claims for compensation. As a result, endowment mortgages have declined sharply in popularity. Relatively few endowments are sold today but there are still hundreds of thousands of policies yet to mature.

Some lenders offer low-start repayment mortgages that are technically known as 'gross profile mortgages'. With such an arrangement the monthly payments are lower in the early years of the term but gradually increase each year so that during the later years they are higher than they would otherwise have been with an ordinary repayment mortgage. These loans are designed for people who, at the time of taking out the loan, are on a tight budget but have expectations of a rising income. Over the full term of the loan, such arrangements are usually more expensive than conventional repayment mortgages. Low-start mortgages should be distinguished from 'discounted' mortgages. Some lenders promoted these in the late 1990s as a way of attracting new business. They involve the mortgagor paying a reduced rate of interest for an initial period (typically a year or so) without the penalty of having to pay higher rates later in the term.

A 'sub-prime mortgage' loan is a loan that is specifically designed for people who are denied prime or standard mortgages by traditional lenders; that is, people who have a poor credit rating or have difficulty proving a regular, reliable income. Higher interest rates are normally charged for these loans to reflect the additional risk for the lenders. In recent years, in the United States, the sub-prime market expanded recklessly. A high proportion of this specialist debt was packaged up and passed on to the traditional banking system at a discount. Mortgage failures in this sector from 2007 led to a loss of confidence causing liquidity concerns for the banking system (the 'credit crunch'). In turn, the liquidity problems fed back into the housing system in 2008, making it difficult for first-time buyers to acquire mortgage *finance* as banks and building societies became risk averse.

interest rates
The following constitute the main ways in which interest rates can be calculated:

- 'Variable rates' require the mortgagor to pay the current going rate and this means that the cost of serving the debt will change when interest rates change.
- 'Fixed rates' require the mortgagee to hold rates for a prescribed period (typically two to five years).
- 'Capped rates' are fixed but if rates fall, the mortgagor then pays the lower rate.
- 'Cash-back deals' provide the mortgagor money back in return for taking out a particular mortgage product. These normally tie the borrower into the scheme and involve a penalty charge if he or she moves to another lender.
- 'Discounted rates' provide the mortgagor a time-limited discount off the lender's variable rate.
- 'Annual review schemes' allow the interest rate to be fixed for

a year so that if there is a change in rates during the year it will be ignored until the following review period (e.g. the following year). If, during the current review period, interest rates are raised then there will be a 'postponed' under-payment owing at the end of the period. In the following review period the repayments are adjusted to take account of this under-payment.

mortgage protection and indemnity insurance

From the late 1990s, both the government and lenders placed more emphasis on 'mortgage payment protection insurance' designed to cover loan service charges if the mortgagor loses his or her job through ill health or redundancy. The reasons for this pressure partly stemmed from the changing socio-economic profile of mortgagors, more of whom were being employed on temporary contracts or were in jobs that did not provide the sort of stable, secure incomes that have historically underpinned owner-occupation. The pressure to take out mortgage protection also stemmed from the general shift in government policy away from sole reliance on the state for safety-net provision to forms of partnership provision with the private sector. A further (and, as it transpired, decisive) reason for pushing these schemes was related to the huge profits being made by the financial institutions offering them. The corporate and sales commissions on individual contracts were eventually exposed by the regulator and the media as being so high that they constituted examples of gross mis-selling and maladministration.

A mortgagor may be asked to pay a 'mortgage indemnity premium' that safeguards the lender against the *value* of the property not covering the value of the outstanding debt in the event of default. Although these are being phased out by a number of the larger lenders, they are still used. They are normally required when a borrower is unable to put down a deposit of more than a specified percentage. Indemnity insurance plans should be distinguished from mortgage protection policies. Although both are charged to the mortgagor, the former are primarily designed to benefit the lender and the latter are, in theory at least, designed to protect the borrower. Mortgage indemnity premiums are being superseded by government-sponsored mortgage guarantees recently introduced to support the growth of *home ownership* and stimulate the construction industry (see *low cost home ownership*).

implications for practice

- Recent research shows that fewer than two in five UK households have property debt (Office of National Statistics, 2013). The ONS figures reveal 9.2 million UK households had property debt in 2010.
- The popularity of interest only mortgages is partially tied to confidence in the *housing market*. In recent years, many borrowers have assumed that the level of house-price inflation would be such that the final cost of paying off the historic debt (the principal) would prove to be a manageable burden. During the recent economic downturn, however, house prices stabilized (in some areas fell) and many wage rates dropped below the rate of general inflation.

KEY TEXT

- Publications by the mortgage industry (banks, building societies and professional bodies such as the Council of Mortgage Lenders)

n

need and demand

SEE ALSO affordability; allocations; asset management; care and support; development; homelessness; housing market; low income households; merit goods and services; partnerships; social housing; value for money

The concept of social need is inherent in the idea of social service. Indeed, the history of the social services is, in large part, the story of how society came to recognize the existence of social needs and then organize itself to meet them.

After 1919, the Liberal Party's election campaign to build 'homes fit for heroes' opened up the debate about whether market forces alone could be relied upon to meet the housing objectives of post-war society. Once the idea of housing as a social service had been mooted, it brought to the fore the question of what distinguishes the social policy concept of 'need' from the market economic concept of 'effective demand'. The twentieth-century concept of housing need gradually emerged as a result of this questioning. By the end of the First World War, the idea was established that the basic housing requirements of the 'working classes' were, in some degree, a concern of central government and should not be left to the vagaries of market forces and the charitable instincts of individual benefactors and parish officials. By requiring all local authorities to prepare plans to meet 'local housing needs', the Town and Country Planning Act 1919 set in place a statutory framework that would allow the provision of basic housing to be treated as a social service.

Today, the primary responsibility for assessing housing needs still resides with local authorities. They are expected to have strategic overviews of the housing needs in their areas. Each local authority is currently required to map patterns of housing need within its administrative area and act as an 'enabler' that identifies needs and establishes plans to close any gap in provision. This no longer means that the authority necessarily has to provide housing and housing-related services itself. Local housing associations and other registered social landlords are expected to work with the authority to help it define its enabling role and to produce solutions to any local needs problem.

The contemporary debate about future national housing need has been shaped, to a large extent, by the findings and recommendations of the 'Barker Review' that was commissioned by the Treasury and which reported in 2004. The review considered what lay behind the lack of supply of housing in the United Kingdom and what might be done to encourage the *housing market* to respond effectively to this shortfall. The report was influential in the *development* of subsequent policies in the fields of planning and housing. Barker suggested that in 2004, just to meet the needs of *social housing*, 17,000 more homes needed to be made available each year. To make real a difference to the backlog of housing need would, it suggested (among other things), require up to 23,000 additional affordable homes every year.

The notion of 'housing need' can apply to an individual household or to a geographical area.

defining the needs of a household

The efficient, effective and equitable provision of any social service is dependent upon an understanding of what constitutes the needs of those who qualify to receive it. 'Social need' is a 'contested concept' in so far as it can mean somewhat different things in different contexts. Jonathan Bradshaw has usefully distinguished between four contrasting categories of social need as used by administrators, politicians and researchers (McLachlan, 1972):

1. 'Normative need' is defined, by some expert or authority, as need in a given situation. It specifies some acceptable norm of provision to which everyone should have access, so that if an individual's or group's consumption falls short of this standard they become identified as being in need. This category is sometimes referred to as 'postulated need' because it defines the taken-for-granted minimum standard that the authority or expert declares should be available to all.

Normative definitions underline the fact that the issue of need assessment is really an aspect of society's desire to establish minimum standards. Such definitions are specific to time and place and are tied to the values and attitudes of those who set the norms. These norms might be postulated by an Act of Parliament, by a local authority, a management committee, an administrator, a professional body, a research group or some other agency claiming authority or expertise. Building *regulations*, Parker Morris space standards, fitness standards, the Decent Homes Standard and point assessment systems all provide housing norm reference points for assessing housing need.

2. 'Felt need' refers to an individual's own assessment of his or her requirements. This category of need is assessed by survey techniques involving questionnaires and interviews. In the private housing sector, for example, volume builders sometimes employ market researchers to carry out consumer preference surveys to find out what type or style of housing is likely to sell well in a particular area. In the social housing sectors, felt need surveys have been employed to guide those producing design briefs for special needs housing such as sheltered schemes for the elderly. Most social landlords use the returns of tenant satisfaction surveys to provide service performance measures that help to check whether the agency is giving *value for money* and addressing people's felt needs.

   The highly subjective nature of felt need means that although it can be used to inform both the strategic planning and the day-to-day operational decisions of social landlords, it cannot be used to establish allocation eligibility criteria.

3. 'Expressed need' is manifested when a felt need is acted upon. The way most people express their felt needs most of the time is by purchasing goods and services. 'Effective demand' is thus a form of expressed need: it is a felt need, or a 'want', expressed in a market by spending money. In the social rented sectors, where a limited supply of *dwellings* and tenancies are allocated rather than sold, would-be occupiers express their felt housing needs via a locally determined applications process (see *allocations*).

4. 'Comparative need' is defined in terms of the characteristics of those who are already in receipt of the service. If other people

in similar circumstances and with the same need characteristics are not in receipt of the service, then they are defined as being in comparative need. This measure underlines the requirement for open and even-handed treatment in the distribution of services to applicants. That is, a housing agency should establish value for money indicators that assess the distributional effects of service provision. Such a measure of VFM is sometimes referred to as 'best value' (see *value for money*). The 'comparative concept' can be applied to the assessment of the needs of geographical areas by the central, regional and devolved governmental authorities.

defining the needs of a geographical area

The Coalition Government revoked the use of regional spatial strategies and returned responsibilities for planning housing provision to local authorities who are now required to prepare 'strategic housing market needs assessments' as part of their local planning frameworks (see *affordability*).

A local housing needs assessment is the normal starting point for devising a housing strategy. Comprehensive and up-to-date information on the nature and scale of current and future housing needs across all *tenures* is required as a basis for identifying priorities, evaluating options, developing programmes and targeting investment.

The cheapest and easiest way of assessing the social housing needs of an area is to refer to the registers of 'expressed need'. Although local waiting lists offer a readily accessible source of information, they provide an inadequate measure of need for a number of reasons. They are seldom up-to-date because when applicants move to some other district or solve their housing problems through the offices of other agencies, they may not bother to withdraw their applications. Since the passing of the Localism Act (2011) and introduction of more local control of allocations (e.g. *choice*-based lettings), waiting lists provide a more accurate measure of current needs. However, lists will still fail to recognize the needs of those who are excluded from registering because they do not possess the appropriate local qualifying characteristics. They fail to register those who are judged to be in need by some normative or comparative standard but who nevertheless do not feel in need. They also fail to account for those who feel in need of re-housing but who do not bother or who mistakenly believe that they do not qualify to register.

As well as being incomplete, waiting lists are time-specific. Because they only register current expressions of need, they cannot be used to assess future requirements. The assessment of future needs for social rented housing requires the employment of a more dynamic methodology that allows policy-makers to project trends in household formation, *tenure* moves and private sector provision so that some crude figure for social demand can be estimated. This estimate can then be compared with current supply projections, planned new social output plus expected re-lets, to determine whether there is likely to be a crude surplus or deficit for the period under review. A more refined estimate of future need can then be sought by adjusting this crude residual to take account of factors such as stock condition, location, household fit and affordability.

Contemporary need assessment exercises are also expected to take account of how housing investment will impact on the government's efficiency and social inclusion agendas.

KEY TEXTS

- Barker, K. (2004) *Review of Housing Supply. Delivering Stability: Securing our Future Housing Needs, Final Report: Recommendations* (London: HM Treasury)
- Bramley, G. (2010) 'Meeting Demand' in P. Malpass and R. Rowlands (eds), *Housing, Markets and Policy* (Abingdon: Routledge)
- Elphicke, N. and House, K. (2015) *From Statutory Provider to Housing Enabler: Review into the Local Authority Role in Housing Supply*. The Elphicke House Report (London: DCLG/HMSO)
- King, P. (2009) *Understanding Housing Finance: Meeting Needs and Making Choices* (London and New York: Routledge), Chapter 2
- Lowe, S. (2004) *Housing Policy Analysis: British Housing in Cultural and Comparative Context* (Basingstoke: Palgrave Macmillan), Chapter 4
- Reeves, P. (2014) *Affordable and Social Housing: Policy and Practice* (New York: Routledge), Introduction and Chapter 1

nudge theory

SEE ALSO choice; housing market; low income households; need and demand; sustainability; value for money

Nudge theory has been a topic of discussion and research amongst psychologists since the 1960s. Its emergence into the fields of sociology and politics occurred in 2008 with the publication of 'Nudge: Improving Decisions about Wealth, Health and Happiness', a book written by Richard Thaler, a behavioural economist, and Cass Sunstein, a legal scholar. The authors argued that by presenting *choices* in certain ways it is possible to encourage people to make more appropriate decisions without them losing their freedom of choice. They gave the example of a school cafeteria: if the healthier food is placed at eye level and is easier to reach than the junk food, individuals' behaviour might be altered – they might pick the fruit and vegetables even though they are still free to pick the chips and cakes. By far the most famous example involves flies and urinals and a man called Aad Kieboom. Rather than putting up a sign in the male lavatories at Amsterdam airport politely asking men to avoid peeing on the floor, he etched the black outline of a fly onto the porcelain at the centre of the urinal to encourage more accurate aiming. Although his methodology of quantification is unclear, he found that 'spillage' plummeted by 80 per cent.

When this socio-psychology is consciously applied in the field of public policy, it is sometimes referred to as 'soft paternalism'. At the theoretical level, political paternalism raises questions of how members of the public should be treated when they are less than fully rational. It is often presented in a negative way and characterized by such pejorative phrases as 'the nanny state'. The history of public policy has taught politicians that there will normally be a negative and vocal reaction from parts of the electorate whenever attempts are made to force individuals to behave more rationally. This is even the case when there is incontrovertible evidence that the behaviour change will save lives or prevent damage to health (e.g. the wearing of seat belts and the banning of smoking in confined public spaces).

Even hard line 'laissez-faire' advocates recognize that the standard neo-classical economic assumption that people in the economy will always act rationally cannot be relied upon in all areas of public life. It is perhaps understandable that right-of-centre democratic politicians would be interested in exploring ways of instigating changes in behaviour without the time, cost and possible critical reactions that result from creating new laws or imposing new and expensive regulatory arrangements. In 2008 Professor Thaler spent some time in Britain where he acted as an unpaid informal adviser to the

Cabinet Office. During this consultancy period he led seminars with ministers and civil servants that attempted to address the classic modern libertarian dilemma of how to promote aspects of social and economic policy without abandoning a political commitment to low taxation and a non-intrusive government. In 2010 the UK Cabinet became the first in the world to set up a dedicated 'nudge unit', known as the Behavioural Insights Team. The team, made up of 13 individuals from academia, management and marketing, focused on a range of policy areas with a view to using the insights from research in behavioural economics and psychology to improve the effectiveness and efficiency in a range of public service areas. They claimed, for example, that a trial with the Courts Service demonstrated that personalized text messages were six times more effective at settling outstanding fines than final warning letters. The Service estimated that this might save hundreds of thousands of bailiff visits and tens of thousands of pounds when rolled out across the country.

Amongst professional service providers, nudge theory is now an established area of debate and is being adopted as an operational tactic in all sorts of ways in all sorts of areas. In 2006 the Treasury commissioned the Varney Report that was clearly influenced by the theory. This considered how communications in the service industries might be improved with a view to both enhancing the customers' experiences and saving money. In 2010, while acting as the government's 'digital champion', Martha Lane Fox published a report that called for the public sector to shift its contact with the public to digital channels. The report said that as well as delivering better services for citizens, moving 30 per cent of government service delivery contacts to digital channels could save the public purse more than £1.3 billion a year. If 50 per cent were shifted to digital methods, some £2.2 billion might be saved annually.

The unit cost savings resulting from what is termed 'channel switching' can be significant. A report produced by Price Waterhouse Coopers for Martha Lane Fox stated that each contact transaction switched to online methods could save the government between £3.30 and £12.00. Recent research into the cost and benefits of channel switching by housing associations indicates that rents paid online cost approximately 3p compared with

£1.60 by contact centre transactions (telephone with paperwork) and £7.91 by traditional face-to-face physical collection methods. Nudge theory is having a direct influence on housing management practices. In 2012 it was featured as a key topic at the CIH National Conference where its principles were explained and its various applications discussed.

Many of the benefits of nudge theory's 'prompting' approach are intuitive and have been utilized in the politics and management of housing prior to its recent prominence in public and business discourses. Throughout this a–z volume, the observant reader will be able to detect numerous examples of its application to housing policy and practice. One of the most overt examples was its application in the changes to the housing benefit qualifying requirements for private sector tenants in 2008. These changes brought in more restrictive rules called the 'local housing allowance' that were intended to provide those entitled to benefit to seek out cheaper accommodation. One of the key principles underlying the introduction of universal credit is making the receipt of benefits by nonworking claimants dependent upon a commitment to seek employment. The new proposed arrangements also require those working claimants who can better themselves to seek to do so (see *low income households*).

Current research trials by local and central government departments indicate that relatively minor changes in the practices of service providers can have a significantly positive impact on the behaviour of service recipients. These minor changes can be cost neutral and simply involve reshaping processes, redesigning forms or using more sensitive language in letters, emails and circulars.

Some *social housing* landlords have used low-profile 'nudges' to reduce tenancy and other types of fraud. It has been found that by requiring people to update personal information by a procedure that reminds them that providing false details is an offence reduces the incidence of fraud. The idea here is that simply asking people whether or not their circumstances have changed is less effective at identifying fraud than requiring them to lie actively.

Higher-profile 'nudges' might produce more dramatic shifts in behaviour. Relating council tax bandings to carbon emissions, for example, might encourage landlords and home owners to upgrade the green characteristics of their properties. The Royal Institution of Chartered Surveyors has suggested that a similar effect might be achieved if rents charged in all sectors were to be explicitly related to energy performance certificates (Epcs).

some more examples of housing-related nudges
development
Government-sponsored nudges can take the form of positive stimuli (usually financial incentives) or deregulating stimuli (usually reductions in bureaucracy). Section 6 of the Localism Act 2011 introduced deregulatory stimuli designed to encourage planning authorities and local communities to engage more positively in the planning process (see *accountability* and *development*). Prior to the Act, the Coalition Government had introduced the New Homes Bonus (NHB) designed to 'nudge' local authorities into building new affordable homes in their areas. The level of NHB depends on the number of net additional homes developed.

housing management
Some Housing Associations (HAs) provide incentive payments to encourage tenants to downsize if they are judged to be over-occupying a dwelling.

help to buy
This is a government-sponsored 'insurance' scheme designed to nudge mortgage lenders into helping those who can only afford a small deposit to buy a home (see *low cost home ownership*).

KEY TEXTS
- The Cabinet Office (Behavioural Insights Team) (2012) *Applying Behavioural Insights to Reduce Fraud Error and Debt*
- Lane Fox, M. (2010) *Directgov 2010 and Beyond: Revolution not Evolution.* A Report by Martha Lane Fox (London: The Cabinet Office, Efficiency and Reform Group)
- Price Waterhouse Coopers (2009) *Champion for Digital Inclusion: The Economic Case for Digital Inclusion.* Report prepared for Martha Lane Fox
- Thaler, R. H. and Sunstein, C. R. (2008) *Nudge: Improving Decisions about Wealth, Health and Happiness* (New Haven and London: Yale University Press)

- Varney, D. (2006) *The Varney Report: Service Transformation: A Better Service for Citizens and Businesses, a Better Deal for the Taxpayer* (London: HM Treasury)
- http://www.theguardian.com/politics/2013/nov/12/government-nudge-theory-budge
- http://plato.stanford.edu/entries/paternalism/

P

participation

SEE ALSO diversity; governance; regulation

The early history of *social housing* provision was characterized by a combination of Christian benevolence and paternalism. Charitable alms houses were established in the pre-industrial world, some as early as the twelfth century. Nineteenth-century industrial philanthropists such as George Peabody, Titus Salt and George and Richard Cadbury were pioneers of ethical capitalism. Their memorials still exist in the form of the model housing and charitable trusts they established to improve the quality of life of the 'artisan class' of their day. To some extent this approach to industrial benevolence mirrored the ideas of enlightened self-interest of the anti-religious Robert Owen (1777–1858), who acted upon the notion that people were moulded by their environments and by education rather than by God. He argued, and to some considerable extent demonstrated, that higher wages and better working and living conditions can increase industrial productivity. It has to be said that these nineteenth-century benefactors had a more than somewhat paternalistic approach to their 'good works'. (Owen in particular might be described as a 'benevolent autocrat'.)

Many of the paternalistic approaches to housing management that persisted into the twentieth century have become associated with the housing campaigner Octavia Hill (1838–1912). While arguing for good conditions and professional housing management, she made it clear in her writings and actions that there should be a sort of 'social contract' between responsible landlords and their tenants. Her 'tough love' approach required tenants to be of good character, disciplined and to follow 'house rules'. She expected tenants who were not in dire circumstances to work to better themselves rather than rely on state or charitable 'hand-outs'.

Her belief in 'professionalism' made her and her influential followers generally unsympathetic to the idea that tenants should become involved in housing management.

Tenant involvement in housing management arguably began as a 'bottom-up' movement that was particularly forceful in the Scottish industrial areas around Glasgow just prior to the First World War. Exploiting housing shortages at a time when resources were being moved out of building and into munitions production, some major landlords put up their rents: an act that led to widespread agitation and a series of *rent* strikes. By December 1915, with strikes threatening shipbuilding on the Clyde, Lloyd-George's government introduced legislation that not only prevented further rent increases in munitions districts but also established national rent levels at pre-war levels for the duration of hostilities.

The experiences of the rent strikes (that were not exclusive to Scotland) began the politicization of tenants, and it might be said that the campaigns left a legacy of experience that allowed for the subsequent formation of organized tenants' clubs and associations. These tenants organizations then provided a platform upon which was built pressure for the greater involvement of residents in the management of their homes.

In the last quarter of the twentieth century, the notions of 'empowerment' and 'tenant participation' became an increasingly prominent aspect of academic and political debates. A series of radical legislative reforms in 1980, 1988 and 1989 transformed the government's 'top-down' expectations of the relationship between tenants and their landlords. As attitudes shifted, the idea of tenant participation gradually became formalized into the *governance* procedures of social landlords and it became a key topic in the training programmes of housing professionals. Tenants' consultation panels and *participation* 'compacts' were supplemented by tenant representation on boards of management and other decision-making committees. Regulators, who actively sought assurances that such involvement was being adopted as a governance objective, reinforced this movement towards tenant involvement. Many landlords sponsored training programmes for tenants who were interested in being involved in monitoring and management, and the Tenant Participation Advisory Service (TPAS) had become an established feature in the housing practice landscape.

conceptualizing participation

In a free enterprise market, consumers are able to take their custom elsewhere if they are not satisfied with the supplier. This is difficult in an administered system like that which operates in *social housing* provision. Therefore, it is argued that governance arrangements should be put in place to ensure that user needs, preferences and opinions are identified and fed into the management decision-making processes. There is, however, no single universally accepted conceptual model of participation and most classifications treat it as a graduated process or continuum that moves from consultation through *accountability* and influence to authority, responsibility and power.

The most often-quoted model is that devised by Sherry Arnstein who, in describing *community* organizations in America in the 1960s, argued that there is a critical difference between going through the 'empty ritual of participation' and having the real power needed to affect the outcome of the process. In developing her argument, Arnstein devised a 'ladder' of citizens' participation in decision-making that progressed from 'non-participation' through 'tokenism' to 'power and control'.

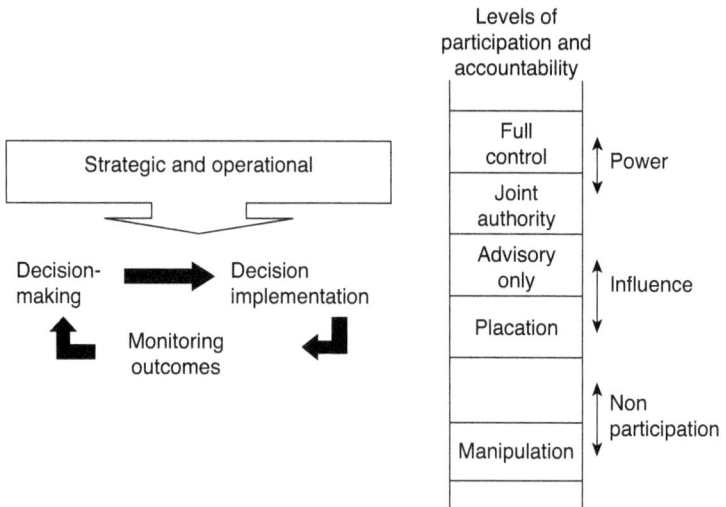

FIGURE 4   *The ladder of participation*

Figure 4 is based on Arnstein's 'ladder' and seeks to summarize the various degrees of resident involvement that might occur in housing organizations.

The 'ladder of participation' draws attention to the fact that key stakeholders (e.g. service users) can become involved in the decision-making processes of the service provider in ways that allow them varying degrees of influence. Figure 4a illustrates the point that key stakeholders can contribute to the processes of decision-making, implementing and monitoring at either or both the strategic and the operational levels of management. Figure 4b illustrates the point that the extent of involvement can be authoritative, powerful, influential, reactive only, consultative only or even cynical and manipulative, depending upon where on the 'ladder' the arrangements are located.

Tenant participation in the decision-making processes of an organization poses a number of governance questions and brings to the fore a number of operational issues. Many of these relate to the role of tenants serving on boards of management. Regulators will look for an appropriate degree of 'bottom-up' involvement by service users. As consumers, the users of the service are well-positioned to judge its effectiveness. It might be said that they are 'experts' in consumption (just as other board members might have expertise in some other fields such as law or *finance*).

The question might be asked, 'If there are tenant board members operating at the top rung of the governance ladder, is there then any need for other mechanisms of tenant involvement (such as tenant forums, committees and working groups)?' The point here is a technical one relating to the nature of 'good governance'. Those serving on governing committees, or boards, carry a brief that is equivalent to that of a company director. They are not serving as representatives so much as non-executive directors. Like any director, their brief is to help steer the organization towards long-term success rather than simply focus on current consumer issues. With their fellow directors, they are expected to take collective responsibility for board decisions. Furthermore, in their leadership role, they will be party to commercially and politically sensitive information and from time to time they will need to be party to decisions that are judged to be in the long-term interests of the organization and of future tenants but not necessarily of current users. These factors make it inappropriate for them to act as a primary two-way channel between the board and the service users. This means that the 'responsive' landlord will have put in place a variety of other mechanisms for identifying the concerns and ideas of the tenants and other stakeholders.

The 2011 Localism Act established an enhanced role for tenants' scrutiny panels that have the function to incorporate tenant views and concerns into the management decision-making processes of social landlords. In terms of Arnstein's ladder, this might be seen as an incremental 'step up' towards joint authority (co-regulation), or even self-regulation.

co-regulation

The concept of co-regulation was introduced by the HCA in April 2010. The idea is that social landlords be managed through a partnership among boards, staff and residents, providing residents with opportunities to shape how services are delivered and to hold boards to account. It is well understood in the profession that tenants, board members and staff need to trust and respect each other for co-regulation to work well, as a high degree of coordination is required. This again brings up questions about how participation arrangements operate in practice at the local level. It also has implications for staff, board and tenant training programmes.

The key question relating to user participation always has been, and still remains, 'What is the appropriate balance between the twin governance objectives of "representation" and "competence"?'

KEY TEXTS

- Arnstein, S. (1971) 'A Ladder of Citizen Participation in the USA', *Journal of the Royal Town Planning Institute*, 176: p. 182
- Cooper, C. and Hawtin, M. (eds) (1998) *Resident Involvement and Community Action, Theory to Practice* (Coventry: Chartered Institute of Housing)
- Lund, B. (2011) *Understanding Housing Policy* (Bristol: The Policy Press), see discussion on 'paternalism'
- Mullins, D. and Murie, A. (2006) *Housing Policy in the UK* (Basingstoke: Palgrave Macmillan)

- Peterman, W. (1998) 'The Meanings of Resident Empowerment' in D. Varady, W. Preiser, and F. Russell (eds) *New Directions in Urban Public Housing* (New Jersey: Rutgers): pp. 47–60
- See also publications of TPAS and HouseMark

partnerships

SEE ALSO anti-social behaviour; care and support; community; need and demand; participation; social returns; value for money

Partnership philosophy is based on the idea that combining the efforts of individuals or organizations that have common interests can result in the achievement of better outcomes than would be the case if they operated on their own. This idea is encapsulated by the often-quoted aphorism, 'The whole is greater than the sum of its parts.'

'Partnership' is a prominent term that is used in current political debates to describe cooperation or collaboration at a formal or informal level between any number of individuals or organizations. There is always an overarching purpose for partners to work together. Their work is typically coordinated through the pursuit of a range of specific objectives. Partnerships can be 'strategic' or 'operational'. Strategic partnerships are concerned with developing coordinated and coherent long-term policies. Operational partnerships are concerned with delivering a particular service in a coordinated and coherent manner.

There is no one model of partnership working. However, experience shows that partnership success is heavily dependent on good communications and relationships (rather than systems and structures), and one of the most common reasons for the failure of a partnership stems from an inability for the key people involved to act as a unified team. Difficulties arise when participants see themselves, not so much as members of the partnership team, but rather as representatives from the various 'parent' teams that constitute the founding partners. Best practice indicates that established partners must expect periodic changes in personnel or in the introduction of new agencies and actors, and for this reason there should be an induction methodology in place. Operational partnerships will commonly focus on more practical aspects and should identify any barriers to effective partnership working from the beginning. Operational partnerships can sometimes overcome potential barriers and create a bonded approach to working together by engaging in well-established brainstorming and project-planning techniques. One technique that is particularly pertinent to partnership working is 'forcefield analysis' that seeks to establish goals and then identify forces, resources and barriers that can help achieve or inhibit these sought-after outcomes.

community planning and partnership

In the area of social service planning and provision (including housing-related services), the arrangement is usually referred to as 'inter-agency working' or 'joined-up working'. Joined-up working involves working in partnership with others, whether in the public, private or voluntary sectors, in order to identify and solve local problems. The government increasingly regards joined-up working as a means of fostering efficiency, effectiveness and *community* engagement in the improvement of service and local government performances.

The advantages of a partnership approach to service users are intended to include the removal of administrative barriers to accessing services; providing more consistent, co-ordinated and comprehensive *care and support*; a one-stop approach to multi-agency issues; and easier and more comprehensive access to training, education and employment opportunities.

The benefits for service providers of partnership working include the ability to develop a 'whole person' approach to dealing with personal needs that should lead to enhanced reputations, better customer relations and administrative efficiencies. It can also extend the range of service support functions that can be offered, facilitate better access to joint research and training facilities for staff and opportunities for joint training. This may achieve more job satisfaction for staff leading to easier staff recruitment and better staff retention. Some joint working can make better use of available resources and open up possibilities for pooling resources.

local strategic partnerships (LSPs)

LSPs are increasingly regarded as the key vehicle for local level strategic decision-making. An LSP is a multi-agency partnership involving key providers and stakeholders in a particular area (usually defined by a local authority's boundaries). Typically an LSP consists of public, private, voluntary and community organizations working together to meet local needs and to improve social, environmental and economic well-being in a particular area. The partners typically comprise local councils, local businesses, health organizations, the police and fire services and senior staff from the major voluntary organizations. LSPs are usually set up and guided by, but not 'owned' by, a local authority and they often act as an 'umbrella' for other existing partnerships and groups.

Local enterprise partnerships (LEPs)

LEPs are the mechanism used by the government to channel monies from a number of European investment funding programmes (together with match funding support) into the regional economies. The key European funds are the European Regional Development Fund (ERDF), the European Social Fund (ESF), the European Agricultural Fund for Rural Development (EAFRD) and the European Maritime and Fisheries Fund (EMFF). The LEPs themselves are expected to work with local partners to set the direction of local growth strategies. This involves each individual LEP setting out the local area's opportunities and challenges, its priorities for spending and the planned outcomes. Its work will form part of the wider economic growth strategy for the area. Both Scotland and Wales have their own *development* agencies that have dedicated budgets and one-stop shop websites that incorporate clear information for investors on areas such as start-ups, partnering and international trade. Similar work is done by the Department of Enterprise, Trade and Investment in Northern Ireland.

reactive partnerships

Not all operational partnerships exist to plan and coordinate a specific service: some are set up (by law or by voluntary action) to deal with complaints, issues and problems. Because housing is so multi-faceted, there exists a great deal of overlap between the services provided by the local council and those provided by a social landlord. In some districts there is often a degree of confusion in the minds of some residents about who is responsible for particular service areas such as pest control, rubbish collection, grass cutting and estates management. This means that calls and complaints that should be directed to the local council end up with the local ALMO or housing association (and 'vice versa'). To prevent residents being summarily told that they have come to the wrong authority, some councils and service agencies have established arrangements that allow the complaint to be passed on to the appropriate authority by the receiving agent.

The proposed 'community trigger' constitutes a more substantial example of 'reactive partnering'. This is an intended mechanism for victims of *anti-social behaviour* to demand that action be taken, starting with a review of their cases. The focus of a 'community trigger case review' is on bringing agencies together to take a more joined up, problem-solving approach to find a solution for the victim. Agencies include councils, the police, local health teams and registered providers of *social housing*. Under this obligation, these agencies have a duty to undertake a case review when someone requests one and their case meets a locally defined threshold. The threshold and procedure for carrying out the case review will be set by the local agencies. For the purpose of the 'community trigger', anti-social behaviour is defined as behaviour that is likely to cause harassment, alarm or distress to any member of the public (see *anti-social behaviour*).

KEY TEXTS
- Glasby, J. and Dickinson, H. (2014) *A–Z of Interagency Working* (Basingstoke: Palgrave Macmillan)
- The Local Government Association publishes guidance on better partnership working, together with case studies that illustrate how partnerships can fail
- Ward, M. and Hardy, S. (eds) (2013) *Where Next for Local Enterprise Partnerships?* (London: The Smith Institute and the Regional Studies Association)

performance monitoring

SEE ALSO business plans; continuous improvement; finance; quality; regulation; risk and uncertainty; value for money

In the free enterprise sector of the economy profit is the measure of success. However, in performance terms, *social housing* cannot simply be treated as a commercial activity. If housing is a 'business' at all, it is a 'regulated social business'. Because of its social and *welfare* outputs, criteria other than profit need to be taken into account in assessing returns on monies directed to its production and consumption. Hence the question 'How is the return on housing spending and investment to be measured and accounted for?' usually takes the form, 'How do we know whether we are getting value for money?'

monitoring and measurement

'Monitoring' and 'measuring' performance are not two ways of saying the same thing: measuring is just one element of monitoring. Monitoring has both formal and informal aspects. Monitoring outcomes on a day-to-day basis is an integral part of informal supervisory activity (line management) and reflective practice (employee awareness of the effects of individual decisions). Formal monitoring usually involves establishing periodic reviews of targets and outcomes that are recorded and then fed back into the wider processes of staff development and strategic and operational planning.

There are three broad, interrelated monitoring approaches. All three are normally employed in the monitoring of housing organizations:

1. 'Spot-checking' typically involves the examination of data and other information relating to a specific time and place (a sort of snapshot of the current position). Annual financial *accounts* and statements are examples of this approach.
2. 'Comparative analysis' involves looking at the organization's performance as compared with other similar organizations. This approach typically involves 'benchmarking' and can lead to the production of 'league tables'. Most housing organizations belong to a benchmarking group of similar agencies. Benchmarking is now extensively used by boards of management and other internal monitoring groups as a mechanism for gauging progress. It can be a vehicle for spreading good practice by asking the question: 'Who is better than us and why?'
3. 'Longitudinal analysis' involves charting progress over a period. Compared with 'spot-checking' this is a dynamic approach and is typically used to determine the extent to which *continuous*

improvement is being achieved. Longitudinal analysis is often referred to as 'trend analysis'.

The formal measurement of outcomes, together with the management of risks, is part of the continuous *business planning* process. As in other areas of regulated service provision (such as health and education), housing managers measure achievements by referencing performance indicators (PIs) that may be collected for local or national purposes.

A distinction is often made between 'general' and 'key' PIs. General performance indicators (GPIs) tend to focus on a range of operational targets and are used to monitor and manage the effectiveness of individuals, teams, projects, processes, procedures and specific areas of policy. Key performance indicators (KPIs) are predetermined quantifiable measurements that focus on the critical success factors of an organization. KPIs are often used by boards, governing committees, executive managers and regulators to check an organization's success against its declared mission and strategic goals.

coordination: scorecards

One recognized danger of the PI approach is the creation of a fragmented and disaggregated monitoring process in which PIs are presented and considered as departmentalized data sets and targets. This lack of connectedness between units of information inhibits the ability of the organization to achieve a properly coherent understanding of its record and prospects. In response to this problem, a management monitoring tool called the 'balanced scorecard' was developed in the early 1990s at the Harvard Business School by Robert Kaplan and David Norton.

The balanced scorecard (BSC) is both theory and method. The method seeks to translate an organization's mission and strategy into a comprehensive set of performance measures that provides a framework for strategic monitoring and management. The original BSC model used a 'four-perspective' approach that coordinates information into an interrelated network embracing the objectives of financial viability, customer needs and expectations, internal business processes and learning and growth. The method is being developed by a number of housing organizations as a way of measuring how each is performing against the totality of its objectives.

Many argue that, in the past, performance figures, particularly when presented as a league table, have failed to take proper account of local circumstances and have therefore been difficult to interpret. For these reasons, their publication often carries 'health warnings' from practitioners, academic commentators and even from the monitoring agencies themselves. However, despite these reservations, it is clear that the drive to achieve 'continuous improvement' requires formal mechanisms of comparison between authorities and associations. Landlords who are required to provide VFM need to carry out systematic self-assessments that can be validated by tenants, funders, internal auditors and external regulators.

KEY TEXTS

- Garnett D and Farrugia, H. (2015) The Idea of *a Balanced Scorecard* at http://leapingfrogpublications.co.uk/housing-society
- Kaplan, R. S. and Norton, D. P. (1993) 'Putting the Balanced Scorecard to Work', *Harvard Business Business Review*, September/October 1993: pp. 133–148, Reprint 93505
- Kotter, J. (1992) *Corporate Culture and Performance* (New York: Free Press)
- http://www.housemarkbusinessintelligence.co.uk/

planning gain

SEE ALSO **affordability; development; private renting; value**

Section 106 of the Town and Country Planning Act 1990 allows a local planning authority to enter into a legally binding agreement or planning obligation with a land developer over a related issue. These obligations are sometimes termed 'value captures', 'section 106 agreements' or 'contractors' contributions'. Such agreements can cover almost any relevant issue and can include the payment of sums of money. These contracted agreements can act as a main instrument for placing restrictions on the developers, often requiring them to minimize the impact on the local *community* and to carry out tasks that provide community benefits.

The Planning and Compensation Act 1991 reinforced the concept of planning obligations. Local planning authorities frequently attach Section 106 requirements for off-site works and financial contributions to planning consents for *social housing developments*. In recent years Section 106 agreements have constituted an important vehicle for providing social housing units within new commercial housing schemes. Registered social landlords must ensure that they are acting within their own rules and complying with regulations when providing such things as community centres not primarily for their own tenants or making financial contributions for non-housing purposes.

The theoretical rationale for planning gain is that by granting planning permission the community (through its planning authority) has created an increase in the *value* of the land and is therefore entitled to receive some return in the form of a community benefit. The phrase 'contractors' contribution', which emerged in the 1980s and reflects an interesting semantic shift in interpretation, implies that developers are 'sacrificing' gains in the community interest rather than the community legitimately sharing the enhanced land values that come with the granting of planning permissions.

KEY TEXT
- Oxley, M. (2004) *Economics, Planning and Housing* (Basingstoke: Palgrave Macmillan)

private renting

SEE ALSO **affordability; finance; homelessness; low income households; proprietary interests; rent; tenancy agreements; tenure**

Private landlords are 'investors in' rather than 'consumers of' housing. A dwelling can be regarded as an item of personal or corporate investment in so far as it is held as a durable asset with a potential to earn a yield in the form of a rental income and/or a capital gain.

Although less than 20 per cent of British households currently *rent* their homes from a private landlord, it is worthy of note that historically most British people depended on private landlords for their accommodation needs. Private renting accounted for some 90 per cent of all *tenure* arrangements before the First World War and even at the end of the Second World War more than 60 per cent of households rented their homes privately. Private renting remained the largest single tenure in Britain until the late 1950s.

The sector's historical dominance, its long-term decline and its recent limited resurgence can be explained in part by people's attitudes towards, and abilities to gain access to, other tenures. Arguably the most significant socio-economic characteristic of housing is that for most households it is expensive relative to disposable income. This has meant that historically even households with above-average incomes have not been able to gain access to owner-occupation without inheriting or borrowing financial resources. This, together with the fact that social renting is a comparatively recent phenomenon, has meant that until the 1940s most people expected that their housing careers would begin and end in privately rented accommodation. These expectations were eventually changed in the immediate post-war period by the development of an increasingly sophisticated and aggressive mortgage *finance* market and a subsidized large-scale council house building programme. From the 1960s, the tenure restructuring away from private renting was further stimulated by government policies that encouraged the development of the housing association movement.

Within the rented sector as a whole, over the past 100 years, the split between private and social renting has fluctuated. In 1918 private renting constituted 76 per cent of all tenures while social renting constituted only 1 per cent. By 1982 social renting accounted for over 30 per cent of all tenures and private renting barely 11 per cent. By 2013 each of the rented tenures was providing about 18 per cent of the total. This resurgence of the sector was to some significant extent the result of the recession that made owner-occupation a more difficult option to achieve for many people. In addition to providing permanent family homes, private landlords are the main providers of both short-term holiday lets (and hotel bed spaces) and employment-related tied accommodation; they are also prominent providers of high class second homes to the 'mobile rich'.

The sector is characterized by high rates of turnover in terms of both tenants and property ownership. This brings with it certain consequences. The 'churn' of ownership can bring uncertainty and insecurity to tenants and the 'churn' of tenants can have a negative impact on the management and maintenance of properties and the motivations of landlords. However, having said this, it is often pointed out that the ease and speed of entry and exit to the sector is one of its positive characteristics. It helps the mobility of labour in the economy as well as providing a non-bureaucratic route into other tenures.

Until recently, a relatively small number of people regarded private renting as a preferred first *choice*. It is treated by many as a temporary stopgap until they can gain access to owner-occupation or to social renting. To others who in the foreseeable future cannot afford, or do not qualify for, access to other tenures it is seen as a permanent 'second-best' arrangement. *Low income households* are a dominant group residing in this sector with a relatively high proportion of lettings going to young couples and singles. Some 20 per cent of private tenants are in receipt of housing benefit or local housing allowance (2015).

In comparison with other European countries, there is a lack of purpose-built private rented accommodation in the United Kingdom. Close to 90 per cent of UK private landlords are individuals. They manage over 70 per cent of the sector's stock. Well over three-quarters only own a single dwelling for rent and well under 10 per cent of all private landlords operate as a full-time business. In some other European countries more private finance goes into the provision of apartments specifically designed as rented accommodation. This allows for one of the potential benefits of private renting namely, the ability to rent modern, newly built accommodation that has just the amount of space needed at just the time it is required.

In the twenty-first century, it would be wrong to describe the provision of market rented *dwellings* as a 'marginal' or 'insignificant' economic activity. Private landlords own hundreds of billions of pounds worth of built assets: these generate an annual rental income of tens of billions of pounds. The sector doubled in size between 1999 and 2014. Dwellings are let in a variety of ways that partly relate to how the properties entered the sector and partly reflect the choices and circumstances of the landlords. Private individual landlords sometimes provide accommodation rent-free to friends or relatives, while corporate landlords sometimes provide accommodation to employees either rent free or with a lower-than-market charge. Most of the dwellings are let on the open market. By 1993 over half of all lettings were assured or assured shorthold and this is now by far the most dominant tenure arrangement (see *tenancy agreements*).

The British private rented stock is dominated by relatively old dwellings many of which have been converted from family residences to accommodate the needs of single people or relatively small households. Compared with social renting, far fewer dwellings in this sector meet the Decent Homes Standard (barely half). New entry landlords, however, are providing a higher standard of accommodation with some three-quarters of this group providing 'decent homes'. In part this is related to the older profile of the sector's properties with some 40 per cent of its stock having been built before 1919, compared to 21 per cent of the housing stock as a whole.

In recent years there has been much debate in Britain about whether private landlords could or should play a more prominent role in the provision of dwellings for households on or below average incomes. It is generally agreed that over the past 60 years or so political, social and economic forces have operated to diminish the role of private landlordism and, if the sector is to be revitalized, some form of intervention in the market is needed to overcome these negative forces.

In 2011 'The Montague Enquiry' was set up by the government to review the barriers to investment in the PRS. It reported in 2012 and proposed a number of changes to planning and funding rules to encourage investment. It made five key recommendations:

1. Local authorities should be encouraged to promote long-term new PRS developments as part of their housing strategies. This would involve waiving the automatic requirement to include new affordable homes in new developments, and using covenants to ensure that homes remained in the PRS for a fixed period.
2. More public sector land should be released for PRS developments.
3. Financial incentives should be provided to encourage large-scale, new-build PRS schemes. These might take a number of forms, such as risk-sharing arrangements or the provision of pump-priming finance in the form of *equity* or debt funding support.

4. A PRS task force composed of officials and inter-disciplinary experts should be set up to help enable investment in this sector. This new agency would work closely with national agencies (such as the HCA) to spread knowledge and information that would be of help to potential investors.

5. High-*quality*, new PRS homes should be given a clear 'kitemarked' identity to distinguish them from units in the existing residential stock. This quality assurance would help stimulate demand and go some way in 'destigmatizing' rented homes in the eyes of young professionals and other groups who have tended to regard the sector simply as a temporary stepping stone to *home ownership*.

Underlying the Montague Report is a general recognition that large-scale institutional investment in private rental housing could not only provide a source of new funding for the housing sector but also provide greater choice for consumers. In line with this view the Homes and Communities Agency (HCA) launched its Private Rental Sector Initiative (PRSI) aimed at encouraging more institutional investors to take an interest in the residential *housing market*.

the owner-occupier landlord and the rent-a-room scheme
There is a long tradition of people letting out rooms in their own homes. The lodger was a common feature of working-class domestic life in the Victorian and Edwardian periods. Lodgers have not had any of the rights that tenants have had under the Housing and Rent Acts. They have no security of tenure and can be evicted without a court order because they share a landlord's property and do not have exclusive use of its facilities.

A tax break was introduced in 1992 that allows home owners to let out spare rooms and pay no tax on the rental income so long as it is less than an official threshold figure. In practice, the scheme is administered by the claimant simply ticking a box on his or her tax return. Landlords can elect for the excess to be taxed in full or, alternatively, they can apply for normal income tax rules for the whole income minus allowable expenses. From the landlord's point of view, participating in the scheme has no implications for capital gains liabilities.

implications for practice
- Compared with social renting, private sector management can be described as 'amateur'. Most landlords have no relevant experience or qualifications and fewer than half of the landlords or their managing agents are members of a professional body or organization related to property or buildings.
- Some owners in this sector can be described as 'reluctant landlords' and are letting out properties that they are having difficulties in selling. These people tend only to remain in the sector temporarily. Longer-term landlords are more likely to have older properties.
- The requirement for deposits is the second most common management and letting practice after written tenancy agreements. The vast majority of landlords require a deposit before letting (typically one month's rent). An authorized deposit protection scheme was introduced in 2007 to provide a fairer system for settling tenancy disputes.
- Some have suggested the introduction of a national register of landlords and a voluntary standards scheme. The idea is to create greater powers for local authorities to tackle the problem of poor-quality housing in the private rented sector, and tougher penalties for 'rogue' landlords. Scotland has a registration scheme operated by the local authorities.

KEY TEXTS
- Country Land and Business Association (2013) *Tackling the Housing Crisis in England: CLA Policy on Securing and Increasing Housing Supply in England 2013–2018* (London: CLA)
- Department for Communities and Local Government (2011) *Private Landlords Survey*
- Fletcher, I. (2009) 'Institutional Investment in the Private Rented Sector' in B. Pattison and J. Vine (eds), *Perspectives on the Future of Housing: A Collection of Viewpoints on the UK Housing System* (Coalville: Building and Social Housing Foundation)
- Kemp, P. A. (2010) 'The Transformation of Private Renting' in P. Malpass and R. Rowlands (eds), *Housing, Markets and Policy* (Abingdon: Routledge)
- Lowe, S. (2004) *Housing Policy Analysis: British Housing in Cultural and*

Comparative Context (Basingstoke: Palgrave Macmillan), Chapter 8
- Smith, M., Albanese, F. and Truder, J. (2014) *A Longitudinal Study of Housing Wellbeing in the Private Rented Sector* (London: Shelter and Crisis)
- Sirr, L. (ed.) (2014) *Renting in Ireland: The Social, Voluntary and Private Sectors* (Dublin: Institute of Public Administration)
- https://www.gov.uk/browse/housing/landlords
- http://www.ons.gov.uk/ons/resources/acenturyofhousing_tcm77–307080.png

proprietary interests

SEE ALSO **business planning; capital and revenue; dwellings; home ownership; low income households; merit goods and services; need and demand; private renting; social returns; subsidies; tenure; value**

That *dwellings* constitute both personal consumption and private investment highlights the point that people have proprietary interests vested in residential properties. The fact that dwellings can be partly or wholly funded from the public purse and that society as a whole is concerned about what happens to the housing stock highlights the point that there are also non-proprietary interests vested in residential properties. Proprietary interests refer to the concerns of those who have a direct and private stake in a property – such as tenants, leaseholders, landlords and owner-occupiers. Non-proprietary interests refer to the concerns that the wider *community* have for the property. These indirect, wider public interests are sometimes referred to as 'externalities'.

proprietorship

When considering the legal and economic relations associated with land and landed property it is often more useful to talk of 'proprietorship' than of 'ownership'. This is because people or organizations other than just the freeholder may have some sort of stake in an individual plot or building.

Legal proprietorship is about *tenure*. In legal terms, a proprietor is someone who has a right or title to something that enables him/her to hold it as property. Although in everyday speech the term 'property' is commonly used to indicate the physical object to which various legal rights relate, in proprietary analysis the word is used to denote the legal, economic and social relations appertaining to such an object. In this way, property is not conceived of as a concrete 'thing' but as a condition of belonging to a person, or persons, and is best thought of as comprising a bundle of rights and interests relating to the possession, use and disposal of an object such as a building.

There may be a number of different legal proprietary interests attached to a particular dwelling. In addition to the freehold interest, individuals may possess *leasehold* or tenancy interests in the dwelling and neighbouring households may have rights to use, enter or cross part of the land or building(s) in order to carry out certain functions. For example, rights of 'easement' establish rights of way or access (e.g. to maintain pipes, wires, fences); rights of 'profits a prendre' establish rights to take something from the property (e.g. grazing rights). Rights and restrictions may also be established by positive or restrictive covenants.

In addition to a legal interest, a proprietor will have private *welfare* and economic interests vested in the property. Whereas a legal interest specifies the nature and scope of a proprietor's rights and authority to use or physically alter a particular dwelling, a welfare/economic interest determines his or her motivation for using or altering it in some way. It can be said that legal proprietary interests are about power and welfare, and economic proprietary interests are about motivation and intent (see Figure 5).

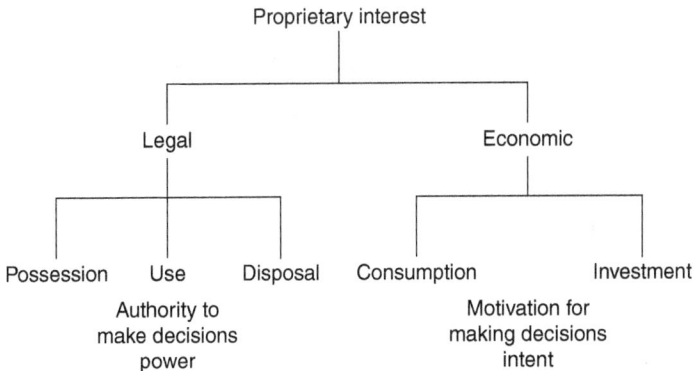

FIGURE 5   *The nature and scope of proprietary interests*

It is welfare and economic interests that underlie a proprietor's attitude towards the property and provide the rationale for making use of it or looking after it in a particular way. The welfare/economic stake that someone has in a dwelling can take the form of a consumption interest or an investment interest.

housing as consumption

A dwelling is a consumer item in that it generates 'utility' (consumer satisfaction) in the form of a stream of housing facilities that individuals and households need or want. Indeed, the primary reason that most people seek access to housing is to consume and enjoy all the various things it provides that together go to constitute a 'home'. These include 'shelter' in the form of protection from the elements, 'location' in the form of convenient proximity to work, shops, schools, countryside and so on, 'physical security' in the form of safety from the outside world and, less tangibly, benefits such as 'status' that may relate to the siting, size or design of the dwelling. It is sometimes said that housing, like food and clothing, is a 'primary' consumer good because without some minimum level of shelter, a reasonably decent life is not possible. In other words, it is argued that some defined level of housing is no ordinary consumer item, but a 'consumer necessity' (see *merit goods and services* and *subsidies*).

In making a decision about where to live, a household will judge each dwelling's 'utility' features in relation to its rental or purchase price. It is important to note, however, that to some extent, these features will be valued in terms of personal preferences. Just as some people like different types of music and some other people like different types of home. This means that in choosing a home, a household will seek to balance a number of factors. On the one hand, they will take account of the price or *rent* of the dwelling and its utility features (whether or not it suits their needs and expectations), and on the other hand they will consider whether or not they can afford to occupy it.

As well as being a home and generating utility, a dwelling will also have the features of an investment and, as such, have the potential to generate a financial or social 'return' on the money capital committed to its production or acquisition.

housing as real capital investment

Investments can be held in the form of paper titles, such as share certificates or bonds, or in the form of physical, usable artefacts, such as plant, machinery or buildings. This latter category of investment is sometimes referred to as 'real capital' or 'fixed capital formation' (see *capital and revenue*).

A dwelling can be regarded as an item of 'personal investment' in so far as it is a durable asset with a potential to earn a yield in the form of a rental income or a capital gain. A dwelling can be regarded as an item of 'social investment' in so far as it has a potential to yield social gains valued by society (see *social returns*). In either case, the *value* of the investment is determined by its potential to generate utility to some current or future end user. This means that its type, size, condition and geographical location will affect an asset's relative value.

The potential of a unit of accommodation to generate utility and a financial or social return affects a proprietor's attitudes towards spending money on its acquisition, improvement or maintenance. What people or organizations choose to do with or to a dwelling depends partly on their financial resources and partly on the nature of their proprietary interests. If the property is regarded as an item of consumption the proprietor will weigh up the price of buying, renting, repairing or maintaining it and compare this with the utility he or she would expect to acquire in return for such an outlay. If, however, a dwelling is regarded as a private or social investment then the proprietor will weigh up any proposed expenditure and compare it with the anticipated yield (including social yield) resulting from the investment outlay.

A tenant will have a predominantly consumption interest in a dwelling and will tend to be motivated to spend money on it with a view to gaining or maintaining its utility as a home. In contrast, a private landlord will have a predominantly investment interest and will be largely motivated to spend money on a dwelling with a view to maximizing its rental income or capital value. An owner-occupier has a consumption and an investment interest in a property and will tend to bear both of these characteristics in mind when purchasing, improving or maintaining it.

Like other proprietors, local authorities and housing associations have clear legal interests in the stock they manage. In contrast with other proprietors, however, their economic 'raison d'être' emphasizes the need to generate politico-welfare returns for public expenditure and charitable investments. These returns are not simply measured in terms of rental flows and capital appreciation, but also take account of how the housing stock serves the needs of low-income or vulnerable households. The aims and policy pronouncements of the authority or association will determine the precise nature of this proprietary interest. Public sector and charitable landlords may regard the return on investment in social and political, rather than commercial, terms. To the extent that these 'returns' are specified (e.g. in the form of statutory duties, mission statements, performance targets), their achievement constitutes part of the organization's proprietary interest. Because such agencies have to balance a number of objectives, such as the well-being of prospective as well as actual tenants, their proprietary interests will not necessarily be the same as those of their current tenants.

The social returns on housing investment extend beyond the specific concerns of the landlords and tenants of *social housing*. People and organizations that have no immediate, direct legal stake in a dwelling may still have concerns about its use or condition. These other-party concerns can be termed 'non-proprietary interests' or 'externalities'. The identification, creation and measurement of politico-welfare returns to social landlords are discussed in the entry on social returns.

KEY TEXT
- Garnett, D. and Perry, J. (2005) *Housing Finance* (Coventry: Chartered Institute of Housing and The Housing Studies Association)

q

quality

SEE ALSO continuous improvement; culture; merit goods and services; performance monitoring; value for money

Henryk Skolimowski (1981) has made the point that 'quality' is a difficult term to define, particularly in professional and business *cultures* that place an emphasis on measurement and quantification. However, both its meaning and identification have to be addressed by professional practitioners because the enhancement of 'quality' is seen to be at the heart of a *value for money* regime. Because of the potential for ambiguity, it is necessary to clarify what is meant by the term when it is being used in a particular management context. In particular, when an organization declares 'the pursuit of quality' as an objective, it should be clear what this implies for those with a responsibility for delivering such a policy.

The following categories represent overlapping ways of classifying the quality of a service. They may apply to the overall experience of service users or to the quality of particular assets employed by the service providers. They do not represent alternative or competing definitions: together they provide a way of thinking about the concept. They are not self-exclusive categories. The good practice organization is likely to be simultaneously pursuing several or all of these approaches to the establishment of 'quality':

1. 'Quality as exceptional': This points to assessments that rank organizations in terms of excellence and identifies those with the 'best' performance. Because it is hierarchical and relative, it also means that the average service provider can never be classed as 'exceptional'. In this classification, quality is seen as something to emulate. It is the notion of quality that underlies the idea of performance league tables.

2. 'Quality as fitness for purpose': This is quite different to 'quality as exceptional' in that it defines quality in terms of non-exceptional 'adequacy'. It is an internal rather than an external measure (i.e. it is not directly concerned with league tables and competitive positioning). It is normally used in assessing the contribution made by fixed assets (e.g. an element of the housing stock or some other physical facility) to the organization's aims and objectives (mission).

3. 'Quality as consistency': What is sought here is 'consistent good practice'. This measure has its roots in industrial production line methods and their associated techniques of quality assurance. In a service context, it places an emphasis on the maintenance of strong management and monitoring procedures and requires lines of *accountability* to be clear.

4. 'Quality as value for money': This emphasizes the efficiency and effectiveness of the service. It focuses on the question of how to make the best use of limited resources. This, of course, begs the question 'What do we mean by "best"?' (see *value for money*).

5. 'Quality as transformation': This places a particular *value* on the organization generating new and creative solutions to old problems and on its ability to encourage and cultivate changes that are in the interest of service users and other stakeholders (innovation).

It has to be re-emphasized that these are not competing definitions of 'quality', but rather different ways of conceptualizing the notion. In achieving one of these quality outcomes (e.g. an exceptional rating), it may automatically bring about one or all of the others. Indeed, there are dangers of over-classifying a notion as complex and subtle as 'quality'. As Robert Pirsig indicated in his cult classic, 'Zen and the Art of Motorcycle Maintenance', real quality cannot be defined, and if we attempt to describe it in any precise way, we will almost certainly be defining something that is less than 'true quality'. However, these ways of thinking about the concept should help the organization to determine an intelligent strategy for improving the outcomes of the services it provides. Once the strategy is in place, the organization must set up mechanisms for monitoring and measuring what is achieved. This brings up the question of *performance monitoring* and evaluation.

KEY TEXTS

- Harvey, L. and Green, D. (1993) 'Defining Quality', *Assessment and Evaluation in Higher Education: An International Journal*, 18 (1): pp. 9–34
- Quality Housing Services Ltd (2012) *The QHS Criteria for Excellence in Communities* (Coventry: QHS)
- http://hqnetwork.co.uk/

r

regulation

SEE ALSO business planning; continuous improvement; culture;
diversity; governance; housing market; participation; performance
monitoring; quality; risk and uncertainty; value for money

A regulation can be thought of as an expectation, requirement or
rule that is used to control, direct or manage an activity or organization. Regulatory rules can be 'obligatory' (required) or 'voluntary'
(recommended as best practice). Obligatory regulation is externally
imposed whilst voluntary regulation stems from the organization's
internal business *culture*.

The underlying rationale for regulation is based on the argument that social service providers and others who are not
subjected to market forces must be answerable to users and
society at large through an alternative mechanism. The regulatory system is a substitute for the market disciplines to which
most private sector firms are subject. Because of their potential power to manipulate the market, large private sector service
firms such as the banks and energy providers are also subjected
to strict regulation.

externally monitored regulations

When a regulation is associated with a specific piece of legislation,
its interpretation and enforcement are usually mandated to a regulatory agency. Housing providers have to engage with a variety of
regulatory agencies, notably the Homes and Communities Agency
in England, the Scottish Housing Regulator, the Northern Ireland
Housing Executive, the Regulatory Board of the Welsh Assembly
Government, the Housing Ombudsman, the Financial Conduct
Authority, the Environment Agency, the Charity Commission, local
planning authorities, Ofsted and nationally focused health care and

quality commissioners (who regulate accommodation for persons requiring nursing or personal care).

Increasingly housing organizations are seeking and acquiring voluntary 'kite-marked' accreditation from governmental and private quality assurance agencies such as Investors in People, the International Standards Organization, Quality Housing Services (now part of Service Matters) and Positive about Disabled People. This normally involves initial inspections and paper investigations and subsequent regulatory checks to ensure that the organization's operations continue to warrant certification. These certificated quality awards can sometimes be incorporated into the obligatory regulatory procedures leading, for example, to 'lighter touch' inspections by the official regulator.

In recent years there has been much discussion about what constitutes the nature and scope of 'good regulation'. This has led to the establishment of a number of generally accepted principles. These indicate that the regulator should seek to achieve the following:

1. 'Accountability': justify its decisions and be subjected to public scrutiny.
2. 'Applicability': take account of differences in the nature and objectives of those who are subject to their scrutiny.
3. 'Proportionality': ensure that any burden or restriction that it imposes on a person, organization or activity is proportionate to the benefits expected as a result.
4. 'Targeted': focus on a clear goal or requirement and minimize any side effects.
5. 'Transparency': exercise its functions as openly as possible and be accessible (with commercial/privacy safeguards) to the regulated *community* and the general public.
6. 'Comprehensibility': devise regulations that are clear, unambiguous and easy to understand.
7. 'Efficiency': use its own resources in the most economical way.

internal self-regulation
The overall approach of internal regulation should be to foster a culture of sensible and appropriate control through the development of coherent strategies and effective management systems.

This should be achieved by maintaining high standards of *governance* and clear lines of responsibility. Organizations are expected to demonstrate that they have in place processes and procedures that manage risks appropriately and produce *value for money* for tenants and other service users.

co-regulation
Co-regulation is the principle by which a social landlord self-regulates in a transparent manner but makes itself subjected to tenant scrutiny and challenge.

implications for practice
- There has been a recent policy shift towards involving residents more in the regulatory process. The current 'co-regulatory' approach puts great emphasis on the role of governing boards and tenant scrutiny panels. Panels typically monitor key performance indicators and progress on complaints. They also advise boards of management on both strategic and operational matters that are of concern to service users. Although a statutory requirement, once in place, tenant scrutiny panels become one aspect of the organization's internal regulatory procedures.
- Currently, all registered providers are required to comply with certain regulated standards. These are classified as 'economic' (covering governance, VFM and *rent*) and 'consumer' (covering tenant involvement, quality of homes, tenancies and community issues).
- Regulatory requirements (introduced in April 2012) identify two broad VFM tests that providers must seek to ensure that they apply. First, they must demonstrate the nature and extent of the returns (including *social returns*) that they are getting from their assets. Second, they must demonstrate that they have clear and effective procedures for driving down costs. These days the housing regulators tend not to set down a prescribed meaning for value for money. There is an expectation, however, that the regulated organization is clear about what it counts as VFM and to have in place procedures and performance indicators for setting and monitoring VFM outcomes (see *performance monitoring*).

- Regulators tend to focus on risk identification and management by scrutinizing the organization's governance and ensuring that the board or governing committee is properly constituted and is effective in scrutinizing its own work. There is an expectation that the board and its sub-committees are competent to monitor strategic risks and appreciate that ultimately it is they who 'own' such risks.
- Under the 'applicability' criterion, there has been a tendency to move away from a universal 'one size fits all' approach to regulation towards a more bespoke and focused approach that takes account of a particular organization's current circumstances. This means, for example, that regulators will scrutinize newly established agencies with a limited 'track record' more rigorously than they do the more 'mature' agencies with an established record of good practice. In the case of well-established landlords, regulators also tend to focus more on outcomes than processes and procedures. However, following governance failures at the Cosmopolitan Housing Group in 2012/2013, the regulators have come under pressure to ensure that post-2015 regulatory arrangements across the United Kingdom become more rigorous and include more prescriptive risk profiling for the sector.

KEY TEXTS

- Bramley, G., Munro, M. and Pawson, H. (2004) *Key Issues in Housing: Policies and Markets in 21st-Century Britain* (Basingstoke: Palgrave Macmillan)
- HM Government (2010) *Reducing Regulation Made Simple: Less Regulation, Better Regulation and Regulation as a Last Resort*
- Housing Quality Network. http://hqnetwork.co.uk/
- Murphy, E. (2013) *The Regulation of Registered Housing Associations* (Belfast: Northern Ireland Assembly). http://www.niassembly.gov.uk/Documents/RaISe/Publications/2013/social_dev/murphy0113.pdf
- National Housing Federation (2012a) *Localism Act 2011: Housing and Planning: A Guide for Housing Associations*
- Smedley, S. (2014) *Briefing: Where Are We Now with VFM Self-assessment?* (HouseMark)
- Welsh Government (2011) *The Regulatory Framework for Housing Associations in Wales*

rent

SEE ALSO affordability; cost of housing; housing market; private renting; subsidies; tenancies; tenancy agreements

The idea of 'rent' comes from early economic theory (e.g. David Ricardo). It was originally used to describe the surplus generated over and above the costs of agricultural production. The greater the surplus (resulting from fertility), the more the landlord could charge the tenant farmer for using the land. In modern society, 'contract rent' is the 'price' paid by a tenant to a landlord for the occupation or use of land, buildings or other property (e.g. cars, mobile phones and televisions can be rented for set periods). When something is acquired on an hourly or weekly basis, it is normally referred to as being 'hired' rather than 'rented'.

market rent

This is the price freely agreed between a landlord and a tenant or leaseholder for a unit of unsubsidized accommodation taking account of factors such as scarcity, condition, location and any restrictive terms set by the owner or the planning authorities. In practice, the market rent is usually derived from a comparison of the current charges made for comparable *dwellings* in the same area.

In commercial settings landlords acting rationally will seek to charge the highest rent that the market will bear. In a free-enterprise economy with no state intervention, the price a landlord can charge will be determined by market conditions. In particular, the ability to fix a rent will be affected by the degree of competition that exists. Economists refer to this traditional approach to rent setting as 'marginal cost pricing', which determines 'market rents'. In practice, rent-setting principles have varied considerably from tenure to tenure and from one period to another (see *tenancy agreements*). Historically, the different rent levels charged by councils and registered social landlords were determined by when and where the housing was built, changes in the *capital and revenue subsidies* given to social landlords and the different rent policies pursued by central government and the landlords themselves.

The rent may also pay for specified services provided by the landlord. These may be paid for separately, in which case they are referred to as 'service charges'. From the tenant's point of view, rents and charges represent the 'price' that is paid in order to acquire these rights of occupancy and associated services.

rent pooling

The old municipal principle of 'rent-pooling' is an example of cross-subsidization of one group of tenants by another. Under rent-pooling arrangements tenants living in established dwellings with small or no debt charges attached to them have their rents increased beyond the historic costs of provision so that tenants occupying newer properties with relatively high historic costs (debt charges) can have their rents reduced to more affordable levels.

rent setting: the 'need–price dilemma'

In the context of rent-setting policy, a 'need–price dilemma' manifests itself as a concern to balance *affordability* with sufficiency. In other words, the problem facing the social landlord is to set a rent that is sufficiently high to cover the costs of provision, yet low enough to be affordable by those deemed to be in housing need. From the landlord's point of view, the rent is an 'income' received in return for making these rights available and for providing the services. 'Total sufficiency rent' (Garnett, 2000) is defined as the level of rent that generates the revenue necessary to cover all of the landlord's costs of provision (see *cost of housing*) without any subsidy inputs. To make rents affordable to poorer households, governments have, at different times, regulated or controlled rent levels and rent increases and provided subsidies to both consumers and producers (see *subsidies*).

Most social tenancies that started before 15 January 1989 are classed as 'secure'. Secure tenants pay what is termed a 'fair rent'. This means that if there is not a rent review clause in the tenancy agreement, then the rent can only be increased by an independent rent valuation officer and this will be the maximum rent the landlord can charge (see *tenancy agreements*).

From April 2011 the government made significant changes to the rules around *social housing*. One of these changes involved the introduction of rents that are nearer to market rents. These are called 'affordable rents' and are intended to be higher than typical secure social rents and lower than market rents. 'Affordable rent' is a technical term tied to legislation (Localism Act 2011) and does not mean that the actual rent charged is affordable as such. In this sense the term is a misnomer. There is no agreement about what in reality counts as an 'affordable rent' in the real (non-technical) sense. Both ministers and the various funding bodies have staunchly refused to give a clear definition. However, in 1988 the then Minister of Housing William Waldegrave said that rents should be 'set and maintained at levels within the reach of those in lower paid employment'.

rent restructuring

By the time of the 2000 Green Paper ('Quality and Choice: A Decent Home for All'), significant differentials had been established between the rents charged by the various types of landlord. These rent differentials were judged to be unsatisfactory as they inhibited the government's dual policy objectives of fairness and *choice*. It was thought to be unfair that people living in similar homes in the same locality should be paying different rents simply because they rent from a different form of social landlord. It was also felt that some tenants were making choices based on the characteristics of the landlord rather than those of the dwelling.

After 2002, as part of its 'rent harmonization policy', the government determined how rents should be set for both housing associations and council properties, by setting out a formula that determined a 'target rent'. This sought gradually to eliminate historic rent differences charged for similar properties in a district. The formula took account of things such as property values, the number of bedrooms and local wage levels. Annual rent increases could then be calculated using a second formula that incorporated the rate of inflation, an allowable increment to the inflation rate (e.g. 1 per cent), plus/minus a fixed sum (e.g. £2). This formula created a 'rent cap'. Rent harmonization has now been abandoned and future rent regimes (from 2016) will not normally allow the setting formula to incorporate a plus/minus adjustment element.

KEY TEXTS

- For a discussion of practice issues refer to Harriott, S. and Matthews, L. (2004) *Introducing Affordable Housing* (Coventry: Chartered Institute of Housing)
- Mullins, D. and Murie, A. (2006) *Housing Policy in the UK* (Basingstoke: Palgrave Macmillan)

- Wilson, W. (2014) *Rent Setting for Social Housing Tenancies (England)*, House of Commons Library, Social Policy Section, Standard Note SN/SP/1090

risk and uncertainty

SEE ALSO asset management; audit; business planning; culture; development; performance monitoring; quality; regulation; sustainability

'Safe as houses' is a phrase of which most of us have heard. Before the Industrial Revolution and the opening up of a vast array of new commercial and industrial investment opportunities, those few individuals with surplus funds had a limited range of activities in which to invest. At that time, overseas trading ventures, land and property represented the most significant outlets. Of these, land and property, including houses, were the most secure. With the emergence of a national industrial economy, huge opportunities for new types of profitable investment arose in factories, canals and, eventually, railways. It is probable that the phrase 'safe as houses' arose when the railway bubbles burst and speculation again favoured land and built structures.

Business risks can have an internal or external origin and can be thought of as anything that threatens the achievement of any of the organization's objectives. Major risks can threaten the organization's very mission. Risk management can be defined as the *culture* and processes that seek to make the most of opportunities that might enhance an organization's objectives and reduce any threats to the achievement of those objectives. It is clearly not possible to run any dynamic venture without taking risks. Indeed, if the firm is committed to innovation, risk-taking will inevitably be fundamental to the ways in which it operates. The goal of risk management is to make sure that the organization only takes those risks that will help it achieve its mission and objectives and that it takes those risks in an informed way.

In housing management the question of risk became an important issue with the introduction of the 1989 housing *finance* regime and the shift away from grant funding towards mixed funding arrangements that involved the necessity for most landlords to borrow money on a commercial basis. In recent years risk management has been given a high profile in all types of organization.

Although people have been managing business risks for decades, risk management's current prominence on organizations' agendas can be traced to the Turnbull Report, published in 1999. This report focused on private business, but much of the content is equally applicable to the public and voluntary sectors. The report advocated a shift in the regulatory focus away from the processes to the outcomes. This implied a move away from a simplistic systems approach to an approach that puts an emphasis on both perform-ance and *quality*. It also underlined the need for effective risk anal-ysis and management. The report stated that risk-management practices should take a holistic approach and be driven by a desire to balance innovation with stability.

A 'risk' is something that is probabilistic with a potential to do harm. It can take the form of an unwelcome occurrence or a missed opportunity. A risk can usually be quantified and its impact assessed. This means that, although it might not be appropriate, most risks can be insured against. Risk-management techniques designed to quantify a risk typically seek to produce a weighted measure based on the calculation 'probability' multiplied by 'impact'. In this way a high risk is identified as being both likely to happen and also to be highly damaging when it does. The standard literature on risk management discusses various ways of creating weighted numerals to represent potential probabilities and impacts. An 'uncertainty' is different from a risk in that it is not possible to calculate the probability of its occurrence and/or its impact cannot be easily assessed. This means that it is not possible to insure against uncertainties.

In housing management a distinction is usually made between general business risks that are embedded in everyday activities and can harm the overall business plan, and project risks that relate to specific *development* schemes. Project risks constitute a particular aspect of business risk and are usually managed on a scheme-by-scheme basis (see *development*).

classifying risks conceptually
Conceptual orderings help to make sense of the world and are necessary in order to develop policies to deal with complex things.

'Risk' is a blanket term and effective risk management needs to begin by classifying risks in a way that aids strategic thinking. Simply producing a list of unclassified risks (the 'bucket' approach) will inhibit the process of strategic thinking and may well produce an uncoordinated and incoherent approach to risk analysis and management that fails to make appropriate connections through time.

To demonstrate that they are thinking and planning strategically, risk managers in housing agencies tend to consider the following dichotomies:

- 'Positive vs negative risks': This emphasizes the need to see a lost opportunity as a risk.
- 'Critical vs non-critical risks': Critical risks are those that could have a major adverse impact on the business; these should be identified and then prioritized.
- 'External vs internal risks': External risks are those that are not in the direct control of the management; these include political issues, exchange rates, interest rates. Internal risks include non-compliance, fraud, information breaches and a vast range of occurrences resulting from poor communications, planning and management.
- 'Warranted vs unwarranted risks': This emphasizes need to manage rather than avoid risks.
- 'Gross vs residual risk': This underlines the need for risk policies that incorporate mitigating activities.
- 'Risk event vs risk effect': This sharpens up the distinction between something happening (e.g. a complaining client writes to the press) and the subsequent consequences (e.g. loss of reputation).
- 'Insurable vs uninsurable': This highlights the distinction between 'probabilistic risk' and 'uncertainty'. (Risks and uncertainties should be managed in somewhat different ways.)
- 'Business vs health and safety risks': This clarifies the distinction between risks that exist in economic space and those that exist in physical space.
- 'Key risks vs hazards': This is another way of expressing the previous category.

- 'Short-term vs long-term risks': This highlights the distinction between those risks associated with the overall business plan and those associated with specific projects or activities within the business plan.
- 'Isolated vs linked risks': This highlights the need for a holistic approach to risk analysis; it also helps to explain why ultimately, the responsibility for risk assessment has to be owned at the corporate rather than the departmental level.
- 'Single vs cumulative risks': This highlights the need for a dynamic rather than a static approach to risk analysis. It also points to the need for risks to be managed at all levels: corporate, departmental, sectional and individual.
- 'Current risks vs emerging risks': This also emphasizes the need for a dynamic approach and to incorporate risk analysis into *business planning.*

In practice, effective risk management begins by identifying the broad operational business categories that have to be managed. This process is usually called 'risk-mapping'. A typical risk map distinguishes between categories such as financial, physical, operational and reputational risks.

general business risks
ownership of risk
In *social housing* agencies there has been a tendency to perceive risk management as a central (top-down) responsibility. That is, it has been seen as a strategic rather than an operational issue. However, because both knowledge of, and attitudes towards, risks vary between stakeholders, it is now generally agreed to be important that everybody in the organization becomes involved in the identification and management of risks. Best practice now indicates that risk awareness should be an aspect of both strategic and operational management.

Most commentators on this subject suggest that effective risk management is grounded in the organization's business culture. It is argued that this is more important than developing extensive policies and procedures. If the management of risk is embedded in the operational practices, all staff will take responsibility for their actions and outcomes. This means that, in a sense, everyone becomes a 'risk manager', and this will result in risk management becoming a natural part of how the organization thinks and works.

risk appetite

Risk appetite is a defined measure of the overall level of risk to which an organization is prepared to be exposed. There is a wide recognition that risk management should not be about making an institution 'risk averse' as this would inhibit innovation. However, some organizations move straight from identifying risk to treating it, without proper consideration of risk appetite. This approach can ignore the context of the risk and can lead to the implementation of costly, ill-conceived and inadequate 'quick fixes'. Such dangers can be prevented through a proper understanding of risk appetite. Often housing organizations acknowledge the need to define a risk appetite, but in many cases, it is seen to be inherent in the way that the institution conducts itself, rather than something that needs to be periodically and formally reviewed and described. In the risk-management literature there are a number of methodologies for defining risk appetite.

Generally speaking, social landlords need to be cautious when taking risks that directly affect the interests of residents. As landlords they are providing 'homes' and they have a duty of care to ensure that these are not put at risk. However, it is generally recognized that an organization's appetite for taking risk will be influenced by its mission, its financial health and its aspirations to expand its range of activities.

options for treating risk

Responses should be designed to treat those risks that are considered unacceptable. A number of options are available:

- avoid the risk,
- transfer the risk,
- retain and manage the risk.

Risk avoidance is achieved through general policy decision-making. Transfer involves ensuring that where possible and appropriate, contracts and agreements with third parties (such as contractors and partnering agencies) require others to take on all or part of the risks in question. For an annual fee, some risks can also be 'transferred' to insurance companies. Registered providers, for example, can now insure against void and bad debt *rent* losses rather than tie up money in internal provisions. Whether this is an appropriate action involves some form of option appraisal. Where the organization takes the final option, to retain the risk, then it should be monitored and, if possible, reduced. Risk-reduction actions turn a 'gross risk' into a 'residual risk'. Residual risk (sometimes called 'net risk') represents the assessment of a risk after anything is done to mitigate it: that is, after controls are put in place.

Best practice suggests that particular attention should be paid to any risk that would have a significant disruptive effect on the business. A 'business impact analysis' predicts the consequences of disruption of a major business function and gathers information needed to develop recovery strategies. Best practice suggests that organizations should identify possible disruption scenarios and have mitigation plans in place. Where the impact of something failing or going wrong is judged to be extremely damaging (or even disastrous), avoidance action might be taken even though the probability of such an event occurring is regarded as unlikely. This is known as 'the precautionary principle'.

dealing with uncertainty
Although uncertainties cannot be quantified, they should not be ignored. Most housing organizations will have access to a network of influential and knowledgeable people who can be consulted with about the possible consequences of uncertainties, such as what would happen if there were to be change in government or a major change in technology. The 'Delphi Method' has been developed to consider such 'unknowns'. This seeks to aggregate opinions from a diverse set of experts whose forecasts are based on their special knowledge. The word 'Delphi' refers to the Oracle of Delphi, a site in Greek mythology where prophecies were passed on.

implications for practice
- The *regulation* of social housing agencies now takes a largely 'risk-management' approach (see *regulation*).
- There will normally be a trade-off between the level of risks and the costs for reducing them. This means that the total

elimination of a risk is seldom the appropriate approach.
- The costs of risk management should be commensurate with the rating of the risks under consideration.
- It is usually argued that any solutions should, where possible, dovetail with the existing work of managers and institutional plans. The integration of risk management into existing processes makes it less likely to be seen as a 'bolt-on' and will allow it to become embedded more quickly and economically.
- Some housing agencies set up a separate 'risk committee' to steer the risk-management procedures. This, however, tends to undermine current guidance that risk management should be 'embedded' in the organization's normal management structures (e.g. monitoring might be done by the Audit Committee).
- Care should be taken that the members of the Audit Committee are, as far as possible, independent from other activities that operate risk procedures. It might, for example, be inappropriate for the chair of the Resources or Finance committees to serve on the Audit Committee.

KEY TEXTS
- Alarm: The Public Risk Management Association. http://alarm-uk.org
- *Risk Management in Higher Education: A Guide to Good Practice*, prepared for HEFCE by Price Waterhouse Coopers, 2005
- *The Turnbull Report: Internal Controls: Guidance for Directors on the Combined Code*, Institute of Chartered Accountants in England and Wales, September 1999

S

social enterprise

SEE ALSO business planning; community; development; diversity; partnerships; social returns

Social enterprises are organizations where the money made is invested in social and *community* projects rather than distributed to shareholders. Although the term is relatively new, social enterprises themselves are not new with many of our prominent institutions having been established on charitable grounds and managed on a not-for-profit basis. Most activities in this sector seek to tackle specific social problems, improve people's life chances or protect the environment. They create shared wealth and give people a stake in the economy. Social enterprise is a growing sector: there are more than 68,000 social enterprises in the United Kingdom, contributing more than £24 billion to the UK economy and employing almost one million people.

Businesses that have social, charitable or community-based objectives can be set up in a variety of formats, including limited companies, business *partnerships*, registered or (if the annual income is less than £5,000) unregistered charities, co-operatives, community benefit societies (previously called industrial and provident societies), community interest companies (a special type of limited company that exists to benefit the community rather than shareholders) or an unincorporated association (typically a small organization such as a sports club or voluntary group that is more of a common interest group than a business). If an organization is run for the benefit of its members it is described as 'mutual'. Some of these arrangements require the organization to be registered by a supervising agency such as Companies House, the Financial Conduct Authority, the Charity Commission (England and Wales), the Office of the Scottish Charity Regulator, the Charity Commission for Northern Ireland and HM Revenue and Customs.

The notion of 'enterprise' is associated with 'entrepreneurship'. In its French origin the word 'entrepreneur' referred to someone who undertakes a significant business venture. Its original use is associated with the writings of the early nineteenth-century French economist Jean Baptiste Say who used the term to describe someone who creates *value* by 'undertaking' to shift economic resources from less-productive to more-productive uses. In the later nineteenth century, economists such as Alfred Marshall expanded this idea by drawing attention to the need to have a coordinating agent at the heart of business activity to undertake the job of bringing together the other 'factors of production' (land, labour and capital) in ways that minimize costs and maximize outputs. In the twentieth century, the idea of entrepreneurship was further expanded. Writers such as Joseph Schumpeter began to define the entrepreneur as the agent in the productive process who took risks and reshaped the patterns of production by adopting new technologies, finding new innovative ways of doing things, searching out new sources of supply and creating new markets. In Schumpeter's portrayal, entrepreneurs became the 'change agents' who moved the economy and society forwards.

Gregory Dees (2001) makes the point that contemporary writers on management theory do not so much emphasize the entrepreneur's function of bringing about change as that of making the most of change when it occurs. In this way, the successful modern entrepreneur is regarded as a resourceful opportunist with a mind-set that sees the possibilities rather than the problems created by change. Dees suggests that successful leaders of social enterprises are 'entrepreneurs with a social mission'.

In commercial businesses the creation of economic wealth is central to their purpose. Once created this wealth is reinvested in the business or distributed to the primary stakeholders (e.g. shareholders or business partners). For social enterprises the published mission is central to their 'raison d'être' and economic wealth is seen as a means to an end and not an end in itself. They are concerned to create social value to be shared with the primary stakeholders (e.g. tenants and local communities). The creation and sharing of 'social value' is now seen as the key idea behind social enterprises (see *social returns* for discussion of 'shared value').

In 2013 the Public Services (Social Value) Act came into force. Its enactment raised awareness of the notion of 'social value' and encouraged its incorporation into the language and practices of procurement appraisal. Under this legislation, for the first time, public bodies are required to consider how the services they commission might improve the economic, social and environmental well-being of the areas in which they operate.

implications for practice
- In recent years there has been an increasing interest in social enterprise in Parliament where there is cross-party support for its development in the context of the 'localism agenda'.
- A number of registered providers have shown an interest in expanding and diversifying their core businesses into wider areas of social enterprise. Many are currently evaluating its potential to support their efforts to counter the negative impact on their residents of the 'welfare reform' programme. This involves considering such things as: how its development might produce goods and services to support the well-being and employment of residents; how it might improve the skills and work readiness of residents and how it could be incorporated into the supply chain to create social value.
- Social investment can be defined as the provision and use of capital to generate social as well as financial returns. There are a number of significant bodies that offer financing to social enterprise. These include Social Finance, New Philanthropy Capital, Big Society Capital, UnLtd, the Charity Aid Foundation, Venturesome, Clearlyso and the Social Investment Bank. Each of these bodies has a slightly different role and obtains funding in different ways.

KEY TEXTS
- Dees, J. G. (2001) *The Meaning of 'Social Entrepreneurship'* (CASE). http://www.caseatduke.org/documents/dees_sedef.pdf
- https://www.gov.uk/set-up-a-social-enterprise

- www.neweconomics.org
- www.socialfinance.org.uk

social housing

SEE ALSO affordability; low cost home ownership; low income households; need and demand; social enterprise; tenancy agreements; value for money

Social housing landlords provide 'affordable' accommodation for people on low incomes or with particular needs. 'Registered social landlord' (RSL) is the technical name for a social housing provider registered with the Homes and Communities Agency (England), the Welsh Assembly Government, the Scottish Housing Regulator or the Northern Ireland Housing Executive. The term 'registered provider' is also sometimes used to describe such agencies. Registration enables landlords to bid for a share of any government financial support allocated to housing provision: in return, the regulators require certain compliance rules to be followed that are designed to ensure that landlords meet specified minimum *quality* standards and provide *value for money* for tax-payers.

Most RSLs are housing associations, but trusts, co-operatives and companies may also come under this heading. To cut through this confusion, the term 'housing association' is now commonly used to describe all non-municipal providers of social housing. Housing associations provide homes for *rent*, leasing, sale and shared ownership.

In the United Kingdom, an arm's length management organisation (ALMO) is a not-for-profit company that provides housing and related services on behalf of a local authority.

KEY TEXTS

- Elphicke, N. and House, K. (2015) *From Statutory Provider to Housing Enabler: Review into the Local Authority Role in Housing Supply*. The Elphicke House Report (London: DCLG/HMSO)
- Reeves, P. (2014) *Affordable and Social Housing: Policy and Practice* (New York: Routledge)

social returns

SEE ALSO business planning; community; culture; development; diversity; dwellings; inclusion and exclusion; partnerships; proprietary interests; social enterprise; value; value for money

The interests in a particular housing *development* and its subsequent management extend beyond the specific concerns of the residents, owners or landlords. People and organizations that have no immediate or direct legal stake in a dwelling may still have concerns about its use or condition. These other-party concerns are variously termed 'non-proprietary interests', 'externalities' or 'social returns', according to the context in which they are being discussed. To the extent that its provision, use and maintenance are seen to be of concern to the wider *community*, housing possesses characteristics that can lead to it being classified as a 'social commodity' in which non-proprietary as well as proprietary interests are vested.

The wider community may have concerns about particular housing that go beyond, or can even be in conflict with, the interests of those with proprietary stakes in the properties. For example, a housing association or a private company may wish to pursue its *welfare* or commercial objectives by developing a plot of land with a view to providing *dwellings* to let: the resultant development might obscure a view, create traffic congestion, destroy a wildlife area, or in some other way affect the interests of others.

Other examples of the ways in which housing might be considered a social good include the following:

1. Because nearly all dwellings in all *tenures* are built to a standard that ensures that they outlive their initial occupiers, housing production caters for future as well as current housing needs and demands. In this sense housing can be regarded as a national social asset, held in trust by one generation for the next.

2. Research findings have long demonstrated a clear link between *homelessness* and poor housing and people's health and vulnerability to crime. Furthermore, there is a recognized, albeit ill-defined, link between housing conditions and educational performances. There has been an historical reluctance on the part of governments to accept the links between poor housing

and social issues. A famous example was the government's rejection in 1980 of the Black Report's finding on the links between poor housing and ill health. Since the 1990s, the links have been more readily accepted, but financial constraints still make it difficult to persuade ministers to invest public funds in housing projects on the basis that such investments will reduce social inequality and its associated problems.

3. Together with roads, schools, hospitals and so on, housing constitutes part of an area's infrastructure and, as such, plays a significant part in the promotion of its economic growth and prosperity. In particular, an appropriate supply of good *quality* housing is needed to attract and retain a skilled and qualified workforce. Regional planning and growth committees, such as the Local Enterprise Partnership boards, generally accept the links between housing investment and economic growth.

4. Because the condition of an individual dwelling has a 'spill-over effect' on the use and exchange values of neighbouring properties, how one proprietor maintains or uses his or her property can affect the interests of neighbouring proprietors. It is in recognition of the interconnected nature of property interests that society gives local planning authorities powers to approve both new construction and alterations to existing buildings. In some instances, the externality interests of neighbours are internalized into the legal interests of a proprietor by means of positive or restrictive covenants.

For all these reasons it is possible to argue that there exist community interests in the housing stock that are external to those with proprietary interests. The existence of external, non-proprietary, community interests in the size and condition of the housing stock is pointed to as one of the reasons for directing public expenditure into the housing system.

social returns and the individual organization

The long-standing issue surrounding the generation of social returns is that many community outcomes are real and important but intangible, difficult to measure and their receipt is spread over the life of the project or the building. By contrast, the investment needed to generate them is front-loaded, tangible and can be measured precisely. This contrast can create a disincentive to invest when it comes to social or community projects.

Any decision to invest in projects in order to generate a social return will always largely be a matter of judgement. Current techniques are designed to provide a transparent, clearly targeted and reasoned case for the investment that is independently verified and does not make exaggerated claims for the resultant benefits. Most of the techniques recommend the active involvement of stakeholders.

SROI (Social Returns on Investment) is an analytic tool developed by the New Economics Foundation to account for (and measure) a much broader area of *value* outcomes than is captured by traditional economic calculations. In particular, it seeks to take into account the social, economic and environmental consequences of economic activity. Its key feature is that it values outcomes by using financial proxies so that VFM decisions can be made using monetary measures. Its application can demonstrate to potential funders and internal decision-makers that, for example, a proposed investment will have a multiplier effect on local economic growth or internal cost savings when social returns are taken into account.

Most *social housing* providers are not-for-profit organizations. The notion of 'not-for-profit' in itself implies that generating a 'social return' is an integral part of the agency's mission. Many social landlords now publicly declare that the pursuit of social returns is a key aspect of their business function. In the housing sector it has long been argued that, just as secure comfortable homes are at the heart of happy family lives, decent affordable houses are at the heart of thriving communities. A number of social housing agencies have extended their activities beyond the traditional landlord function to provide a variety of other services as part of their commitments to the wider communities in which they operate. The examples of such investments are legion and often involve some form of partnership arrangement. They range from things such as the provision of dog fouling notices and collection boxes to helping with the provision or refurbishment of community assets such as village halls and youth centres.

the emerging idea of 'shared value'

The commitment to the creation of social value is intrinsically a matter of business *culture*. In recent years a significant shift in business thinking around the notion of 'shared value' has been developed. Based on research and analysis carried out at the Harvard Business School, new ideas are emerging about the appropriate relationship between business and society.

Many firms declare a commitment to 'corporate social responsibility' (CSR). This can be thought of as an approach to business that actively seeks to make a positive contribution to society. In practice the term can refer to a wide range of actions that companies may take, from donating to charity to reducing carbon emissions. The Harvard approach argues for the efficacy of instigating more fundamental changes in business thinking and suggests that in the political and commercial climate following the 'financial crisis' of the late 1980s, successful companies need to review their relationships with society. The criticism of CSR is that it does not represent a full cultural commitment to being a valued part of society but rather that it maintains an 'old-fashioned' (and increasingly inappropriate) view of benevolent capitalism of the nineteenth and twentieth centuries. Because the creation of social value is not embedded in the business plan, the advocates of 'shared value' argue that the 'good works' of the corporately responsible firms are little more than 'bolt-ons' to their traditional ways of working.

Social organizations and government entities often see success solely in terms of the external (e.g. community) benefits achieved or the money expended. The concept of 'shared value' can be defined as 'policies and operating practices that enhance the competitiveness of a company while simultaneously advancing the economic and social conditions in the communities in which it operates'. This approach moves away from a business model in which the firm donates a small proportion of its distributable profits to 'good causes' to one in which proper recognition is given to the fact that the addressing of societal concerns yields direct productivity benefits to the firm (see 'implications for practice').

measuring and declaring a 'social dividend'
There does not yet exist an agreed approach to the measurement of social returns that is equivalent to the International Accounting Standards Board. However, the current operating climate for social landlords is increasingly challenging, and it is now regarded by many as being important that organizations can demonstrate to

funders, governing boards, regulators and stakeholders the value of what is being delivered. Building homes is easy to quantify but many valuable social returns are more opaque. This has led many agencies not to attempt to declare a 'social dividend'. A number of housing associations, however, are currently experimenting with ways of measuring (or at least describing) the social returns that are being generated by their activities.

implications for practice
- In a housing context, a 'shared value' approach might, for example, give recognition to the fact that providing advice on household budgeting not only helps the physical and mental well-being of residents, but also reduces the bad debts of the organization. Investing in job-creation projects might produce similar benefits for the organization.
- Similarly, when a company invests in a wellness programme, this not only enhances the lives of employees and their families, but also benefits the firm by minimizing absenteeism through ill health and improves staff morale and loyalty which, in turn, will have an impact on productivity, staff recruitment and retention.
- Increasingly land development and service provision contracts are being awarded to firms and agencies that can demonstrate a commitment to 'shared value'.
- The 'SROI Network' (Social Returns on Investment) includes the Charities Evaluation Services (CES), New Economics Foundation (NEF), New Philanthropy Capital (NPC) and the National Council for Voluntary Organisations (NCVO). In a related SROI project in Scotland, CES helps to design and evaluate accredited SROI training.

KEY TEXTS
- Porter, M. E. and Kramer, M. R. (2011) 'Creating Shared Value', *Harvard Business Review*, January–February 2011
- Sally Cupitt (CES) has edited the *Guide to Social Return on Investment* and Jean Ellis had has edited the *SROI Network's Guide to Commissioning for Maximum Value*. These can be downloaded from the SROI Network website
- Trotter, L., Vine, J., Leach, M. and Fujiwars, D. (2014) *Measuring the Social Impact of Community Investment: A Guide to Using the Wellbeing*

Valuation Approach (London: HACT)
- http://www.thesroinetwork.org/sroi-analysis/the-sroi-guide
- http://www.housing.org.uk/policy/investing-in-communities/deciding-your-direction#sthash.lBjLfnıI.dpuf
- http://www.ces-vol.org.uk/services
- www.socialenterprise.org.uk

subsidies

SEE ALSO cost of housing; equity; finance; low income households; mortgages; need and demand; nudge theory; planning gain; proprietary interests; social returns; tenure

The word 'subsidy' comes from the Latin 'subsidium', a word that originally referred to troops stationed in reserve in the third line of battle who stood ready to provide assistance if and when needed. The front-line troops would be at the battle front; the second-line troops would be the reserves that could be called upon quickly to support the front-line; and well behind the battle front would be the third-line troops – the auxiliaries or 'subsidium' – who were settled down and waiting to 'assist'. (It is interesting to note that this feature of 'settling down' also gave rise to the notion of 'building subsidence' referring to the physical settling down of a structure.) From this application it came to be applied to a sum of money paid by one prince or nation to another to purchase the services of auxiliary troops. It was then used more generally to mean 'extraordinary aid in money' rendered by subjects to a sovereign, usually to pay for wars. It was then further extended to refer to a sum of money granted by the state or a public body to help an industry or business to keep the prices down or to aid an undertaking held to be in the public interest. Finally its use was fully generalized to its current meaning of a monetary sum passed from one individual or organization to support the functioning of another.

In contemporary financial parlance, the word has come to have a more focused technical meaning that is derived from economic theory.

economic subsidy
In market theory a subsidy is said to exist if a good or service is sold below its market price. Thus the term 'subsidy' is used to

describe a deficit between the price that is actually charged for a good or service and the higher price that would have been charged by the market. The idea here is that if a good or service is sold at a price that fails to cover its costs of production, including profit, the consumer is said to be enjoying an 'economic subsidy'. This is a rather theoretical view of subsidy and, in practice, it is difficult to determine the extent of economic subsidy when goods and services are provided outside of competitive markets. The *social housing* system has evolved out of *welfare* rather than market arrangements and, for this reason, it is often more sensible to conceive of subsidy in this sector as a 'money transfer'.

money transfer (cash flow) definition
The cash flow approach to defining subsidy seeks to measure and track money transfers between people and organizations. This is the way in which subsidy is measured and traced in official statistics and *accounts*. The most common transfers take the form of public sector grants or allowances to certain qualifying housing providers or consumers. It should be recognized, however, that some important housing subsidies do not involve a tangible transfer of funds: current *rent* pooling and *planning gain* are notable examples of economic subsidies that do/did not involve direct cash payments.

The question of housing subsidies became an issue once the state began to intervene to establish minimum standards of housing provision as part of its drive to improve public health. The law prevented free market forces from adjusting housing standards downwards in line with the limited incomes of working-class people. As a result, a more obvious gap emerged between the rent-paying capacity of many households and the rent levels that needed to be charged by the market to provide less over-crowded and better-*quality dwellings*. Simply put, once the state had intervened to improve housing standards, it brought to the fore the question of how the improved conditions should be paid for. It became clear that to realize fully the government's health and housing policy objectives would require additional interventionist measures in the area of housing subsidies.

After 1914, three broad strategies were adopted: rent control and *regulation*, the public provision of subsidized housing for the 'labouring classes' and the encouragement of area-based slum-clearance schemes. In addition, later in the century, financial assistance was also directed to the housing association movement and tax concessions, and income augmentation measures were introduced to help people meet their housing-related expenses. In this way it can be argued that the social rationale for intervention was tied to society's desire to increase both the quantity and quality of the nation's housing stock and to help *low income households* gain access to decent homes that are necessary for them to live healthy, active and productive lives.

It is sometimes said that housing, like food and clothing, is a 'primary consumer good' because without it, a reasonably decent life is not possible. In other words, it is argued that housing is no ordinary consumer item, but a consumer necessity. This argument is, however, limited as the quantity and quality of the housing enjoyed by many better-off households are more than that needed to satisfy what society currently regards as its minimum housing standards. Over the past 100 years or so society has used central and local government machinery to establish and enforce minimum housing standards and it is the desire to maintain such standards that is the underlying explanation of why housing is subsidized.

Part of the argument for subsidizing the consumption of housing is that it is expensive relative to disposable incomes. The ratio of house prices (including rents) to incomes has long been a political issue. Compared with many other developed economies, housing in Britain is expensive relative to household budgets. This fact is important because it impacts on the structure of the UK benefits system, the mobility of labour and thereby the economy in general. The price of a house is almost invariably equivalent to a multiple of the purchaser's annual income and, for those who rent, the rental charge is likely to represent a high proportion of their expenditure relative to other items in their household budgets.

The recognition of the fact that some minimum standard of housing is necessary for all people, and that it is expensive relative to income, has had a profound effect on the way in which the system of housing *finance* has evolved. When households with a preference for ownership are unable to purchase outright, they must either rent their homes from landlords or borrow the money for purchase. Two consequences resulting from the nature of housing as a consumer commodity have been the establishment of rented sectors, and the *development,* alongside the market for owner-occupied housing, of a parallel money market providing long-term loans to purchasers in the form of *mortgages.* Over the years both rented and owner-occupied housing have been subsidized in a wide variety of ways.

ways of subsidizing

Historically, all of the following have been used as mechanisms for subsidizing housing at different times:

- price control and regulation;
- council house building and slum-clearance programmes;
- the provision of building grants to the providers of social housing;
- revenue support grants to social housing providers;
- tax relief on mortgage interest payments;
- home improvement grants;
- mortgage guarantees;
- rent rebates, housing benefit allowances and other forms of income augmentation;
- right-to-buy discounts;
- the use of 'planning gain' (contractor contributions) to support the production of affordable homes in mixed development schemes;
- rent pooling (cross-subsidy).

In recent times, the benefits system has borne much of the strain of subsidizing those classified as being in housing need. The idea of support arrangements such as 'housing benefit' is to provide financial help in the form of income augmentation to qualifying households to enable them to acquire and enjoy housing or housing-related services that they need but could not otherwise afford.

The precise operational form of a subsidy will largely be determined by its intended function(s). This means that in seeking to assess the effectiveness of a subsidy it is necessary to establish its function.

the function of a subsidy

Where the issues of acceptable standards and *affordability* are brought together in housing policy, the question of 'subsidy' is bound to arise. Arguably the most obvious reason for subsidizing housing is to counteract market failure. In particular, the purpose is to overcome any 'demand deficiency' in the market that prevents low income households acquiring decent affordable homes in line with government policy objectives (see *merit goods and services*).

It is also argued that present and future generations have an interest in ameliorating the social and economic costs associated with bad housing. At different times subsides have been used to encourage investment in housing that would not otherwise take place. The argument here is that society at large has an interest in encouraging owners and tenants to renovate, or in some other way improve, their properties. These non-proprietary interests, or positive externalities, may include factors such as environmental enhancement, safer communities and economic growth (see *proprietary interests* and *social returns*).

Fiscal policy is not simply concerned with raising funds to pay for public activities and to support the worthy and the needy. Throughout history governments have used taxes and subsidies to achieve wider economic and social objectives by deterring certain activities through taxation and encouraging other activities through subsidization. For example, at different times, subsidies have been used to foster the development of a particular form of *tenure* (e.g. see *low cost home ownership*).

Where the market fails to promote society's politically determined objectives, subsidies may be used to promote greater social efficiency by altering patterns of production or consumption, and/or social justice by altering the distribution of real income. In this way, politicians see subsidization as a policy instrument for altering what gets produced and consumed and by whom.

Gibb and Munro (1991) distinguish between the 'formal' and the 'effective' incidence of a subsidy. The distinction enables the point to be made that those who formally receive the benefit can pass its financial impact or 'effect' on to others. A social landlord, for example, may receive a capital grant that reduces the total scheme costs of a housing development (formal incidence) and, as a result, the tenants enjoy lower rental charges (effective incidence).

It has to be recognized that a subsidy may have consequences beyond those that have been planned for. In particular, subsidies in one tenure are likely to have implications for other tenures. The ultimate beneficiary of a subsidy may turn out to be other than those for whom it was intended, or it may produce an unintended, undesirable effect in another sector of the economy. This aspect of housing subsidization is seldom discussed but has been long recognized:

> No thoughtful man will advocate the letting of houses below their economic rent, by means of subsidies ... because ... wages follow rents, and therefore that policy would only result in providing capitalists with cheap labour at the expense of the general body of ratepayers. (Nettlefold, 1908, p. 55)

Because housing finance policy has developed in the context of political and administrative concerns that are tenure-specific (e.g. concerns to encourage owner-occupation and concerns to make social rented housing more affordable), most subsidies are tied to specific tenures. Although understandable, this tenure specificity has inhibited rational discussion about how the subsidy system might be reformed with a view to enhancing cross-tenure efficiency, effectiveness and *equity*.

ways of categorizing housing subsidies

'Fiscal and non-fiscal': Subsidies that are derived from the state and are an aspect of government policy are termed as 'fiscal subsidies' (from the Latin 'fiscus', meaning 'public money'). Subsidies that arise as a result of one private citizen or organization aiding the production or consumption of some other private citizen or organization and are not directly derived from government policy can be described as 'non-fiscal subsidies'. In the field of housing, examples of non-fiscal subsidies are rent pooling (tenant-to-tenant subsidies) and grants from charities to help provide or manage dwellings for special needs groups such as the elderly or the disabled.

'Cross-subsidy': This occurs when administrative arrangements require one housing account, activity or group to aid some other housing account, activity or group. Before 1990 local authorities could make transfers from the General Fund to the Housing Revenue Account (HRA), and vice-versa. Many councils used this power to lower rent levels without the HRA being forced into deficit. This ability to cross-subsidize one account with another was made illegal by the Local Government and Housing Act 1989.

The old municipal principle of 'rent pooling' is an example of cross-subsidization of one group of tenants by another. Under rent pooling arrangements tenants living in established dwellings with small or no debt charges attached to them have their rents increased beyond the historic costs of provision so that tenants occupying newer properties with relatively high historic costs (debt charges) can have their rents reduced to more affordable levels.

'Planning gain': This is another example of cross-subsidy. Under a development proposal requiring planning permission, it is possible for a local authority to grant permission, subjected to an agreement with the developer that part of the profits from the sale of the properties on the open market will be used to subsidize the provision or improvement of a number of social housing units that are associated with the primary development (see *planning gain*).

'Visible and hidden': A subsidy can be said to be 'visible' if its existence and nature are widely known and understood. All direct grants and benefits, or money transfers, are openly publicized, reported on and accounted for in expenditure statistics that are in the public domain. Not all subsidies are so clearly perceived and understood. If a subsidy's existence is obscured by administrative arrangements, or its cost to the Exchequer is not openly discussed, it can be said to be 'hidden'. It is sometimes said that subsidy received through tax exemption is less obvious than subsidy provided through the receipt of grant or benefit. It may be that the 'hidden' nature of the old mortgage interest tax relief and capital gains tax exemptions protected the main subsidies going to owner-occupation from the scrutiny and criticism to which more 'visible' subsidies were subjected. Similarly, by controlling or regulating prices at the point of consumption the old Rent Acts effectively required landlords to provide a hidden economic subsidy to their tenants.

'Universal and targeted': A subsidy is said to be 'universal' if it is available to a whole class of people (e.g. a tenure group), irrespective of their individual incomes or normative needs. As the term implies, 'targeted' subsidies are aimed at specific households on the basis of some assessment of need and/or income and savings. The means testing involved in the distribution of targeted subsidies makes them relatively more complex to administer than universal subsidies. However, by concentrating limited funds on those in most need, they are usually regarded as being more rather than less socially efficient (see *equity*). Housing benefit is the most prominent targeted aid available to help with housing costs.

As well as targeting financial support at individual households through the application of means tests, it is also possible to target state resources at specific geographical areas through the application of needs indices (see *need and demand*).

supply-side and demand-side subsidies

Throughout the twentieth century, there has been a continuous debate about the most appropriate way of subsidizing the housing needs of low income households. In essence this is a debate about whether it is better to subsidize supply or demand. Any support measure that has the effect of influencing production and provision can be termed a 'supply-side subsidy', and any measure that influences consumption can be termed a 'demand-side subsidy'.

Provider (supply-side) subsidies are formally directed at landlords or developers with the intention of aiding them to provide quality accommodation at less-than-market rents. Where the grants in aid are provided to help cover the capital development, or redevelopment costs, they are sometimes referred to as 'bricks and mortar subsidies'. Provider subsidies can take the form of either capital or revenue aid: such subsidies invariably take the operational form of a money transfer.

Market economists tend to argue that supply subsidies to housing are only really justifiable in times of national emergency such as periods of war or post-war reconstruction. This is because, at such times, national priorities are such that the free market economy is abandoned or severely disrupted by a shift towards command economics. If housing is needed at these times, then the state may have to intervene directly and help pay for its production. In contrast, advocates of the welfare state tend to argue that, at all times, the housing needs of some vulnerable groups have to be guaranteed by the state and, consequently, suppliers should be aided to ensure that such needs are met (see *merit goods and services*). Proponents of this approach point out that the 'universal' nature of supply subsidies makes them less complex to administer than means-tested personal assistance. It is also argued that they are less socially divisive because, as a general subsidy, they are less inclined to stigmatize the recipients.

Consumption (demand-side) subsidies are directed at the users of housing with the intention of giving qualifying recipients additional income with which to pay for a standard of accommodation that would otherwise be beyond their means. They are sometimes referred to as 'personal' subsidies. By far the largest amount of personal subsidy is channelled through the housing benefit system. Critics of demand-side subsidies argue that the imperfect nature of the *housing market* means that the additional money demand may not get translated into more or better housing but lead to house price inflation, whereas supply-side subsidies are more likely to be directly converted into 'bricks and mortar'. Critics of supply-side subsidies argue that they are inefficient and distort the market. They are deemed to be wasteful of public money because their universal nature helps people whether they are in need or not. They distort the market by producing rents that are not related to either the 'true' costs of provision or to the current *value* of the property. By contrast, means-tested, demand-side assistance can be tightly targeted at those in most need and also allow the authorities and associations to set rents that are more in line with provision costs or current values (see *cost of housing* and *value*). In this way, the flow of rental income into the housing system is not diminished as a result of policies designed to aid low income households.

Since 1980, there has been a gradual but emphatic change in policy emphasis towards the demand-side arguments that has resulted in a shift from supply-side (particularly 'bricks and mortar') subsidies to demand-side, or 'personal' subsidies. As a consequence of this shift in emphasis rents have risen and the housing benefit budget has expanded. By 2013–2014 it totalled £23.8 billion, or almost 30 per cent of the entire welfare bill.

The current subsidy arrangements were not so much designed as evolved. As a result there clearly exist a number irrationalities and inequities in the system. One barrier to reforming and rationalizing the system is the 'subsidy ratchet effect'. This means that there is usually only limited resistance to the introduction or extension of subsidies because they tend to create identifiable beneficiaries. Once these beneficiaries have been created, however, they have a vested interest in seeing the measures retained and this causes both political and administrative difficulties in bringing about reforms.

KEY TEXTS

- King, P. (2009) *Understanding Housing Finance: Meeting Needs and Making Choices* (London and New York: Routledge)
- Lowe, S. (2011) *The Housing Debate* (Bristol: The Policy Press, University of Bristol), Chapter 1
- Lund, B. (2011) *Understanding Housing Policy* (Bristol: The Policy Press)
- Marsh, A. and Mullins, D. (eds) (1998) *Housing and Public Policy: Citizenship, Choice and Control* (Buckingham and Philadelphia, PA: Open University Press)
- Mullins, D. and Murie, A. (2006) *Housing Policy in the UK* (Basingstoke: Palgrave Macmillan)

sustainability

SEE ALSO culture; development; equity; fuel poverty; low income households; nudge theory; private renting; value for money

Given the extent to which the notion of 'sustainability' currently permeates so many journalistic, academic, management and political debates about a diverse range of policy topics, it is perhaps surprising that, as a word, it first entered everyday speech as late as 1965 and was not used widely in its current meanings until the 1970s. The long-standing meaning of 'sustainable' is to be capable of being maintained, continued or stabilized at some prescribed rate or level (originally from the seventeenth-century meaning, 'supportable from beneath').

The global 'sustainability' debate was launched with the publication of an influential report by a self-appointed group of concerned academics, diplomats and industrialists who came together in 1968 to form the Club of Rome. The report called 'Limits to Growth' (1972) produced computer-generated simulations indicating the impossibility of the ecological, biological and social systems supporting projected industrial and developmental growth trends. The subsequent 'limits to growth' debate stimulated a great deal of interdisciplinary research and comment, and the idea of 'sustainability' has now been extended from concerns about population growth, resource depletion and environmental degradation to embrace stability concerns in a wide range of policy areas, including housing *development* and use.

With the extension of its application has come imprecision about its meaning. In many ways it has become a loaded word that is used to mean different things to different people in different contexts. We might say that in many policy debates, the notion of 'sustainability' is a 'contested concept'. In its simplest conception, a 'sustainable decision' might be thought of as 'one we do not live to regret'.

In the area of housing policy, the notion of sustainability has tended to focus on the so-called green agenda, reflecting the fact that the provision and consumption of housing in all *tenures* impacts strongly on environmental and ecological concerns. The term 'green buildings' refers to structures that are designed and built in ways that minimize any negative impacts on human well-being and the natural environment. In housing, added emphasis is given to the green agenda because of the high incidence of *fuel poverty* amongst tenants.

It is generally accepted that improving the green credentials of existing buildings is more difficult than is the case for new buildings. However, many green construction principles can be applied to retrofit work as well as new construction. Retrofitting refers to the addition of new technology or features to older systems.

Houses, like most buildings, have an economic and physical existence that extends beyond those of their current occupiers. This longevity means that costs-in-use represent a relatively high proportion of all the associated whole life costs. The economic significance of this is illustrated by work done by the Royal Academy of Engineering that indicates that the typical costs of owning a building for 30 years are represented by the following ratios: 1 for construction costs; 5 for maintenance costs and 200 for building operating costs.

Although a 'rough and ready' measure, this ratio underlines the importance of seeing a 'green' building as one that has a low negative impact during its occupation. The single biggest green housing policy initiative in the United Kingdom has been the official push to increase investment in energy conservation (particularly higher levels of insulation and more efficient appliances). Domestic housing is responsible for between 25 and 30 per cent of total greenhouse gas emissions. In recent years the Code for Sustainable Homes (the national standard for the sustainable design and construction of new homes) has sought to reduce carbon emissions and promote higher standards of sustainable design above the current minimum set out by the building *regulations.*

A number of Organisation for Economic Co-operation and Development (OECD) countries now officially declare a commitment to pursue 'sustainable building practices'. These can range from using recycled materials carried by low-polluting forms of transport in construction, to maximizing energy efficiency in a finished building through, for example, improved insulation and solar-powered energy installations. A number of policy approaches are now being used to minimize the negative impacts of buildings through their life cycles. These cycles include (i) the planning, procurement and development periods; (ii) the period of occupation; (iii) the retrofit, renewal and redevelopment period and (iv) the demolition event.

sustainable development

As a phrase, 'sustainable development' was introduced in 1987 by the World Commission on Environment and Development (The Brundtland Report) that proposed it as a key international political and moral issue for the twenty-first century. The Report made the point that future generations have legitimate interests in present-day decisions. It famously articulated this by arguing that current decision-makers have an obligation to achieve development outputs that 'meet the needs of the present without compromising the ability of future generations to meet their own needs'. As well as raising concerns about the distribution of future costs and benefits of current development activities (questions of intergenerational justice), the Commission also pointed to the need to consider the balance of interests between the developed and developing worlds (questions of regional justice). The regional issue focuses on the need to find a means of allowing economic growth (particularly in so-called underdeveloped economies) whilst sustaining the natural world and maintaining stable democratic arrangements.

The broad Brundtland principles are easily postulated, but their prosecution is bedevilled by 'application imps' (see 'introduction'). When applied to a real-life development proposal, it becomes apparent that agreeing to what counts as 'sustainable' can be open to severe disagreement. Indeed, the term has been adopted by commentators and lobbyists who have significantly divergent values and interests. An internet search of the term indicates that for some who reference the wider environmental debate, it is regarded as an oxymoron, while for others it is used narrowly to mean 'commercially viable development'. In other words, it is the sort of term that can be appropriated by interlocutors in the same debate who then use it to mean quite different things.

implications for practice
- No matter how sustainable a building may have been in its design and construction, it can only remain so if it is operated responsibly and maintained properly. Behaviour change studies have shown that if occupiers alter the ways in which they operate domestic appliances and purchase energy supplies, household bills can be reduced by up to 50 per cent. More alarmingly, these studies (largely by individual landlords) also indicate that a lack of understanding, and consequent misuse, of new technologies can increase household bills.
- Where feasible, many social landlords now use local contractors and materials as part of their declared commitment to their local economies and to reduce 'carbon miles' from the transportation of materials and people to a minimum.
- Launched in 1990, BREEAM (Building Research Establishment Environmental Assessment Methodology) is the world's longest established and most widely used method of assessing, rating and certifying the sustainability of buildings.
- Building regulations have long played a central role in improving energy efficiency through the use of policy instruments for reducing CO_2 and other greenhouse gas emissions. These, however, only apply to new buildings.
- Building regulations are under constant review and energy performance is now a key element within the regulations.
- The European Energy Performance of Buildings Directive requires all new building to be nearly zero energy buildings from 2020.
- The Code for Sustainable Homes is voluntary. It is not a set of regulations and should not be confused with zero carbon policy or the zero carbon target.
- To comply with the 2016 Building Regulations, new zero carbon homes will have to meet on-site requirements for

Carbon Compliance (achieved through the energy efficiency of the fabric, the performance of heating, cooling and lighting systems and low and zero carbon technologies). Any remaining CO_2 emissions, from the use of regulated energy sources in the property, must be reduced to zero. This requirement can be met either by over-performing in other areas or by investing in off-site carbon reduction projects via a cost-sharing vehicle called 'allowable solutions'.

- The Zero Carbon Home standard will be set at Level 5 of the Code for Sustainable Homes, but the legislation will allow developers to build to Level 4 as long as they offset through the 'allowable solutions' scheme to achieve Code 5.
- Homeowners and landlords in all sectors are increasingly investing in eco-upgrades through such measures as installing photovoltaic (PV) panels on roofs that generate electricity. By making this particular capital investment, the occupier is able to earn a fixed income return on every kilowatt hour of electricity generated, whether it is used in the home directly or exported as a surplus to the National Grid. Although the 'feed-in tariffs' (FITs) were reduced in 2011, the costs of purchasing and installing the panels continue to fall, making the investment worthwhile for many (particularly better off) households (see *equity*).

KEY TEXTS
- BREEAM Centre at the Building Research Establishment (BRE) under contract to the Department for Communities and Local Government
- Communities and Local Government (2010) *Code for Sustainable Homes: Technical Guide*
- Department of Energy and Climate Change website for current projections and other statistical information
- Dobson, A. (ed) (1999) *Fairness and Futurity: Essays on Environmental Sustainability and Social Justice* (Oxford: Oxford University Press)
- Helweg-Larsen, T. (2009) 'Act Immediately to Limit the Effects of Climate Change' in B. Pattison and J. Vine (eds), *Perspectives on the Future of Housing: A Collection of Viewpoints on the UK Housing System* (Coalville: Building and Social Housing Foundation)
- Killip, G. (2008) *Transforming Britain's Housing Stock* (Oxford: Environmental Change Institute, University of Oxford for the

Federation of Master Builders)

- Meadows, D. H., Dennis, L. and Meadows, D. (2004) *The Limits to Growth: The 30-Year Update* (Verrmont: Chelsea Green Publishing and Earthscan)
- OECD (2003) Policy Brief: Environmentally Sustainable Buildings: Challenges and Policies
- Reported by Local Government Task Force and the Housing Forum (2002) *20 Steps to Encourage the Use of Whole Life Costing*
- https://www.gov.uk/government/policies/providing-effective-building-regulations-so-that-new-and-altered-buildings-are-safe-accessible-and-efficient
- https://www.gov.uk/government/publications/code-for-sustainable-homes-technical-guidance
- http://www.greendealinitiative.co.uk/
- http://www.zerocarbonhub.org/zero-carbon-policy/zero-carbon-policy
- http://www.zerocarbonhub.org/sites/default/files/resources/reports/ZCHomes_Nearly_Zero_Energy_Buildings.pdf

t

tenancy agreements

SEE ALSO home ownership; leasehold; private renting; proprietary interests; rents; social housing; tenure

A tenancy agreement is a contract between an occupier and a landlord. It sets out the legal terms and conditions of the occupancy arrangements. It can be written down or oral. A tenancy can be of fixed-term (running for a set period of time) or periodic (running on a week-by-week or month-by-month basis).

In the *social housing* sector, it is now usual for new tenants to be given a probationary or 'starter' tenancy prior to establishing a longer-term agreement. A probationary tenancy typically runs for 12 months. At the end of this period the landlord has the option to establish a firm tenancy agreement, extend the probationary period or evict the occupier.

secure and assured tenancies

Under the provisions of the Housing Act 1988, most tenancies granted by housing associations were removed from the remit of the 1985 Housing (Local Authority Tenancies) Act, and instead fell within the scope of the new legislation, with the housing associations becoming 'registered social landlords'.

The 1988 Act created differences between the rights of council and housing association tenants. Prior to the Act, the rights of council and housing association tenants were broadly the same. The 1988 Act changed the status of housing associations by putting them into the 'independent rented sector' and changed the status of new housing association tenants from 'secure' to 'assured' (with effect from January 1989). Although associations can no longer grant secure tenancies to new tenants, residents whose tenancy has been transferred from a local authority with a secure status can retain their existing tenancy rights. Nearly all council tenants have secure tenancies. Different tenancy arrangements may be in place for a small number of council tenants who are in temporary accommodation or whose homes go with the job.

Compared with assured social tenants, secure social tenants have more rights and greater security of *tenure*. The rights of secure tenants are set out in the Housing Act 1985 and include the following:

- The right for certain close relatives as well as the husband or wife to inherit the tenancy.
- The right to sub-let part of the home (with the council's consent).
- The right to re-charge the council for repairs when there has been a long delay in carrying them out.
- The right to buy the home at a discount (dependent upon the period of the tenancy; see *low cost home ownership*).
- The right to be charged a 'fair rent'.

'Fair rents' are a form of *rent* control applicable to most private sector rented accommodation without a residential landlord let before 15 January 1989. The Rent Act 1977 provides the rules for setting fair rents and the Rent Acts (Maximum Fair Rent) Order 1999 limits the amount of rent that can be charged by linking increases to the Retail Prices Index. Private sector secure tenancy agreements have to be registered with the local Valuations Office. The fair rent regime limits the timing of any rent increases to a two-year review period and once set, this becomes the maximum rent that the landlord can charge until the it is reviewed again or cancelled. A 'fair rent' is generally lower than the rent that could be charged as a market rent for a similar tenancy. It is estimated that there are still more than 100,000 secure tenancies operating in the United Kingdom (2012).

assured and fixed-term tenancies
As mentioned earlier, prior to January 1989 many housing association residents were secure tenants but from that date the law changed. At the end of any starter tenancy the tenant will now normally be offered either an 'assured' or a 'fixed-term' tenancy.

Until recently, the typical fixed-term tenancy ran for a period of five years and an assured agreement gave tenants security of tenure for life. Until 2014, 'assured' tenants were charged a 'target rent' set by a government formula based on inflation, location, bedroom size and other factors. Target rents were introduced with the intention of gradually bringing all the sector rents in line and eliminate (or reduce) local differences between landlords that had evolved over time. This policy of 'rent convergence' was abandoned in 2013. The new regime also allows associations more freedom to set the length of tenancy terms.

flexible tenancies

The Localism Act 2011 brought in a number of significant changes to the ways in which social housing is provided, administered and regulated. It provided, for the first time, the use of 'flexible' tenancies as an alternative to open-ended 'lifetime' tenancies that have always been the rule in the sector.

private sector tenancies

The Housing Act 1988 introduced two new types of tenancy into the private sector, namely, the 'assured tenancy' and the 'assured shorthold tenancy'. Most private sector rents are no longer controlled (see 'fair rents', p. 191).

assured shorthold tenancies (ASTs)

The most common form of private sector tenancy is an assured shorthold tenancy (called 'short assured tenancies' in Scotland). Most new tenancies are automatically of this type. During the term of the tenancy a landlord can seek repossession on one of a number of specified bases (e.g. rent arrears), and at the end of the term has an absolute right to repossess the property.

A tenancy can be an AST if all of the following conditions apply:

- It is in the private rented sector (the landlord is not a local council or housing association).
- The tenancy started on or after 15 January 1989.
- The property is the tenant's main accommodation.
- The landlord does not live in the property.
- The rent is less than £100,000 and more than £250 a year (£1,000 in London).

- It is not a business tenancy or tenancy of licensed premises.
- It is not a holiday let.

Assured and shorthold tenancies allow landlords to charge a full market rent (unlike previous forms of regulated tenancy). Shorthold tenancies also allow a landlord to let a property for a short period only and to get it back if they wish after six months. When originally introduced, these tenancy formats were seen as part of a process of deregulating the private rented market and thus encouraging more investment in the sector. In other words, the provisions of an assured tenancy agreement were specifically designed to enhance the 'proprietary investment interests' of the landlord while, at the same time, maintaining a degree of security of tenure which is regarded as a key 'proprietary consumption interest' of the tenant (see *proprietary interests*).

Other tenancies
In addition to regulated (fair rent) and assured shorthold tenancies, there can be other, less common private sector arrangements, including assured (see above) and excluded tenancies or licences (see *leasehold*).

If the landlord has a lodger living in his or her home and rooms are shared (typically a kitchen or bathroom), they may operate under an 'excluded tenancy' or 'licence'. These arrangements recognize that the property is the landlord's home and, as such, provides the lodger with less protection from eviction than other types of agreement.

KEY TEXTS
- Department for Communities and Local Government (2011) *Private Landlord Survey 2010* (CLG)
- Department of Communities and Local Government and the Welsh Assembly (2007) *Assured and Assured Shorthold Tenancies: A Guide for Tenants*
- Publications by Shelter and Shelter Cymru, Shelter Scotland and the Housing Rights Service
- http://www.leeds.gov.uk/docs/Tenants'%20Tenancy%20guide.pdf
- https://www.gov.uk/renting-out-a-property/landlord-responsibilities
- https://www.gov.uk/tenancy-agreements-a-guide-for-landlords/tenancy-types

- http://england.shelter.org.uk/get_advice/social_housing/housing_association_tenancies/assured_tenancies
- http://www.housinglaw.org.uk/Ass%20Ten.htm

tenure

SEE ALSO dwellings; need and demand; private renting; proprietary interests; rent; subsidies

The legal terms on which a dwelling is held as property is referred to as its 'tenure'. The word derives from the Old French 'tenir' 'to hold' (Latin 'tenere'). The use of the word to refer to property rights (land tenure) is long-standing and traceable back to the thirteenth century. Its application to the holding of an occupational or authority or position (e.g. president of a country and chair of a housing association) is also well established (fourteenth century). Its meaning 'guaranteed tenure of office' (as in a university) is recorded from the late 1950s.

Its derivation ('to hold') underlines the point that land tenure is about the 'holding of rights and interests'. There may be a number of different legal *proprietary interests* attached to a particular dwelling. In addition to the freehold interest ('fee simple'), individuals may possess *leasehold* or contractual tenancy interests in the dwelling and neighbouring households may have rights to use, enter or cross part of the land or building(s) in order to carry out certain functions. The term 'fee' comes from the Anglo-Saxon 'feoh' meaning cattle – cattle being in early times a chief part of a person's possessions and a common medium of barter or exchange and, as such, came to signify transferable property. A freehold interest is the nearest thing to an absolute, transferable ownership of real estate (see *home ownership*). A leaseholder has temporary possession of the land and building(s) for a term of years from a freeholder or superior lease-holder who may be a private individual or an organization, a local authority or a housing association (see *leasehold*). Other contracted tenancy rights are established by a tenancy agreement (see *tenancy agreements*).

For the purpose of analysis, the academic and practice literatures on land use distinguish between three broad tenure arrangements: owner-occupation (freehold or long leasehold), short leasehold and rented (secure, assured and assured shorthold). These three broad tenure sectors can be classified further by reference to the proprietary interests that individuals and organizations have in a particular dwelling (see *tenure* and *proprietary interests*).

At the start of the twentieth century *private renting* was by far the largest tenure. The rapid growth of *home ownership* (less than 10 per cent at the outbreak of the First World War) was matched by both a decline in private renting and a rise in *social housing* provision. There is a popular view that Britain has a relatively high rate of owner-occupation compared to other European nations. This is not the case. In 2002, when the rate peaked, Britain ranked 17th highest among the 27 EU countries, and lower than that of Bulgaria, Ireland, Italy and Romania.

The details of Britain's tenure structure are captured by the various census returns and other periodic surveys. In 2011, there were 23.4 million households in England and Wales: the majority (15 million or 64 per cent) were owner-occupied. The remaining 8.3 million (36 per cent) were rented, either privately from a landlord or letting agency or from a social landlord, such as a local authority, housing association, housing co-operative or charitable trust. Of the 15 million owner-occupied households in 2011, 7.2 million homes were owned outright while the remaining 7.8 million were being bought with a mortgage. Of the 8.3 million households renting, there were similar numbers renting privately to those renting from social landlords at 4.2 million and 4.1 million, respectively. Among those households in socially rented homes, 2.2 million were renting from local authorities, and 1.9 million from other social landlords.

Since 1981, the tenure shift towards home ownership in Scotland has been particularly dramatic. In 1981, less than 40 per cent of Scotland's stock of *dwellings* was owner-occupied. By 2004, this had risen to 62 per cent. As in England and Wales, this percentage fell slightly to about 60 per cent in 2012.

Of the just over three-quarters of a million dwellings in Northern Ireland (2012), some 488,000 were in owner-occupation and just over 29,000 were owned by the Northern Ireland Housing Executive. Some 3.8 per cent of the total stock was under housing association management. Private Rented and 'Other' dwellings increased sharply in the ten years from 2001/2002 to 2011/2012: jumping from 44,000 to 114,800 over this period – an increase of 161 per cent. The Private Rented and Other category accounted for 15.1 per cent of the total housing stock, compared to just 6.6 per cent in 2001–2002. In this category, 'Other' properties include *rent*-free properties.

tenure neutrality
The introduction of tenure neutrality into fiscal arrangements is a topic of debate amongst academics, particularly economists. Some argue the need to reform the system of housing taxes and *subsidies* to reduce any advantages or disadvantages that the system provides to particular tenures. The idea here is to make the overall housing tenure arrangement as efficient as possible so that people's *choices* of tenure are not distorted by any 'artificial' fiscal benefits or penalties.

KEY TEXTS

- Communities and Local Government and Homes and Communities Agency (2011) *2011–15 Affordable Homes Programme – Framework*
- Lowe, S. (2004) *Housing Policy Analysis: British Housing in Cultural and Comparative Context* (Basingstoke: Palgrave Macmillan), Chapter 6
- Orr, D. (2009) 'It's Time to Redefine "Social Housing"' in B. Pattison and J. Vine (eds), *Perspectives on the Future of Housing: A Collection of Viewpoints on the UK Housing System* (Coalville: Building and Social Housing Foundation)
- Scottish Government Communities Analytical Services: Housing Statistics
- Williams, P. (2009) 'Future Tenure Mix and Flexible Tenure' in B. Pattison and J. Vine (eds), *Perspectives on the Future of Housing: A Collection of Viewpoints on the UK Housing System* (Coalville: Building and Social Housing Foundation)
- http://www.ons.gov.uk/ons/guide-method/census/2011/index.html
- http://www.scotland.gov.uk/Topics/Statistics/Browse/Housing-Regeneration/TrendTenure
- http://www.dsdni.gov.uk/northern_ireland_housing_statistics_2011–13.pdf

V

value

SEE ALSO accounts; asset management; business planning; cost of housing; housing market; low cost home ownership; social returns; value for money

The word 'value' comes from the Latin 'valere' – to be strong – to be relied upon – to have worth. Philosophically speaking, it is possible to say that something has 'intrinsic value' if it has qualities that go beyond usefulness. If something is intrinsically valuable then it is worthy in its own right without having any reference to how it might be used or marketed. In the world of human affairs, however, the notion of value tends to be tied to usefulness. So the 'value' of something is usually thought to be that attribute that makes it, in some sense, worthy of use. If something has no use it tends to be regarded as worthless and if it is worthless, it tends to be regarded as having no social or economic value.

The economic value of any capital asset is composed of three inter-related factors, namely, its potential selling price (its exchange value), its potential usefulness (its 'utility' or use value) and its potential to yield a return on money capital committed (its investment value). At any time, a building's exchange value will be determined by the perceptions of potential purchasers about its current use and/or future investment value. The real, underlying, fundamental social and economic value of a building is determined by what it does – its usefulness, and in the final analysis, this determines both its investment value and its exchange value. In the end, all social and economic value is grounded in current or potential use value.

The exchange value of a building is represented by its selling price. Exchange is the mechanism by which use or investment values are realized. By selling a property its use and investment values are exchanged for cash; that is, they are 'liquidated'.

open market value (OMV)

The OMV is defined as the value that the freely competitive market would determine for the property. It is the usual way of valuing properties for sale in the owner-occupied and private rented sectors.

existing use value (EUV)

EUV is a common way of valuing buildings that are not likely to be marketed. It is sometimes referred to as the 'going concern value'. A housing association, for example, holds a stock of properties mainly in order to provide a service for current and future tenants. Although it will at times dispose of individual properties as part of its business plan, it is not in the business of buying and selling properties 'per se'. This means that if the organization were to be taken over by another social landlord for some reason, it would be inappropriate to value the acquired properties in open market terms. It would be more appropriate to value them by referencing their potential contribution to the new owner's business plans. Like the current owner, the new owner would be particularly interested in the value of the net capitalized income the *dwellings* would generate as this will allow them to value the acquisition as 'a going concern'. The Royal Institution of Chartered Surveyors has developed methods of calculating EUV using the net present value methodology.

net present value (NPV)

When people buy income-producing assets, they are buying the net revenue that these assets will generate in the future. Similarly, when people sell these assets, they lose the regular net income the assets will produce in the future.

NPV measures the difference between the present value of future cash inflows (e.g. from rents and other incomes) and the present value of future cash outflows (e.g. for cost of repairs, maintenance, voids, debt servicing and management). NPV is used in capital budgeting to analyse the profitability of an investment or project.

NPV analysis is sensitive to changes in inflation and assumptions about future interest rates. It is also sensitive to the reliability of estimated future cash inflows that an investment or project will yield and future costs that it will impose. The calculation has to take account of the changing purchasing power of a unit of money over time as measured by a 'discount rate'. A pound today is worth more than a pound in the future (because it can be used or invested in the interim to earn a return). This means that future anticipated income flows have to take this into account and 'discount' future values back to an equivalent present value. This has to be done because decisions that have future consequences will have to be made in the present. NPV is an analytical tool that helps decision-takers to make a rational judgement about the present financial viability of a proposed purchase or project that has future financial consequences.

If the NPV of a prospective project is positive, it could rationally be accepted as potentially viable. However, if the NPV is negative, the project should probably be rejected because net cash flows will be negative. For example, if a property investment firm was considering purchasing a group of existing rented houses, it would first estimate the future net cash flows that the estate would generate, and then discount those cash flows into one lump-sum present value amount – say £10 million. If the disposing landlord was willing to sell for less than £10 million, the purchasing company would, all other things being equal, reasonably consider going ahead with the deal because the offer presents a positive NPV investment.

As well as informing acquisition strategies, this way of estimating value is also used to guide a housing agency's disposal policies. For example, consider two houses with the same rental income – but one has significantly higher projected maintenance costs. From the point of view of the landlord's 30-year business plan, although generating the same rental income, one property has a lower value (NPV) than the other. This sort of value measure is used to help inform the building and disposal plans of landlords. It can have interesting results. Some social landlords deem it worthwhile to dispose of houses that are relatively expensive to maintain, at prices that might be described as 'nominal'. In 2014, for example, as part of its redevelopment strategy, Stoke on Trent Council (with central government approval and support) advertised some derelict properties for sale at prices well under £3,000 with some being offered for as little as £1.

added value and the idea of a 'valuation gap'
Because of its primary function as a home, most decisions to improve an owner-occupied dwelling are designed to add 'utility'

(comfort and convenience). However, an improvement is also likely to add to the property's exchange value. Precisely how much is added to the exchange value will depend on the nature of the improvement and the location of the property. Estate agents often make the point that it is possible for an owner to 'over invest' in their homes. In making this point, they are considering the improvement expenditure from a strictly investment point of view. The argument centres on the notion of what land economists refer to as the 'neighbourhood effect value' (NEV). The NEV is defined as that part of a property's total value that is determined by its location. Because location is such a powerful determinant of property value, it may turn out that an investment in improvement will not be fully 'capitalized' into the dwelling's exchange value. This means that if the purpose of the improvement is to increase the market value of the property, account has to be taken of the neighbourhood in which the dwelling is located. For instance, a £60,000 annex on a house worth £200,000 in a district where the maximum selling price for similar properties is £220,000 is unlikely to increase the property's value to £260,000. The extent to which improvement expenditure gets capitalized into the exchange value depends on the nature of the expenditure, as well as the location of the property. Some property experts suggest that central heating is the principal improvement that is likely to guarantee a reasonable recoupment of outlay, and the modernization of a kitchen or bathroom is also likely to add value, although with these types of improvement the owner is unlikely to get back all the expended costs: there is likely to be a 'valuation gap'.

the 'carrying value' of property
This is the value of an asset as it appears in the company's balance sheet (see *accounts*). This measure is based on the original cost of the asset (sometimes referred to as 'the historic cost value') minus any depreciation, amortization or impairment costs made against the asset (see *accounts*). This is different from exchange (i.e. market) value, as it can be higher or lower depending on the circumstances, the nature of the asset in question and the accounting practices that affect them. In many cases, the carrying value of an asset and its market value will differ greatly. This is because, in accordance with accounting rules, the assets are carried in the books at a value

that is based on original costs. In particular, if a company holds land that was purchased (say) 50 years ago, it holds it at the cost paid. Over time, however, this real estate will probably have gained in value.

right to buy valuations
Social dwelling are valued differently for different purposes. The Right to Buy (RTB) policy was included in the Housing Act 1980 and the Tenants' Rights etc. (Scotland) Act 1980. The initial legislation established the principle that a secure tenant opting to purchase is entitled to a discount on the market value of the property, and that this discount should be dependent on the previous length of the tenancy. The idea is that those who have been paying *rent* over many years should be able purchase their homes more cheaply than short-standing tenants. The *regulations* require a minimum residency period, and they put a ceiling on the total amount of discount that can be granted to any one purchaser. RTB discounts can be thought of as 'purchase grants' to those who enter owner-occupation by this route. The right to a discount is like having a gifted cash deposit: it gives automatic *equity* in the property – something that takes years to accrue in the private sector, and/or it enables the purchaser to borrow more to carry out improvements.

social value
There is a growing recognition in government that the local social, economic and environmental impacts that public and voluntary bodies make as part of their work should be valued. The Public Services (Social Value) Act became operational in 2013. This legislation makes it a requirement for commissioners of public services to take consideration at pre-procurement stage of how the services they commission can improve the economic, social and environmental well-being of their areas.

KEY TEXTS
- Garnett, D. (1996) *Building Obsolescence* (Bristol: UWE). Republished: Garnett (2015) at http://leapingrogpublications.co.uk/housing-society
- Oxley, M. (2004) *Economics, Planning and Housing* (Basingstoke: Palgrave Macmillan)
- Russell, S. (2013) *Journey to Impact: A Practitioner Perspective on Measuring Social Impact* (Coventry: HouseMark/Midland Heart)

value for money

SEE ALSO asset management; audit; business planning; continuous improvement; development; governance; nudge theory; performance monitoring; proprietary interests; quality; regulation; risk and uncertainty; social returns; value

'Value for money is achieved when limited financial resources are spent or invested in ways that produce the greatest long-term beneficial effects'. Defining VFM is easy enough, but identifying and delivering it is quite a different matter. In the academic literature, VFM is treated as a 'contested concept'. This means that what is regarded as VFM is determined, to some degree, by the predispositions, interests, values and attitudes of the person or organization making the judgement.

As well as being a contested concept, VFM can also be regarded as a relative notion. In particular, what counts as VFM will depend on the political, economic and social environments appertaining to a specific place at a specific time. In other words, VFM judgements are influenced by the operating context of the particular individual or organization seeking its achievement. The judgement will, to some considerable extent, be influenced by factors such as the availability of resources, any requirements or duties imposed by the law or by the regulators, market forces, views about the current and future state of the economy and the current and future needs and aspirations of proprietors and stakeholders. It might also be argued that in the housing field, VFM is, to some extent at least, tenure-specific. What counts as a VFM decision to an owner-occupier may not be seen as such by a landlord, and what is regarded as VFM by a private landlord may not be seen as such by a social landlord. This is because VFM is in part determined by the specific consumption and investment interests that the decision-maker has vested in the property (see *proprietary interests*).

Because of the concept's contested and relative nature, VFM is usually measured against declared, time-specific hoped-for outcomes, goals or targets, or against a set of agreed benchmarks. Measurement of this kind is now a regulatory expectation and for many years the regulators have required housing providers and their employees to ensure that a value for money approach is adopted when developing and delivering services. All social landlords that are in receipt of public subsidy are required to deliver services that 'perform well at the best possible cost'. In so doing they must have in place mechanisms that set and monitor *quality* and performance standards that will allow auditors, regulators and stakeholders to ask the question, 'In your organization, how is the return on housing spending and investment measured and accounted for?'

Housing cannot simply be treated as a commercial activity. Because of its social and *welfare* outputs, criteria other than profit need to be taken into account in assessing returns on monies directed to its production and consumption. For this reason the question 'How is the return on housing spending and investment to be measured and accounted for?' usually takes the form (implicitly), 'How do we know whether, taking everything into account, we are maximizing the long-term net benefits from the monies being spent and invested?' It is generally agreed that in the provision of public services, VFM has to be judged in terms of a number of *value* considerations; typically these include efficiency, effectiveness, fairness (or *equity*) and responsibility (including responsibility to stakeholders and society at large). To these four considerations, some commentators add a fifth – economy (see Figure 6).

Historically regulators have placed a particular emphasis on user satisfaction, which bridges the considerations of 'effectiveness' and 'responsibility'. Because of this emphasis, many agencies identify the 'experience' of service users as a separate major category in their VFM assessments (see Figure 7). All of these considerations are tied together in the overall cycle of production (from investment to consumption) as shown in Figure 7.

efficiency and VFM

Figure 7 indicates that efficiency is determined by considering the relationship between inputs and outputs. The idea of efficiency has its roots in engineering where the efficiency of an engine is calculated in terms of how much energy input is needed to generate a unit of power output. Indeed, some contemporary management theorists use the term 're-engineering' when referring to the processes of restructuring corporate arrangements with a view to enhancing an organization's efficiency. Like an engine, an organization is deemed to be operating below its optimum level of efficiency if either it could produce the same output with fewer resources or

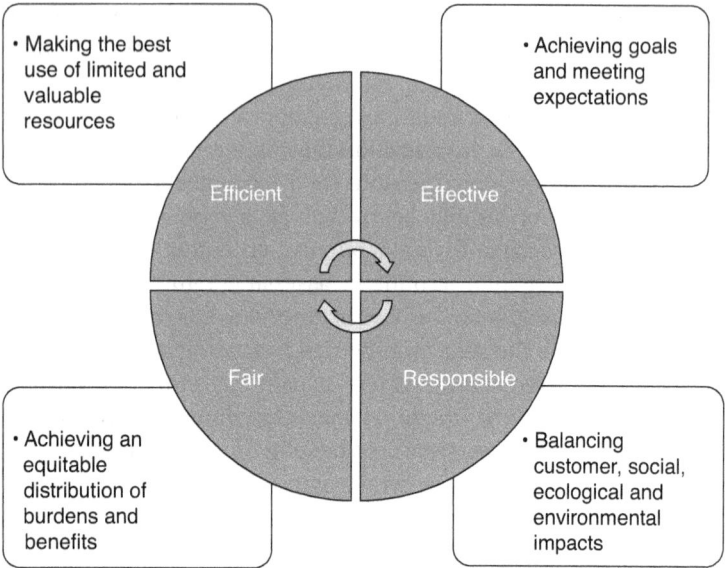

FIGURE 6 *The components of value for money*

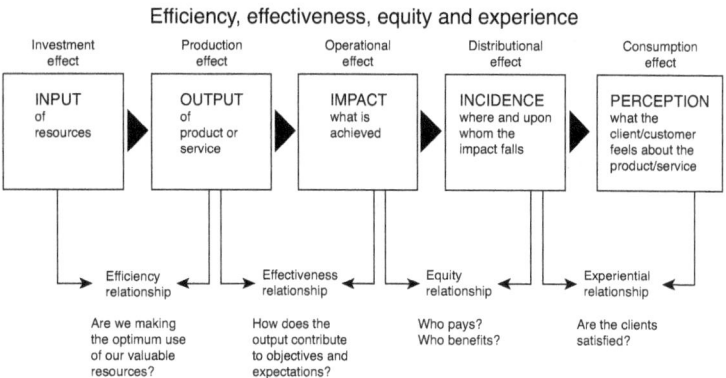

FIGURE 7 *The production of value for money*

if, with the same resources, it could produce a greater output. In the context of providing goods and services, quality as well as quantity is regarded as an aspect of 'output'. This means that a better quality service or product would constitute an increase in output just as much as would a service expansion or an increase in the number of units produced.

In traditional economic thinking, an assumption is made that if measured in terms of market values, any additional employment of resources ('marginal costs') produces a more than proportional increase in goods and services ('marginal benefit'), then some improvement in efficiency has taken place. In the public sector the marginal benefit might be seen as some form of social return (e.g. better health, fewer crimes or more affordable homes) and the marginal cost is seen as the private and/or public expenditure committed.

It is sometimes argued that, in the context of public and welfare services, current debates about the need for greater efficiency have a hidden political dimension. The contention is that as a justifying notion, 'efficiency' is intellectually sympathetic to free-enterprise market]attitudes and many of those who are calling for 'more efficiency' in the running of public services are seeking to ally themselves with the core values of the private sector. In this way the notion of 'efficiency' has been used, it is said, to impose business management and budgetary arrangements on public sector and other welfare agencies. The concerns here are twofold. First, when welfare organizations are reformed with 'efficiency savings' in mind, this occurs in a managed rather than a free-enterprise market, and when detached from the discipline of real market forces, the application of business management ideas can become procedural and unresponsive. A managed market is insulated from the warning signals of falling profits and other market indicators that exist under proper free enterprise arrangements and, as a result, there is a danger that changes justified in terms of private sector management theory may be inappropriate. The second concern is that efficiency criteria tend to measure success in a relatively short-term time frame, giving undue weight to current cost savings and under-valuing longer-term effectiveness.

effectiveness and VFM

Concerns such as those mentioned earlier mean that the achievement of VFM involves more than making an 'efficient' use of valuable resources. Most organizations are concerned to assess the output against its impact as well as against the quantity of resources used up in its production. The effectiveness of an output is assessed in terms of how well it contributes to the key business goals, including the reasonable expectations of those with some interest in the organization's operations (see Figure 7).

Increasingly, effectiveness criteria are prescribed by society in the form of explicit *regulations*, laws and externally imposed perform-ance targets. 'Effectiveness' is not the same as 'efficiency' and is assessed by referencing the outcomes that the organization's efforts have in relation to its planned-for objectives. Clearly a housing agency might be able to demonstrate increases in efficiency whilst failing to achieve its goals (and 'vice versa').

equity and VFM

Any consideration of effectiveness is likely to bring to the fore ques-tions of fairness. In cases where public money, or the public interest, is involved there is likely to be a particular concern about the distri-bution of costs and benefits that result from an employment of resources. Most major decisions made by *social housing* agencies have to be demonstrably fair as well as effective and efficient.

Economic and financial decisions change situations: they have an 'impact'. As a result, some people are made better off and some people will almost certainly be made worse off. The positive and negative outcomes of such decisions (marginal social costs and benefits) are distributed differentially to different interest groups.

Assessing the impact of policy decisions brings up questions of time and inter-generational justice. Costs and benefits associated with housing decisions tend to come on stream at different times, so it is possible for one generation of tenants or occupiers to enjoy or pay for the spending decisions made at some other time. This can be illustrated by reference to the issue of paying for major repairs. If future repairs are paid for by means of a sinking fund set up before the expenditure occurs, then the burden will fall on current *rent* payers. If, on the other hand, they are paid for by a loan taken out at the time of the works, then future loan charges will displace the cost burden onto the rents of future tenants.

experience and VFM

There is an old Swiss proverb that says, 'Don't ask the doctor, ask the patient.' Regulators insist that service providers should never lose sight of the fact that consumption is the ultimate purpose of all economic activity in this and other welfare services. What the customer or client feels about the service or product is of prime importance. In the free-enterprise sector of the economy, market forces operate to reward those firms whose output is in demand (wanted and bought) and commercially punish those whose products are not in demand. In recent years public sector and other welfare organization have made a conscious effort to monitor user satisfaction and feed the results into their policy-making processes. The argument here is that if users are unsatisfied there must be doubts about whether the organization is achieving *value for money*.

'best value'

'Best value' is a term that is sometimes used to highlight the need to seek more than simple efficiency savings in the pursuit of VFM outcomes. It is also used to shift the emphasis in VFM decision-making away from narrow 'short-termism'. For example, if a proposed building project is put out to tender with minimum specification requirements, the cheapest tender can be said to be the most 'cost-effective'. Of course, a more costly tender that offered a higher specification might, in the longer term, prove to be cheaper to run and maintain or it might provide a wider range of tangible and intangible benefits to the service provider or its clients. This means that this limited view of 'cost effectiveness' is not necessarily the same thing as 'value for money'. The argument is that the 'responsible' agency will seek 'best value' outcomes in VFM assessments (see *continuous improvement*).

economy and VFM

In discussing value for money, some commentators make reference to the need for 'economy'. In so doing, they are referring to the act of acquiring resources and are making the point that raw materials and other factors of production should be bought as cheaply as possible so long as they are commensurate with minimum specifications. Economy is about 'cost effectiveness' or achieving the least cost to produce a defined outcome. Best value theory suggests that cost effectiveness is not the same thing as 'value for money'. As economy is concerned with the price of inputs, it is probably more sensible to treat it as an aspect of 'efficiency' than as a separate category.

implications for practice

- In recent years a number of sophisticated but easy-to-use computer packages have been developed to help social landlords collect, organize and evaluate tenant priorities.
- Along with 'probity' and 'good governance', the pursuit of VFM is a central theme of the regulatory system (see *regulation*).
- In addition to the regulatory requirements, a battery of research findings from government departments and independent bodies also influences the VFM strategies of social landlords. In 2006, for example, the Varney Report set out the importance of moving contact events to 'lower cost channels' as a way of contributing to the savings target of £21.5 billion identified in Sir Peter Gershon's review (2004) of public sector efficiency (see *nudge theory*).

KEY TEXTS

- For current official approaches to determining VFM, refer to the HCA website (search 'Regulatory Framework')
- Garnett, D. and Perry, J. (2005) *Housing Finance* (Coventry: Chartered Institute of Housing and The Housing Studies Association)
- HM Treasury (2004) *Releasing Resources to the Frontline: Independent Review of Public Sector Efficiency* – known as 'the Gershon Report' after its chair Sir Peter Gershon (HMSO: Norwich), July 2004
- In the housing association sector, the two current key regulatory documents are: (1) The Regulatory Framework and (2) Regulating the Standards
- Oxley, M. (2004) *Economics, Planning and Housing* (Basingstoke: Palgrave Macmillan), Chapter 3
- Smedley, S. (2011) *Embedding Value for Money* (Coventry: HouseMark)
- Smedley, S. (2014) *Briefing: Where Are We Now with VFM Self-assessment?* (Coventry: HouseMark)

W

welfare

SEE ALSO affordability; care and support; continuous improvement; equity; housing market; inclusion and exclusion; low income
households; merit goods and services; social returns; subsidies

Welfare is a composite word combining 'well' (in its contemporary
meaning) with 'fare' (from the Old English 'faran'), meaning a
state of being. The elements can, of course, be reversed to form the
departure phrase 'farewell'. In housing practice the term 'welfare'
is used to reflect social concern for the well-being of individuals and
groups. It is often applied to specific vulnerable categories such as
the elderly, the unemployed or those on low incomes. This application of the term first appeared in the early twentieth century and,
with the development of the modern welfare and social security
arrangements, its use has now become ubiquitous in both popular
and academic writing.

'welfare' as ideology

During the past 100 years, welfare principles have played a significant part in the development of housing policy. These principles
have contrasted (one might almost say 'competed') with economic
market principles as rationales for housing reform (see *housing
market*).

'Welfare ideology' is grounded in the belief that certain commodi-
ties have a social importance that is so great that the state should
guarantee some minimum standard of provision for everyone. It
emphasizes the notion of 'need' rather than that of 'demand', and it
represents the *value* system that underlies what is popularly referred
to as 'the welfare state'. It has been instrumental in developing the
concept of welfare rights and, in the housing field, is associated
with the proposition that every household should have a decent
home at a price it can afford.

It might be argued that, as well as 'Squalor', poor housing was, in various ways, historically implicated in the creation of the other four of Beveridge's 'Giant Evils' that plagued the pre-welfare state society of the 1940s: 'Want', 'Disease', 'Ignorance' and 'Idleness'. Since Beveridge there have been more than a generation of reforms that have clearly recognized a relationship between decent affordable homes on the one hand and improvements in wealth, health, educational performance and employment on the other. The precise relationship between housing policy and the post-war emergence of the 'welfare state' is complicated and much discussed in the academic literature.

welfare reform

By the start of the second decade of the twenty-first century, in the context of a recessionary economy and a hugely expensive, complex and largely uncoordinated welfare system, the Coalition Government postulated the need for radical welfare reform. From 2012 a series of welfare reforms was systematically introduced that were intended to encourage self-reliance, increase employment and cut the total government spend on welfare. These reforms are outlined in the entry *low income households* (refer to the sections: 'specific fiscal measures: housing benefit, council tax support and the introduction of universal credit'). The reforms remain highly controversial. Their introduction brings to the fore fundamental issues about the nature and purpose of state-provided welfare support.

The reform agenda brought to the surface once again a long-standing debate about the legitimacy of large-scale welfare funding. This debate has periodically been given prominence in academic, political and popular argument ever since the creation of the modern 'welfare state'. The influential German philosopher and writer Jurgen Habermas suggested that the expanded activity of the state was bound to produce the need for what he termed 'new legitimation'. The point being made is that the extension of state involvement in social life disrupts old, established cultural 'legitimations' (e.g. market theory, capitalist ideology and self-help philosophy) and therefore it has to be continuously justified to bring about a new cultural acceptability and make it politically sustainable. Socialist writers such as Jean Meynaud and Ralph Miliband have made the same point in more explicitly political terms. In his 1970s critique of capitalist society, Miliband suggests, for example, that government interventions through the tax and welfare systems that have the effect of redistributing wealth from the rich to the poor inevitably bring forth a barrage of complaints from vested interests about the undermining of the 'economic orthodoxy' and the dangers to society at large resulting from the additional burdens on 'wealth producers' (Miliband, 1973). More recently, Brian Lund points to how justifications for welfare reforms have been popularized by selective press stories highlighting 'inappropriate' support for individual households (such as former asylum seekers) who, at the taxpayers' expense, have moved into expensive homes at a time when 'hard-working families' were struggling to 'make ends meet'.

Despite continuing underlying political disagreements about what counts as legitimate, fair and effective welfare interventions by the state, there has emerged over the years a degree of cross-party consensus on some general points of principle. For example, there are almost 300,000 households in the United Kingdom where none of the adults has ever worked (2014), and 300,000 children have parents with serious drug problems. Children in families affected by these problems have reduced chances of success in their lives. There is now a general agreement that the state has a legitimate role in helping to make society function better by providing the support and tools to help turn lives around. There is also general agreement that this approach involves engaging with poverty in all its forms and is not about income poverty alone. In particular, most politicians agree that the state should intervene to help 'troubled' people out of drug dependency and into stable employment. Part of the declared rationale for combining in- and out-of-work benefits within the new universal credit is to make the transition from benefits to work easier. Other areas of general agreement include the need for a more active and coordinated approach to deal with mental health issues, and the need to reduce child poverty. The Child Poverty Act 2010 set income targets for 2020.

The key political divide remains. This might be summarized by reference to the question: 'Should state-sponsored welfare programmes be collectively regarded as a 'safety net' or as an integral element in a modern developed economy?'

KEY TEXTS

- Diacon, D. (2009) 'Decent Housing for All' in B. Pattison and J. Vine (eds), *Perspectives on the Future of Housing: A Collection of Viewpoints on the UK Housing System* (Coalville: Building and Social Housing Foundation)
- Ham, C. (2009) *Only Connect: Policy Options for Integrating Health and Social Care* (London: Nuffield Trust)
- Health and Social Care Bill: www.gov.uk/dh
- Lund, B. (2011) *Understanding Housing Policy* (Bristol: The Policy Press), Chapter 10
- Malpass, P. (1990) *Reshaping Housing Policy: Subsidies, Rents and Residualisation* (London: Routledge)
- Malpass, P. (2004) 'Fifty Years of British Housing Policy: Leaving or Leading the Welfare State?', *European Journal of Housing Policy*, 4 (2): pp. 209–227
- Oxley, M. (2004) *Economics, Planning and Housing* (Basingstoke: Palgrave Macmillan)
- Thistlethwaite, P. (2011) *Integrating Health and Social Care in Torbay: Improving Care for Mrs Smith* (London: The King's Fund). http://www.kingsfund.org.uk/sites/files/kf/integrating-health-social-care-torbay-case-study-kings-fund-march-2011.pdf
- https://www.gov.uk/government/policies/simplifying-the-welfare-system-and-making-sure-work-pays
- https://www.gov.uk/government/policies/reducing-drugs-misuse-and-dependence
- https://www.gov.uk/government/policies/making-mental-health-services-more-effective-and-accessible--2
- https://www.gov.uk/government/policies/raising-the-achievement-of-disadvantaged-children
- https://www.gov.uk/government/publications/welfare-reform-communications-toolkit

bibliography

Adams, R. (2003) *The Successful Business Plan.* 4th edn (London: The Planning Shop)

Adamson, D. (2001) *Management of Project Risk.* Unpublished paper, UWE 7 April 2001

Aldrich, H. (2004) *Organizations Evolving* (London: Sage Publications)

Aldrich, H., Kenway, P., MacInnes, T. and Parekh, A. (2012) *Monitoring Poverty and Social Exclusion 2012* (York: Joseph Rowntree Foundation)

Altair Consultancy and Advisory Services Ltd (2014) *Cosmopolitan Housing Group: Lessons Learned* (London: Altair)

Arden, A. and Dymond, A. (2012) *Manual of Housing Law.* 9th edn (London: Sweet and Maxwell)

Arnold, M. W. (1869/1963) *Culture and Anarchy* (London: Cambridge University Press)

Arnstein, S. R. (1969) 'A Ladder of Citizen Participation', *Journal of the American Institute of Planners*, July, 35 (4): pp. 216–224

Atrill, P. and McLaney, E. (2012) *Accounting and Finance for Non-specialists* (Hemel Hempstead: Pearson)

Barker, K. (2004) *Review of Housing Supply. Delivering Stability: Securing our Future Housing Needs, Final Report: Recommendations* (London: HM Treasury)

Barker, K. (2006) *The Barker Review of Land Use Planning: Final Report (December 2006)* (London: HM Treasury)

Balchin, P. and Rhoden, M. (2002) *Housing Policy: An Introduction* (New York: Routledge), Chapter 14

Baldry, D. (1998) 'The Evaluation of Risk Management in Public Sector Capital Projects', *International Journal of Project Management*, February, 16 (1): pp. 35–41

Beardshaw, J. and Palfreman, D. (1990) *The Organisation in its Environment* (London: Pitman)

Berger, P. and Luckmann, T. (1966) *The Social Construction of Reality* (New York: Penguin Books)

Blewitt, J. (2010) *Understanding Sustainable Development* (London: Earthscan)

Bourdieu, P. (1977) *Outline of a Theory of Practice* (London: Cambridge University Press)

Bradshaw, J. (1972) 'The Taxonomy of Social Need' in G. McLachlan (ed.), *Problems and Progress in Medical Care*, 7th series (London: Nuffield Provincial Hospitals Trust, Oxford University Press)

Bramley, G., Munro, M. and Pawson, H. (2004) *Key Issues in Housing: Policies and Markets in 21st-Century Britain* (Basingstoke: Palgrave Macmillan)

Brantingham, P. J. and Faust, F. L. (1976) 'A Conceptual Model of Crime Prevention', *Crime and Delinquency*, 22: pp. 284–296

Brundtland Report – see to the World Commission on Environment and Development (1987)

Burke, E. (1968) 'Citizen Participation Strategies', *Journal of the American Institute of Planners*, September, 34: pp. 287–294

Burney, E. (2009) *Making People Behave: Anti-social Behaviour, Politics and Policy* (Devon: Willan Publishing)

Cabinet Office (Behavioural Insights Team) (2012) *Applying Behavioural Insights to Reduce Fraud Error and Debt*

Chartered Institute of Housing (2013) *Welsh Housing Review 2013* (Coventry: CIH Cymru)

Coleman, A. (1985) *Utopia on Trial: Vision and Reality in Planned Housing* (London: Hilary Shipman Ltd). Revised edition now available

Collins, P. and Blake, R. (2005) 'Finance, Procurement and Marketing of Housing' in A. Golland and R. Blake (eds), *Housing Development: Theory, Process and Practice* (London: Routledge)

Connor, D. M. (1995) 'A Generic Design for Public Involvement Programmes' in M. Hermann (ed.), *Resolving Conflict* (Washington: International City Management Association)

Cooper, C. and Hawtin, M. (eds) (1998) *Resident Involvement and Community Action, Theory to Practice* (Coventry: Chartered Institute of Housing)

Country Land and Business Association (2013) *Tackling the Housing Crisis in England: CLA Policy on Securing and Increasing Housing Supply in England 2013–2018* (London: CLA)

Deal, T. E. and Kennedy, A. A. (1982) *Corporate Cultures: The Rites and Rituals of Corporate Life* (Harmondsworth: Penguin Books)

Dees, J. G. (2001) *The Meaning of 'Social Entrepreneurship'* (CASE). http://www.caseatduke.org/documents/dees_sedef.pdf

Denman, D. R. and Prodano, S. (1972) *Land Use: An Introduction to Proprietary Land Use Analysis* (London: Allen & Unwin)

Department of Communities and Local Government (2010) *Code for Sustainable Homes: Technical Guide*

Department for Communities and Local Government (2011) *Private Landlords Survey*

Department for Communities and Local Government (2012a) *A Plain English Guide to the Localism Act, November 2011*

Department for Communities and Local Government (2012b) *Review of the Barriers to Institutional Investment in Private Rented Homes*

Department of Communities and Local Government and Homes and Communities Agency (2011) *2011– 2015 Affordable Homes Programme – Framework*

Department of Communities and Local Government and the Welsh Assembly (2007) *Assured and Assured Shorthold Tenancies: A Guide for Tenants*

Diacon, D., Pattison, B. and Vine, J. (2009) *The Future of Housing: Rethinking the UK Housing System for the Twenty-First Century* (Coalville: Building and Social Housing Foundation)

Dobson, A. (1999) *Fairness and Futurity: Essays on Environmental Sustainability and Social Justice* (Oxford: Oxford University Press)

Eliot, T. S. (1948) *Notes Towards the Definition of Culture* (London: Faber and Faber)

Elphicke, N. and House, K. (2015) *From Statutory Provider to Housing Enabler: Review into the Local Authority Role in Housing Supply*. The Elphicke House Report (London: DCLG/HMSO)

Financial Reporting Council (March 2013), *FS102: The Financial Standard applicable in the UK and Republic of Ireland*

Fisher, I. (1907) *The Rate of Interest: Its Nature, Determination and Relation to Economic Phenomena* (New York: Macmillan)

Garnett, D. (1996) *Building Obsolescence* (Bristol: UWE). Republished: Garnett (2015) in *Housing and Society* (Leaping Frog Publications). http://leapingrogpublications.co.uk

Garnett, D. (2000) *Housing Finance* (Coventry: Chartered Institute of Housing)

Garnett, D. (2006) *Redevelopment v Rehabilitation* (Bristol: University of the West of England). Republished as *The Needleman Rule* (2015) by Leaping Frog Publications under *Housing and Society* at: http://leapingfrogpublications.co.uk/

Garnett, D. and Farrugia, H. (2015) *The Idea of a Balanced Scorecard* (Leaping Frog Publications) under *Housing and Society* at: http://leapingfrogpublications.co.uk/

Garnett, D. and Perry, J. (2005) *Housing Finance* (Coventry: Chartered Institute of Housing and The Housing Studies Association)

Gershon Report (2004) *Releasing Resources to the Frontline: Independent Review of Public Sector*, HM Treasury July 2004

Gibb, K. and Munro, M. (1991) *Housing Finance in the UK: An Introduction* (Basingstoke and London: Macmillan)

Giddens, A. (2003) (ed.) *The Progressive Manifesto* (Oxford and USA: Polity Press with Blackwell Publishing)

Glover, J. and Clewett, N. (2011) *No Fixed Abode: The Housing Struggle for Young People Leaving Custody in England* (Ilford: Barnardo's)

Golland, A. and Blake, R. (eds) (2004) *Housing Development: Theory, Process and Practice* (London and New York: Routledge)

Habermas, J. (1976) *Legitimation Crisis* (trans. McCarthy, T.) (London: Heinemann)

Ham, C. (2009) *Only Connect: Policy Options for Integrating Health and Social Care* (London: Nuffield Trust)

Handy, C. B. (1985) *Understanding Organizations*. 3rd edn (Harmondsworth: Penguin Books)

Harriott, S. and Matthews, L. (2004) *Introducing Affordable Housing* (Coventry: Chartered Institute of Housing)

Harvey, L. and Green, D. (1993) 'Defining Quality', *Assessment and Evaluation in Higher Education: An International Journal*, 18 (1): pp. 9–34

Hills, J. (2007) *Ends and Means: The Future Roles of Social Housing in England* (The Hills Report, CASE Report 34, February 2007) (HCA: The Hills Report)

Hills, J. (2012) *Getting the Measure of Fuel Poverty*. Final Report of the Fuel Poverty Review, CASE Report 72 March 2012

HM Government (2014) *Practice Guide 27: The Leasehold Reform Legislation*. https://www.gov.uk/government/publications/the-leasehold-reform-legislation

Home Office (March 2013) *Policy Statement 'Reducing and Preventing Crime'*

Institute of Fiscal Studies (2013) *Living Standards, Poverty and Inequality in the UK: 2013*. IFS Report R81

Johnson, G., Scholes, K. and Whittington, R. (2011) *Exploring Corporate Strategy: Texts and Cases*. 9th edn (Harlow: Prentice Hall)

Joseph Rowntree Foundation (2013) *Distribution of Carbon Emissions in the UK: Implications for Domestic Energy Policy*

Kandola, R. and Fullerton, J. (1994) *Diversity in Action: Managing the Mosaic* (London: Chartered Institute of Personal Development)

Kaplan, R. S. and Norton, D. P. (1993) 'Putting the Balanced Scorecard to Work', *Harvard Business Review*, September/October 1993, pp. 133–148, Reprint 93505

Kearns, A. and Mason, P. (2007) 'Mixed Tenure Communities and Neighbourhood Quality', *Housing Studies*, 22 (5): pp. 661–691

Kenna, P. (2011) *Housing Law, Policy and Rights* (Dublin: Clarus Press)

Killip, G. (2008) *Transforming the UK's Existing Housing Stock* (Oxford: Environmental Change Institute, University of Oxford for the Federation of Master Builders)

King, P. (2009) *Understanding Housing Finance: Meeting Needs and Making Choices* (London and New York: Routledge)

Lane Fox, M. (2010) *Directgov 2010 and Beyond: Revolution not Evolution*. A Report by Martha Lane Fox (London: The Cabinet Office, Efficiency and Reform Group)

Lindsay, J. (1962) *Cause, Principle and Unity* (trans. Bruno, G.) (London: The Diamon Press)

Lowe, S. (2004) *Housing Policy Analysis: British Housing in Cultural and Comparative Context* (Basingstoke: Palgrave Macmillan)

Lowe, S. (2011) *The Housing Debate* (Bristol: The Policy Press, University of Bristol), Chapter 1

Lowry, I. S. (1960) 'Filtering and Housing Standards: A Conceptual Analysis', *Land Economics*, 36 (4): pp. 362–370

Lund, B. (2011) *Understanding Housing Policy* (Bristol: The Policy Press)

Macauley, A. (November 2013), 'A Perfect Match', in *'Asset Management Supplement' to Inside Housing*

Maclennan, D. (2005) *Housing Policies: New Times, New Foundations* (York: Joseph Rowntree Foundation)

Malpass, P. (1990) *Reshaping Housing Policy: Subsidies, Rents and Residualisation* (London: Routledge)

Malpass, P. (2004) 'Fifty Years of British Housing Policy: Leaving or Leading the Welfare State?', *European Journal of Housing Policy*, 4 (2): pp. 209–227

Malpass, P. and Rowlands, R. (eds) (2010) *Housing, Markets and Policy* (Abingdon: Routledge)

Marsh, A. and Mullins, D. (eds) (1998) *Housing and Public Policy: Citizenship, Choice and Control* (Buckingham and Philadelphia, PA: Open University Press)

Marshall, A. (1890) *Principles of Economics* (London: Macmillan) (1959)

Matthews, R. and Pitts, J. (eds) (2001) *Crime, Disorder and Community Safety: A New Agenda?* (London and New York: Routledge)

McCluam, M. (1951) *The Mechanical Bride: Folklore of Industrial Man* (NY: The Vanguard Press). (Reissued by Ginko Press 2002.) Magic that Changes Mood, *The Mechanical Bride*, 1951

Meadows, D. H., Dennis, L. and Meadows, D. (2004) *The Limits to Growth: The 30-Year Update* (Vermont: Chelsea Green Publishing and Earthscan)

Miliband, R. (1973) *The State in Capitalist Society: The Analysis of the Western System of Power* (London: Quartet Books)

Mills, E. S. (1990) 'Housing Tenure Choice', *Journal of Real Estate Finance and Economics*, 3: pp. 323–331

Mullins, D. and Murie, A. (2006) *Housing Policy in the UK* (Basingstoke: Palgrave Macmillan)

Murphy, E. (2013) *The Regulation of Registered Housing Associations* (Belfast: Northern Ireland Assembly)

Myers, D. (1994) *Economics & Property: A Coursebook for Students of the Built Environment* (London: Estates Gazette)

National Housing Federation (2012a) *Localism Act 2011: Housing and Planning, A Guide for Housing Associations*

National Housing Federation (2012b) *Code of Conduct: With Good Practice for Members*

National Housing Federation (2013) *Rising to the Challenge: How LEPs can Deliver Growth Strategies*. NFH submission to the APPG on local growth

National Housing Federation (2014) *The Lyons Housing Review: Mobilising across the Nation to Build the Homes Our Children Need*

Nettlefold, J. S. (1908) *Practical Housing* (Letchworth: Garden City Press)

Newman, O. (1973) *Defensible Space: People and Design in the Violent City* (London: Architectural Press)

Niskanen, W. A. (1971) *Bureaucracy and Representative Government* (Chicago: Aldine-Atherton)

Norris, M. and Redmond, D. (eds) (2007) *Housing Contemporary Ireland: Policy, Society and Shelter* (Dordrecht: Springer Science)

O'Connell, C. (2007) *The State and Housing in Ireland: Ideology, Policy and Practice* (New York: Nova Science)

OECD (2003) *Policy Brief: Environmentally Sustainable Buildings: Challenges and Policies*

ONS (May 2013) *The Burden of Property Debt in Great Britain, 2006/08 & 2008/10*

Oxley, M. (2004) *Economics, Planning and Housing* (Basingstoke: Palgrave Macmillan)

Paris, C. (ed.) (2001) *Housing in Northern Ireland – and Comparisons with the Republic of Ireland* (Coventry: Chartered Institute of Housing)

Park, R. E. and Burgess, E. (eds) (1925) *The City* (Chicago: University of Chicago Press)

Parker, M. (2000) *Organisational Culture and Identity* (London: Sage Publications)

Pattison, B. and Vine, J. (eds) (2009) *Perspectives on the Future of Housing: A Collection of Viewpoints on the UK Housing System* (Building and Social Housing Foundation)

Peace, S. and Holland, C. (eds) (2001) *Inclusive Housing in an Ageing Society, Innovative Approaches* (Bristol: Policy Press)

Porter, M. E. and Kramer, M. R. (2011) Creating Shared Value, *Harvard Business Review*, January–February 2011

Power, A. (1993) *Hovels to High Rise: State Housing in Europe since 1850* (London: Routledge)

Price Waterhouse Coopers (2009) *Champion for Digital Inclusion: The Economic Case for Digital Inclusion*. Report prepared for Matha Lane Fox

Price Waterhouse Coopers (2011) *Hard Times, New Choices: A New Deal for Housing Associations*

Quality Housing Services Ltd. (2012) *The QHS Criteria for Excellence in Communities* (Coventry: QHS)

Redmond, D. and Norris, M. (2014) 'Social Housing in Ireland' in D. Redmond and M. Norris (eds), *Social Housing in Europe* (London: Wiley-Blackwell)

Reeves, P. (2005) *An Introduction to Social Housing* (London: Elsevier Butterworth, Heinemann)

Reeves, P. (2014) *Affordable and Social Housing: Policy and Practice* (New York: Routledge)

Robinson, P. (2003) *Leasehold Management: A Good Practice Guide* (Coventry: Chartered Institute of Housing, National Housing Federation and The Housing Corporation)

Ruskin, J. 1894 (1860) *Munera Pulveris: Six Essays on the Elements of Political Economy* (New York: Greenwood Press)

Russell, S. (2013) *Journey to Impact: A Practitioner Perspective on Measuring Social Impact* (Coventry: HouseMark/Midland Heart)

Sampson, R. J. and Raudenbush, S. (1999) 'Systematic Social Observations of Public Spaces: A New Look at Disorder in Urban Neighbourhoods', *American Journal of Sociology*, 105 (3): pp. 603–651. Referred to by King, G. L. in R. Matthews and J. Pitts (2001) *Crime, Disorder and Community Safety: A New Agenda?* (London and New York: Routledge)

Schein, E. H. (2004) *Organizational Culture and Leadership* (San Francisco: Jossey-Bass)

Schon, D. A. (1983) *The Reflective Practitioner: How Professionals Think in Action* (New York: Basic Books)

Silver, S. (1995) 'Three Paradigms of Social Exclusion' in G. Rodgers, C. Gore, and J. B. Figueiredo B (eds), *Social Exclusion: Rhetoric, Reality, Responses* (Geneva: International Institute for Labour Studies)

Sirr, L. (ed) (2014) *Renting in Ireland: The Social, Voluntary and Private Sectors* (Dublin: Institute of Public Administration)

Skolimowski, H. (1981) *Eco-Philosophy: Designing New Tactics fir Living* (Boston and London: Marion Boyars)

Smedley, S. (2011) *Embedding Value for Money* (Coventry: HouseMark)

Smedley, S. (2014) Briefing: Where Are We now with VFM Self-assessment? (Coventry: HouseMark)

Smith Institute (2011) *Making the Most of HRA Reform* (London: Price Waterhouse Coopers). www.psrc.pwc.com

Smith, M., Albanese, F. and Truder, J. (2014) *A Longitudinal Study of Housing Wellbeing in the Private Rented Sector* (London: Shelter and Crisis)

Smith and Williamson (2014) *Finance Demystified: A Guide for Housing Association Board Members and Non-finance Executives* (London: NHF)

Thaler, R. H. and Sunstein, C. R. (2008) *Nudge: Improving Decisions about Wealth, Health and Happiness* (New Haven and London: Yale University Press)

Thistlethwaite, P. (2011) *Integrating Health and Social Care in Torbay: Improving Car for Mrs Smith* (London: The King's Fund)

Thomas, R. R. (1990) 'From Affirmative Action to Affirming Diversity', *Harvard Business Review*, March–April, pp. 107–117

Tilley, N. (2005) *Handbook of Crime Prevention and Community Safety* (Devon: Willan Publishing)

Tilley, N., Smith, J., Finer, S., Erol, R., Charles, C. and Dobby, J. (2004) *Problem-solving Street Crime* (London: Home Office)

Titmuss, R. (1968) *Commitment to Welfare* (London: Allen and Unwin)

Trotter, L., Vine, J., Leach, M. and Fujiwars, D. (2014) *Measuring the Social Impact of Community Investment: A Guide to Using the Wellbeing Valuation Approach* (London: HACT)

The Turnbull Report (1999) *Internal Controls: Guidance for Directors on the Combined Code* (Institute of Chartered Accountants in England and Wales), September 1999

Tylor, E. B. (1871) *Primitive Culture: Researches into the Development of Mythology, Philosophy, Religion, Language, Art, and Custom.* 2 vols (London: John Murray)

United Nations Economic and Social Commission for Asia and the Pacific (2005) *Human Settlements*

Varney, D. (2006) *The Varney Report: Service Transformation: A Better Service for Citizens and Businesses, a Better Deal for the Taxpayer* (London: HM Treasury)

Ward, M. and Hardy, S. (eds) (2013) *Where Next for Local Enterprise Partnerships?* (London: The Smith Institute and the Regional Studies Association)

Wilcox, S. (1996) *Housing Finance Review 1996/1997* (York: Joseph Rowntree Foundation)

Wilcox, S. and Pawson, H. (eds) *UK Housing Review 2013* (Coventry: Chartered Institute of Housing)

Williams, R. (1976) *Keywords: A Vocabulary of Culture and Society* (London: Fontana)

Wilson, J. Q. and Kelling, G. L. (1982) 'Broken Windows: The Police and Neighbourhood Safety', *Atlantic Monthly* (March): pp. 29–38

Wilson, W. (2014) *Rent Setting for Social Housing Tenancies (England)*, House of Commons Library, Social Policy Section, Standard Note SN/SP/1090

Woods, F. (2009) *Book-Keeping and Accounts* (London: Financial Times/Pitman)

World Commission on Environment and Development (1987) *Our Common Future*. The Brundtland Report (Oxford: Oxford University Press)

index

___

Note: references to main content entries are in bold type.

accountability, **1–2**, 19, 22, 74–76, 83, 124, 128, 150, 153

accounting period, 3–5, 16, 28

accounts, 1, **2–6**, 16, 19, 20, 26–28, 31, 66, 68, 135, 176, 197, 200, 221

accrual accounting, 5–6

added value, 199–200

affordable home ownership, **6–7**, 83, 99–100, 124, 169

affordability, xiv, **6–9**, 38, 51, 77, 79, 95, 97–100, 119–120, 157, 169, 178, 209

affordable homes, 7–10, 52, 58–59, 68, 100, 117, 124, 141, 158, 169, 172, 178, 205

allocations, 9–12, 36–38, 80–81, 118–119

ALMOs, 1, 68, 74–75, 134, **169**

amortization, 111, 200

annual efficiency statements, 20

annual statement on internal control, 20

anti-social behaviour, xiv, **12–16**, 31, 57, 134

Arnold, Matthew, 46

Arnstein, S., 128–130

ASBOs, 14–15

asset Management, **16–19**, 27–28, 57, 70, 170, 197–198

assets, 3, **16–18**, 26–30, 53, 60, 63, 68–69, 100, 140, 150, 154, 198, 200

assignment, 92

assured shorthold tenancies, 140, 190–194

assured tenancies, 140, 190–194

AST, *see* assured shorthold tenancies

audit, 2, 5, **19–21**, 137, 165, 203

bad debts, 164, 174

balanced scorecard, 136–137

balance sheet, 3, 29–30, 68, 200–201

banks, 67–68, 110–115, 152

Barker Review, 86, 117

Bateson, Gregory, 47

bedroom tax, 17, 64, 105, *see also* under occupancy charge

behavioural economics, 9, 122, 187

benchmarking, 135

best value, 64–65, 119, 149–150, **207–208**

Beveridge, William, 210

Big Society, 40, 69, 168

Black Report, 171

Bonds, 16, 68–69, 70, 146

BREEAM, 187

Bricks and mortar subsidies, 182–183

Brundtland, 186

building regulations, 85, 118, 185, 187

business culture, *see* culture

business impact analysis, 20, 47, 123, 160–164, 174, 205–206

business planning, 3–4, **22–25**, 28, 75, 135–137, 161–162

Cadbury, George and Richard, 126

capital, xiv, 3, 6, 8, 16, **26–31**, 52–54, 63, 66–70, 78–79, 99, 110–112, 144–148, 167–168, 197

capital appreciation, 99, 148

capital budgeting, 27, 31, 112, 198

capital expenditure, 26–28, 30, 66–67, 147, 200

capital gains, 27, 63, 138, 142, 147–148, 181

capital income, 27–28, 30, 67, 198

capital market, 68–70, 110–115

capital receipt, 27–28, 67, 69

capitalism, 126, 173, 180, 210–211

capitalization, 198, 200
capping, 105, 113, 158
carbon emissions, 70, 123, 173,
    185–188
care, **31–36**, 59, 108, 132, 153
care and repair agencies, 100
care homes, 33–35
care in the community, 32–36, 132, 153
Care Standards Act (2000), 33
carrying value, 29, **200–201**
cash accounting, 4–5
CBA, *see* cost-benefit-analysis
change agents, 167
channel switching, 122
Charity Commission, 152, 166–167
Chartered Institute of Housing, 50
Child Poverty Act (2010), 211
choice, 10–11, **36–39**, 85, 87, 121, 140,
    142, 158, 196
choice-based lettings, 10–11, 38, 119
CIH, *see* Chartered Institute of
    Housing
citizenship, 38, 74, 108, 128
climate change, 72
Code for Sustainable Homes, 187–188
coincidence of categories, 84, 86
commonhold, 93–94
Commonhold and Leasehold Reform
    Act (2002/14), 93–94
community, 12–15, 22, 32, 34, **39–41**,
    47, 49, 52, 62, 69, 74, 78, 128, 132,
    133–134, 137–138, 144, 154, 166,
    170–174
community benefit societies, 166
community funding, 32, **69**, 133
Community Housing Cymru, 4
community interest companies, 166
community planning and partnership,
    13, **132**
community safety partnerships, 13,
    15, 74
community trigger, 14, 134
competition, 84–86, 156
component accounting, 4
compulsory competitive tendering, 64
consumer sovereignty, 87
contested concepts, 117, 185, 202
continuous improvement, 20, **41–45**,
    135–137, 207

contract risk, 19, 33, 53, 55, 163
conveyance, 85, 92, 110
co-operatives, 166, 169
co-regulation, 2, **130**, **154**
corporate social responsibility, 49, 173
Cost-Benefit-Analysis, 18, 33, 44, 62,
    65, 122, 186, 203, 205–207
cost of housing, 5–9, 16, 18, 24, 27,
    29–30, 33, **45–46**, 52, 55, 58, 62,
    63, 65, 67, 68, 77, 94–95, 97–100,
    101–104, 113–115, 157, 175, 179–183,
    185, 198–201
costs in use, 5–6, 7, 18, 24, 30, 67, 99,
    102, 104, 154, 167, 185, 198–199
council tax, 67, 104–105, 123, 210
council tax support, 67, 104, 105, 210
credit crunch, 113
crime, 12–15, 54, 90, 102, 170, 205
Crime and Disorder Act (1998), 13
Crime and Policing Act (2014), 14
cross-subsidy, 58–59, 67, 157, 178,
    180–181
CSR, *see* corporate social responsibility
culture, xiv, 23, **46–50**, 149, 152, 159,
    162, 172

debt, 1, 3, 16–17, 27–28, 30, 32, 63, 66,
    67–68, 69, 70, 99, 103, 110–111,
    113–115, 141, 157, 164, 174, 180–181,
    198
decent homes, 52, 118, 141, 158, 172,
    177, 178, 210
Dees, J Gregory, 167
Delphi method, 164
demand, 10, 11, 17, 29, 52, 59, 78,
    83–88, 98, **116–120**, 142, 170,
    178, 182–183, 207, 209
demolition, 53, 186
Department for Work and Pensions,
    102, 104
deposit protection scheme, 143
depreciation, 4, 16, **28–29**, 200
development, 31, 41, 49, **51–55**, 58, 68,
    69–70, 82, 93, 124, 133, 138, 141,
    160, 170, 174, 178, 179, 181, 184,
    186, 199, *see also* redevelopment;
    refurbishment; renewal
development risk, 31, **52–53**, 55, 68,
    141, 160

devolution, x, 69, 103
digital inclusion, 90–91, 122
disability, 34, 37, 57, 90
Disability and Discrimination Act
    (1995), 58, 64
discounting, 6, 96–97, 113, 178, 191,
    198–199, 201
discrimination, 57–58, 64, 90
disposable income, xiii, 71, 87, 99,
    108, 139, 177
diversification, 53, 56, 57, 59, 168
diversity, xv, 40, **56–60**, 75
dwellings, xiii, 16, 17, 28, 53, 54,
    60–61, 79, 84, 85, 87, 98–99, 109,
    138, 140–141, 144–148, 158, 170, 171,
    176, 194–201
DWP, *see* Department for Work and
    Pensions

easement, 78, 145
ecology, 39, 184–185, 204
economic life of a building, 18, 28–29,
    171, 185–186
economy, 203, 207, *see also* market
    economy
effective demand, 87–88, 118, 202
effectiveness, 4–5, 18, 44, 46, 65,
    75, 122, 129, 132, 136, 150, 180,
    203–207
efficiency, 20, 42, 44, 58, 65, 67, 120,
    122, 132, 150, 153, 203–208, *see also*
    energy efficiency; social efficiency
elderly, 31, 33, 97, 118, 180, 209
Eliot, T. S., 47
empowerment, 38, 127
endowment, 110–112
energy, 7, 9, 18
energy efficiency, 7, 9, 18, 64, 71–72,
    124, 185–188
energy performance certificates, 124,
    187
ENR, *see* expected net return
entrepreneur, 167–168
environment, 15, 40, 54, 126, 133, 152,
    166, 168, 172, 179, 184–187, 201,
    202, 204
equal opportunities, 57, 64, 82
equality, *see* inequality
Equality Act (2010), 57, 64

equity, 8, **62–65**, 93, 97, 141, 180, 181,
    188, 201, 203, 204, 205
equity loans, 62–63
equity release, 62–63
ERDF, *see* European Regional
    Development Fund
ESF, *see* European Social Fund
estate agents, 84, 85, 86
ethics, xiii, 23, 63–64, 74, 75, 126
Europe, 7, 69–70, 133, 140, 187, 195
European Energy Performance of
    Buildings Directive, 187
European Regional Development
    Fund, 69–70, 133
European Social Fund, 69–70, 133
EUV, *see* existing use value
exchange value, 28–29, 46, 54, 78, 99,
    171, **197**, 200
exclusion, **98–91**, 101–102
exclusive possession, 94
existing Use Value, **198–199**
ex-offenders, 31
expected net return, 16
externalities, 144, 148, 170, 179
extra care, 33–34

facilities management, 58
fair rent, 157–158, 191, 192, 193
fairness, 64, 71–72, 93, 158, 203, 206,
    see also equity
FCA, *see* Finance Conduct Authority
fee simple, 78, 92, 194
feed-in tariffs, 188
filtering, 87
finance, xiii, 1, 9, 30, 52, 53, 62, 63,
    66–70, 98, 109, 113, 139, 140, 141,
    159, 168, 177, 180
financial assets, 16–17
Financial Conduct Authority, 8, 111,
    152, 166
financial crisis, 77, 173
Financial Reporting Council, 4, 28
fiscal policy, 67, 79, 99, **104**, 179, 180,
    196, 210
Fisher, Irvin, 83
fit for purpose, 17, 53–54, 150
FITs, *see* feed-in tariffs
fixed capital, 26–29, 63, 147
fixed term tenancy, 81, 141, **190–192**

flexible tenancies, 38, **192–193**
forcefield analysis, 132
fraud, 123, 161
freehold, 77–78, 92, 94, 144–145, 194
fuel poverty, **70–72**, 101, 185, *see also* poverty

Gershon Report (2004), 208
Gibb and Munro, 179
governance, 4, 19, 20, 48, **73–76**, 127, 128, 129, 130, 154, 155, 208
GPIs, *see* performance indicators
green agenda, 124, 185, 187–188
green buildings, 124, 185, 187–188

Habermas, Jurgen, 210
Hall, Stuart, 47
Handy, Charles, 48
HCA, *see* Homes and Communities Agency
health, 7, 10, 14, 31, 34–36, 38, 42, 78, 90, 102, 108, 114, 121, 133, 134, 136, 137, 152, 161, 170, 174, 176–177, 205, 210, 211
Health and Social Care Act (2012), 35
Help to Buy, 98, 124
HFC, *see* Housing Finance Corporation
Highland and Islands Enterprise, 54
Hill, Octavia, 126
Hills Report (2007), 103
historic cost, 115, 157, 181, 200
home improvement agencies, 100
home ownership, 7–8, 62, **77–80**, 92, 96–100, 142, 144–145, 194–195, *see also* low cost home ownership; owner occupation
homelessness, 52, **80–82**, 170
Homelessness Acts (1996/2002), 81
Homes and Communities Agency, 52, 142, 152, 169
horizontal integration, 58
household fit, 17, 120
Housing Act (1980), 77, 96, 201
Housing Act (1985), 190–191
Housing Act (1988), 190, 193
Housing Act (1996), 96
housing associations, 1, 4, 8, 10–11, 14, 31, 34, 36, 38, 39–40, 52, 58–9,

65–70, 74–75, 96, 100, 104, 117, 122, 124, 137, 139, 155, **169**, 170, 174, 176, 190–192, 195, 198
housing benefit, vii, 32, 56, 67, 82, 91, 101, **104–106**, 123, 140, 177, 178, 181, 183, 196, 210
housing finance, *see* finance
Housing Finance Corporation, 68
housing law, xiii, **82–83**, 93–94, 191, 206
housing management, 49, 93, 159, *see also* property management
housing market, 1, 8, 10, 46, 57, 59, 63, 78–79, **83–88**, 92, 96–98, 108–109, 113, 115, 116–119, 140–143, 156–157, 175–179, 181, 198, 209
housing need, *see* need
housing renewal, *see* renewal
housing revenue account, 29–30, 52, 66–67, 180
HRA, *see* housing revenue account

IASB, *see* International Accounting Standards Board
ideology, 78, 109, 209, 210
impact analysis, 65, 72, 120, 123, 137, 160–161, 164, 168, 174, 179, 185–186, 201, 204–206
impairment, 3, **29**, 200
implementation imps, xv, 106, 186
improvement, 17, 19, 27, 53–54, 63, 100, 147, 178, 181, 200–201, *see also* continuous improvement
inclusion, 54, 70, **89–91**, 101–102, 120
industrial and provident societies, 69, 166
inelasticity, *see* price elasticity
inequality, 64, 171
information management, 20, 22, 123, 129, 135, 136, 161, 164
injunctions, 14
innovation, 50, 57, 70, 150, 159, 160, 163
Institute of Fiscal Studies, 103
Institute for Public Policy Research, 37
institutional culture, *see* culture
inter-agency working, 13, 132
interest rates, xiv, 7, 77, 86, 99, **113–114**, 115, 161, 198

intergenerational justice, 65, 75, 186, 202

International Accounting Standards Board, 173

International Standards Organization, 153

investment, xiii, 5, 6, 16, 27, 30, 31, 42, 54, 59, 61, 65, 67, 69, 70, 79, 103, 112, 119, 120, 133, 135, 138, 141–142, 144, 145–148, 159, 168, 171–172, 179, 185, 188, 193, 198, 199–200, 202–204

investment value, 54, 147, 197–200

Investors in People, 153

IPPR, see Institute for Public Policy Research

Ireland, 4, 195

Irish Council of Social Housing, 4

ISO, see International Standards Organization

Kaizen, 42

Kieboom, A., 121

KPIs, see performance indicators

laissez faire, 93, 121

Lane Fox, M., 122

Langlands Report, 74

LAP, see local action plans

Law, see housing law

leasehold, 22, 63, 77–78, **92–95**, 97, 144–145, 156, 193, 194

Leasehold Reform Act (1967), 93

legitimation, 210

LEP, see Local Enterprise Partnership

licenses, 94–95

life cycles, 52, 186

liquidity, 27, 30, 63, 113, 197

Lindsay, Jack, 51

living will, 60

local action plans, 8, 52

local authorities, 1, 3, 28, 34, 66, 68, 74, 81, 96, 104, 116–118, 133–134, 137, 152, 169, 181, 190, 194, 195

local connections, 10

local development strategies, **52**, 133, 141

Local Enterprise Partnership, 54, 69, **133–134**, 171

Local Government Act (2000), 40–41

Local Government and Housing Act (1989), 180

local housing allowance, 104–105, 123, 140

local housing strategies, see local development strategies

local planning framework, 8, 40, 51–52, 54, 116, 119

local strategic partnerships, 74, 116, 132

localism, 11, 28, 38, 39–40, 51, 67, 81, 82, 119, 124, 130, 157, 168, 192

Localism Act (2011), 11, 51, 67, 81, 82, 119, 124, 130, 157, 192

location, 17, 19, 39, 84, 90, 120, 146–147, 156, 192, 200

longitudinal analysis, 135–136, see also trend analysis

low cost home ownership, 63, 77, 94, **95–100**, 114, 124, 179, 191

low income households, vii, 7, 64, 66, 71–72, 87, 89–90, 100, **101–107**, 112–113, 123, 140–141, 148, 157, 169, 176–177, 179, 182–183, 209–210

Lowry, I.S., 87

LPF, see local planning framework

LSPs, see local strategic partnerships

Lund, Brian, 211

maintenance, 8, 17–19, 28, 49, 53–54, 97, 109, 139, 147, 185, 198, 199

marginal benefit, 65, 205–206

marginal cost pricing, 156

marginal costs, 65, 156, 205–206

marginal owner occupiers, 98, 100

marginal social costs and benefits, 65, 205–206

market economy, 2, 10, 86, 87, 108, 121, 134, 140, 156, 159, 166–167, 177, 179, 182, 202, 207, 210, 211

market failure, 128, 152, 175–179, 182–183, 210

market forces, 37, 191, 193, 197, 202

market rent, 7, 8–9, 10, 46, 58, 59, 83–84, 139–143, **156–157**, 176, 182, 191, 193

marriage value, 94

Marshall, Alfred, 167

matching principle, 5
Mead, Margaret, 47
means testing, 104, 106, 181, 182–183
merit goods and services, 108–109,
146, 179, 182
Meynaud, Jean, 210
Miliband, Ralph, 210–211
minimum wage, 103
mission, 17, 23, 44, 48, 69, 70, 75–76,
136, 148, 150, 159, 163, 167, 172
MITR, *see* Mortgage Interest Tax
Relief
mobility of labour, 10, 140, 177
money capital, 16, **26–31**, 68, 70, 99,
146–147, 197–198
Montague Report (2012), 141–142
Morris, William, 47
Mortgage Interest Tax Relief, 96, 99
mortgage protection, 114
mortgages, 7, 8, 62–63, 77–79, 87, 96,
99–100, **109–115**, 124, 139, 177, 178,
181, 195
multiple occupation, 60–61, 93
mutual, 166

nanny state, 121
National Housing Federation, 4, 40,
90
National Planning Policy Framework,
8, 54
need-price dilemma, 157
needs, 8, 9–11, 17, 32, 33–36, 37, 44,
52, 59, 67, 77, 80–81, 85, 86, 87–88,
89, 100, 102, 108–109, **116–120,**
128, 132, 133, 136, 138, 141, 146, 148,
157–158, 169, 170, 177, 178, 180–183,
186, 202, 209–210
negative equity, 8, 63
neighbourhood, 12, 13–14, 39, 40–41,
200
neighbourhood effect value, 200
net present value, 17, 38, **198–199**
Nettlefold, J.S., 180
NEV, *see* neighbourhood effect value
New Economics Foundation, 172, 174
New Homes Bonus, 124
new public management, 10, 37
NHB, *see* New Homes Bonus
NHS, 35, 74

NIHE, *see* Northern Ireland Housing
Executive
NIMBY, 41
Northern Ireland, 4, 52, 98, 103, 133,
152, 167, 169
Northern Ireland Department of Social
Development, 52
Northern Ireland Federation of
Housing Associations, 4
Northern Ireland Housing Executive,
152, 169, 195
Norton, David, 136
not-for-profit, 3, 40, 46, 69, 100, 166,
169, 172
NPPF, *see* National Planning Policy
Framework
nudge theory, 54, **120–125,** 208

obsolescence, 29, 53
OECD, *see* organisation for Economic
Co-operation and Development
Office for National Statistics, 71, 99,
115
Ofsted, 152
Ombudsman, 152
OMV, *see* open market value
ONS, *see* Office for National Statistics
open market value, 198
opportunity cost, 18, 27, 99
Organisation for Economic
Co-operation and Development, 186
organisational culture, *see* culture
overcrowding, 7, 81, 176
Owen, Robert, 126
owner occupation, **7–8, 79–80,** 93, 97,
114, 139–140, 180, 181, 194–195, *see*
also home ownership

Pareto, Vilfredo, 42–43
Parker, Morris, 118
participation, 126–131
partnerships, 13, 40, 49, 54, 69, 74,
114, **131–134,** 166, 171, 172
paternalism, 1, 121, 126
Peabody, George, 126
performance indicators, 36, 154
performance monitoring, 17, 20, 22,
25, 44, 118, **134–137,** 148, 149, 150,
154, 187, 203

PFI, *see* private finance initiative
Pirsig, Robert, 150
PIs, *see* performance indicators
Planned maintenance, 17
planning, 8, 15, 40–41, 51–52, 54, 78,
    82, 86, 116–119, 124, 137–138, 141,
    152, 156, 171, *see also* business plan-
    ning; planning gain
Planning and Compensation Act
    (1991), 137
planning gain, **137–138**, 176, 178, 181
politics, xiii, 1, 9, 12, 37, 39, 56, 64, 79,
    83, 84, 86, 89–90, 93, 95, 98, 102,
    103, 105, 109, 121–123, 127, 129, 141,
    147–148, 161, 173, 177, 179, 180, 183,
    186, 202, 205, 210–211
Positive about Disabled People, 153
postcode lottery, 40
poverty, 89–90, 101–103, 211, *see also*
    fuel poverty
power, x, 3, 14, 35, 37, 38, 40, 48–49,
    56, 73, 89, 93, 96, 105, 128, 129,
    143, 145, 152, 171, 180, *see also*
    empowerment
precautionary principle, 164
present value, 17, 38, 198–199
preserved right to buy, 96
price elasticity, 86, 98
private finance Initiative, 53
Private Rented Sector Initiative, 59,
    142
private renting, 59, **138–144**, 147, 193,
    195
probity, 20, 208
procurement, 53, 55, 82, 168, 186, 201
project risk, *see* development risk
property management, 34, 58, 94,
    100, 139, 143, *see also* housing
    management
proprietary interests, 61, 66, 77, 79,
    93, 98, **144–148**, 170–171, 179, 193,
    195, 194, 202
PRSI, *see* Private Rental Sector
    Initiative
psychology, 12, 57, 121, 122
public choice theory, 36
public expenditure, 42, 75, 147, 171,
    176, 181, 101, 105, 205, 206
public goods and services, 109

Public Services (Social Value) Act
    (2012), 168, 201
Public Works Loans Board, 68
PWLB, *see* Public Works Loans Board

quality, xv, 6, 20, 26, 27, 37, 41–42,
    44, 53–54, 67, 85, 87, 90, 108, 142,
    143, **149–155**, 158, 160, 169, 171,
    176–177, 182, 203, 204
quality of life, 12, 57, 126

Rawls, John, 64
real assets, *see* real capital
real capital, 16, 27, 30, 99, **146–147**, *see
    also* fixed capital
real estate, 78, 110, 197
real income, 99, 104, 179
redevelopment, 18, 53, 186, 199
reflective practice, 50, 135
refurbishment, 16, 28, 37, 53–55, 172
regional development, 67, 69–70, 119,
    133, 171, 186
registered providers, *see* registered
    social landlords
registered social landlords, 1, 4, 96,
    117, 134, 138, 154, 156, 164, 168, 169,
    190
regulation, xiv, 1, 2, 4, 20, 22, 27, 29,
    38, 41, 49, 59, 76, 84, 85, 92, 96,
    105, 114, 118, 121, 124, 127, 129, 130,
    135, 136, 137, **152–155**, 157, 160, 164,
    169, 173, 176, 178, 181, 185, 187,
    192–193, 201, 202, 203, 206, 208
rehabilitation (buildings), 18, 53
rehabilitation (people), 34
renewal, 18, 53–54, 186
rent, 7, 8–10, 16, 17, 30, 33–34, 38, 46,
    49, 58, 65, 67, 83, 84, 87, 92, 97,
    104, 122, 124, 127, 138–144, 146,
    147, 148, 154, **156–159**, 169, 176,
    177, 178, 179, 180–184, 191–193,
    195–196, 198, 199, 201, 206
Rent Acts, 181,191
rent arrears, *see* bad debts
rent control, 157, 176, 178, 181, 191, 192
rent convergence, 192
rent equalisation, *see* rent convergence
rent harmonisation, *see* rent
    convergence

rent pooling, **157**, 176, 178, 180
rent setting, 156, **157–159**, 191
rent-a-room scheme, 142
repairs, 8, 17, 18, 19, 27, 30, 53–54, 58, 65, 66, 97, 100, 109, 147, 191, 198, 206
reputation, 18, 53–54, 59, 132, 161, 162
residency qualifications, 9, 96
residential care, 9, 32–34
resource accounting, 5, 28, 67, 68
retrofit, 185, 186
revenue, xiv, 3, 5–6, 16, 20, **26–31**, 32–3, 46, 52, 58, 59, 63, 66–67, 147, 156, 157, 178, 180, 182, 198
Ricardo, David, 156
right to acquire, 96
right to buy, 77, 96, 178, 191, 201
right to manage, 92, 93–94
right to purchase, 92
risk, 19–20, 31, 33, 38, 52–53, 55, 59, 60, 68, 74, 111, 112, 113, 136, 141, 154, **159–165**, 167
risk appetite, 38, 59, 113, 163
risk map, 162
rough sleepers, 81, 87
Royal Academy of Engineering, 185
RSLs, *see* registered social landlords
RTB, *see* right to buy
running costs, *see* costs in use
Ruskin, John, 47

Salt, Titus, 126
Say, Jean Baptiste, 167
Schon, Donald, 50
Schumpeter, Joseph, 167
Scotland, x, 34, 71, 96, 98, 105, 127, 133, 143, 174, 192, 195, 201
Scottish Enterprise, 54, 69
Scottish Federation of Housing Associations, 4
Scottish Government, 52
Scottish Housing Regulator, 152, 16
scrutiny panels, 37, 130, 154, *see also* co-regulation
Section 106 agreements, *see* planning gain
Secure by Design, 15
secure tenants, 96, 157, 190–191, 194, 201

security of tenure, 93, 142, 191, 192, 193
self-financing, 52, 67
service charges, 30, 32, 67, 69, 156–157
Sex discrimination Act (1975), 58
shared equity, 63, 97–98
shared ownership, 34, 93–94, 97–98, 169, *see also* shared equity
shared value, 168, **172–174**
sheltered Housing, 19, 33–34, 97, 118
shortage, 17, 85–86, 127
short-term, 23, 25, 64, 68, 139, 162
short-termism, 207
silo management, 49
sinking fund, 65
Skolimowski, Henryk, 149
Smiles, Samuel, 42
Smith, Adam, 37, 85
social business, 22, 24, 40, 69, 75, 134–135, 166–168, 172–174, *see also* social enterprise
social dividend, 173–174
social efficiency, 179–180
social enterprise, 22, 24, 69, **166–168**, 171
Social Exclusion Unit, 90
social investment, 42, 69–70, 120, 133, 135, 146–148, **168**, 171–172, 179, 203
social justice, 63–64, 71–72, 179, 186, 206
social mobility, 79, 101, 103
social returns, 22, 31, 42, 135, 146, 147, 148, 154, 168, **170–174**, 179, 203, 209
social returns on investment, 172, 174
social services, 1, 10, 34–38, 36–37, 40, 42, 62, 64, 75, 89–90, 116, 117, 122–123, 132–133, 152, 168, 201, 205
social value, 5, 22, 147, 167–168, 170–174, 197, 201, 203–205
SORPs, *see* Statement of Recommended Practice
special needs, 118, 180
SROI, *see* social returns on investment
stakeholders, 22, 44, 48, 49, 74, 75, 76, 129–130, 132, 150, 162, 167, 172, 173, 202, 203

standards, 17, 33, 54, 85, 87, 118, 143, 153, 154, 169, 173, 176, 177, 178, 185, 203

Statement of Recommended Practice, 4

stigma, 101, 142, 182

strategic housing market needs assessments, 118–119

strategic thinking, 12, 35, 44, 50, 83, 149–150, 161, 172–173

structure and agency, 48

sub-prime, 113

subsidies, vii, 3, 9, 30, 46, 58–59, 66–67, 79, 109, 146, 156–157, **175–183**, 196, 203

subsidy ratchet effect, 183

supply, 10, 52, 54, 67, 83–88, 98, 117, 118, 120, 167, 171, 182–183

supply chain, 168

supporting People, 32

sustainability, **184–186**, 210

sustainable building practices, 186–187

sustainable communities, 40

sustainable development, **186**

sustainable energy, 64, 72, 188, *see also* Code for Sustainable Homes

tangible assets, 16–17, 26, 28–29, 53

taper, 105

target rent, 156, 192

tax credits, 101, 13, 103–104, 105, 106

taxation, 3, 38, 58, 61, 66, 69, 79, 82, 96, 98, 99, 101, 122, 142, 176, 178, 179, 181, 196, 211, *see also* bedroom tax; council tax

tenancy agreements, 31, 78, 81, 93, 96, 123, 141, 143, 145, 156, 157, **190–193**, 194, 201

tenant Management, 75, 127–129

Tenant Participation Advisory Service, 127

tenant relations, *see also* reputation

tenant satisfaction, 17, 31, 118, 203, 207

Tenants' Rights etc. (Scotand) Act (1980), 96, 201

tenants' scrutiny panels, *see* scrutiny panels

tenure, 7, 8, 53, 57, 58, 77–80, 84, 86, 93, 119, 120, 138–144, 156, 179, 180, 181, 191, 192, 193, **194–196**, 202

tenure choice, 38, 53, 196

tenure diversity, 52, 53, 57, 86, 103, 119, 139–140, 194–195

tenure neutrality, 38

tenure restructuring, 58

Thaler, R., 121

time-cost dilemma, 18

Titmuss, Richard, 37

TMOs, *see* tenant management

total quality management, 45

total sufficiency rent, 157

TPAS, *see* Tenant Participation Advisory Service

TQM, *see* total quality management

trading down/up, 63, 87

trend analysis, 120, 136, *see also* longitudinal analysis

Trussell Trust, 103

Turnbull Report, 19, 160

Tylor, Edward B., 47

uncertainty, *see* risk

under occupation, 17, 64, 105

under occupancy charge, 105, *see also* bedroom tax

undeserving poor, 42, 64

universal credit, vii, 64, 91, 104, **106**, 123, 210, 211

use value, 28, 29, 54, 197–200

utility, 31, 146–147, 197, 199

valuation, 94, 157, 191, 199, 200, 201

valuation gap, 199, 200

value, 3, 4, 5, 17–18, 20, 28–30, 38, 46, 54, 62, 63, 78, 87, 92, 94, 96, 97, 99, 111, 114, 138, 147, 158, 167, 168, 171, 172–174, 183, **197–201**, 205, *see also* best value; value for money

value capture, *see* planning gain

value chain analysis, 45

value for money, xv, 5, 20, 45, 46, **64–65**, 118, 119, 135, 149, 150, 154, 169, 202–208

Varney Report, 122, 208

vertical integration, 58, 59

voice, 37

waiting lists, 10–11, 81, 119–120
Wales, 40, 57, 71, 98, 105, 133, 166,
     195, *see also* Welsh Assembly
     Government
welfare, 1, 17, 31, 32, 36, 37, 42, 43, 62,
     64, 75, 89, 135, 145, 146, 147, 148,
     168, 170, 176, 182, 183, 203, 205,
     207, **209–212**
welfare economics, 12, 43
welfare reform, 17, 32, 64, 168, **210–212**

welfare state, 42, 89, 105, 182,
     209, 210
Welsh Assembly Government,
     35, 52, 152, 169
whole life costs, 185
Wilcox, S., 99
Williams, Raymond, 46

zero carbon homes,
     187–189

.